The **Real** Power of **Parenthood**

How To Find and Use It Successfully

The **Real** Power of **Parenthood**

How To Find and Use It Successfully

A. Lynn Scoresby, Ph.D.

Knowledge Gain Publications
703 South State Street, Suite One
Orem, Utah 84058
(801) 225-9588
Fax (801) 225-9498
http://www.familyadv.com

Grateful acknowledgement is made to Nancy Heaton De Loach for editing this book, Kathy Foulger and Ashley Hibdon for designing, typesetting and proofing, and to Dan Scoresby for cover design.

Printed in the United States of America
ISBN 1-884518-19-2

TABLE OF CONTENTS

Chapter One:
The Real Power of Parenthood: How To Find It   **1**
Try Learning a Few Things   26

Chapter Two:
The Developmental Perspective   **27**

Chapter Three:
The Power of Your Family Environment   **48**
Family Environment   91
Family Environment Case Studies   93

Chapter Four:
Clear and Consistent Leadership   **95**
Adaptation Principles   130
Observing Yourself   132

Chapter Five:
Family Beginnings   **135**
Summary of Developmental Tasks (Children 0-5)   163
    Summary of Adapting the Family Environment   165
Create a Balanced Family & Achieve a Good Fit
        with Each Child   166

Chapter Six:
Family Consolidations   **167**
Summary of Developmental Tasks (Children 6-11)   210
Summary of Adapting the Family Environment   213
Applying Leadership Skills   216

Chapter Seven:
Family Flexibility **218**
Summary of Developmental Tasks (Children 12-18) 274
Adolescent Case Studies 281
Love and Emotional Support 283

Chapter Eight:
Family Launching **284**
Summary of Developmental Tasks (Young Adults) 317

Chapter Nine:
**Your In-Laws: Loving the People Your
        Children Love** **321**

Chapter Ten:
Grandparenting **341**

Chapter One

THE POWER OF PARENTHOOD

HOW TO FIND IT

The awesome moment of holding your first newborn child is shortly followed by a clear recognition that life has been created and is now in your hands. Your baby is vulnerable and dependent. It is also intelligent and organized, poised to unfold into a future created by a combination of experience and genetic potential. Family scientists tell us that those first few moments can begin a lasting attachment so strong that you and your infant are forever tied to each other. We learned many years ago that this attachment means both parent and child will be influenced by each other. What you do or do not do can make a real difference. As a parent you do not exert total control over what happens to this child, but there is no mistake that you are very influential. If you do not decide what kind of parent to be then it is quite likely that your children will decide for you.

As the months pass the child grows and you are faced with more than the basic care of feeding, dressing, and bathing. Soon you are faced with getting this child to follow your instructions, comply with your rules, accept the ideas you teach, and come to value at least some of what you value and believe what you believe. At first you probably want to know what to do when a child hits and bites, needs to be toilet trained, runs away, and makes big messes. How do you get him or her to eat, to stay in bed and sleep at night, and play nicely with friends? What will happen if you ask your child to stop or start something and he won't? What if she takes her clothes off in some public place or gets lost in the grocery store?

Later you probably will want to know how to keep this child at home when he or she wants to play at another's house. Then, when you allow your child to play with friends, how do you get the child to return home on time? How do you get a child to come and eat when called? How do you help your child use correct language and avoid using words you dislike? What if your child lies or is selfish and mean? How do you get bedrooms cleaned, homework done, and settle arguments and conflict? What about wearing the right clothes? What should you do when a child reveals a private family matter and embarrasses you or when something is stolen from school?

What influences which friends are chosen, activities participated in, and what should a child know about sex and when should it be taught? What about allowances, driving the car, curfews, and consequences? What do you do when too much time is spent with a friend and not enough with other responsibilities? How do you handle depression and anxiety? What if the child is shy, has few friends, and avoids spending time with others?

You are the parent. These questions and many others require that you answer. What are you going to do? In the practical realities of family life these questions are about power, the power to influence, and what you believe is the best application of it. You can do little or nothing with your power, of course. You may not know what to do or fear doing the wrong thing. You may avoid the responsibilities these questions imply and spend your time elsewhere. There are many who have followed this path and given neglect and rejection full meaning. You can have a reactive power and respond mostly when your children do something you do not like. This is expressed in the form of spanking, yelling, scolding, criticizing, restricting, removing privileges, and/or isolating. All of these may be in your parental bag of options and used at one time or another.

If you choose to use power in this way, like many other parents, discipline and child management has become the chief and most important part of what you do. You will operate on the belief that power comes from your ability to make rules and enforce them. This will lead you to power struggles where real contests between you and your child characterize your relationship. You may escalate your power through leverage, loud voices, and threats that you feel obligated to carry out in order not to lose. So you do not win, your child may do exactly the opposite of what you want him or her to do. In extreme cases the child may leave. The reconciliation, if there is one, comes many years later.

If you emphasize this form of power, however, you may find like many other parents that these methods are not powerful at all. They may work temporarily or when children are young, but they tend to be less effective as children mature. In fact, your efforts to impose control using these methods may actually reduce the amount of influence you exert.

There is a third alternative. You can find the real power of parenthood and use it successfully. Your words and stories will be listened to. Your children will explain their actions by saying something like, "Dad said we should...." or "because Mom asked me to...." There will be sacrifice, attention, and great effort. Your life as a parent will be balanced between the idea that your children are what is most important to you and your encouragement of their own efforts to bring about success. You typically will have little conflict with your children because you have taught them what you hope will be good for them. You talk and communicate instead. Your family life can be expected to include love, compassion, comfort, and sacrifice. Your life as an individual will include time for them and a struggle to find time for you. You will laugh at their antics, cheer at their triumphs, and sorrow in their defeats. When they have gone, the memories you have of them will be among the best of your life.

> **You can find the real power of parenthood and use it successfully.**

The real power of parenthood helps your children overcome their fears and go out into the world confident they can find their own place in it. It motivates them to excel where they have talents. It carries them across chasms of disappointment where, for a moment, they do not believe in themselves or other people. When they fail or have been hurt by something or someone, this power enables you to give hope again. They pick themselves up and look again to the future, believing in something positive because you say it is there.

Neither you nor they are perfect, but you are not finished yet. You are never finished. This is because you have used your power to exert influence toward their positive development, toward the growth of children into mature and successful adults. They are still developing and growing. When power is used in this manner, the ability to make and enforce rules through some form of discipline is still important but less important than teaching and encouraging them. Control is still important but is less necessary because you have created companionship and communication. Your limits for them are followed because they want limits too, being convinced that your efforts are for their welfare.

Among the chief benefits this power creates is the ability to make parenthood more rewarding at the same time it gives you real and lasting influence on your children. Instead of being afraid of it, find it and learn to create it. Instead of abusing it, mete it out carefully and wisely. Parents with real power have more actual influence than parents who do not. In some paradoxical way those who have the most power use it sparingly. Because children come with their own freedom to choose, it does not guarantee that you will be equally successful with all children. It does promise, however, that when your children leave home you will know you have done most, if not all the best things parents can do to ensure the success of their children.

Finding the Real Power of Parenthood

Busy Parents

Parents are usually very busy people. You have many things that occupy your time. Child care often has to compete with other priorities. There may be involvements with your children's schools, religious activities, community service, and friends. In addition, economic necessity takes its portion, demonstrated by the survey finding that more than seventy percent of American children between the ages of six and seventeen live in families in which both parents work outside the home. Almost twenty-eight percent of American children are being reared by one parent. Collectively, this means that our children, though deserving of our attention, may be thought of as only one priority among many. Parenting is often emotionally demanding. It is understandable why you may think of child care as an obligation instead of a desire.

> There is a great premium on high-quality parenting.

As always though, there is a great premium on high-quality parenting. In our current world there is added importance to make parenting positive, practical, and effective. It needs to be powerful enough to succeed. Busy parents need an approach that helps them find greater rewards in the process of rearing children. If parenthood is not rewarding, finding something else to do in a world filled with many options is easy. That many parents do not find rearing children rewarding is no insignificant matter.

There is an accelerated emphasis on individual expressiveness and opportunity as the "right" of each adult. When marriage or family life appear to impair or suppress this possibility, many adults option out of their marriage and family responsibilities. This can be considered a symptom of a pervasive social problem. Research presented by Barbara Whitehead in the March 1994 *Atlantic Monthly* indicates that some adults may benefit, at least temporarily, from the escape of what to them may be a stifling family climate. However, it is consistently and painfully clear that their children do not share the benefit.

If you are busy and do not treat your children as you would like to because of it, your choice may be despair and guilt or parenting out of a sense of obligation that makes parenting a burden. In contrast to both of those options, it is possible to learn how to be powerful enough to bring success to your children and satisfaction to you. A little common sense suggests that the right use of power will be found in a positive approach—one that combines the wisdom of the past with the demands of the present, while being usefully linked to desirable future objectives. Such an approach should enthrone parenthood as an important opportunity that challenges and fulfills—an opportunity worthy of the commitment of one's best talents. It should make family life a more positive experience for parents and children. Further, the right type of power should provide confidence that effort will produce quality results and not be based on fear of failure. Then we will know that when we try hard and commit ourselves fully, we will have a better chance of succeeding.

All of this is possible if we find the real power of parenthood and use it successfully. The ideas of power and parenthood may seem like an oxymoron but the truth is that the most successful parents typically have a great deal of power and they use it judiciously meting out care, nurturance, and guidelines. It takes this kind of power to promote the successful development of children all the way through their young lives until they arrive at the positive shores of happy adulthood. It takes real power to focus enough attention on our children and make them the priority they deserve while we are rearing them.

This is not just giving ourselves to providing and protecting. Using the real power of parenthood means that beyond providing basic care, we promote children's development and our sense of achievement. Such a method of parenthood can reduce its strain and increase its fulfillment. Again, we need to remind ourselves of an obvious truth. As in previous generations, today's children will have many problems to solve, and they do not need the extra burden created by neglect, rejection, or mistreatment. As parents, we can improve what we do to prepare children for the times in which they live. They deserve our best effort so that they can, in turn, make the same investment in their children. Instead of passing on our mistakes, they can pass on our methods of contributing toward the development of high-quality people.

"The Children, the Children"

The origin of the power of parenthood lies in the nature of our children and our willingness to understand them. Anna, in the musical *The King and I*, gives life to a familiar idea by saying, "The children, the children, we can't forget the children." Those words have different meanings to different people. I hope they mean to you that thinking of your children means to improve what you know about them.

All of us become parents without knowing much about the best way to organize a family and care for children. As a result, many think some strange things about parenthood. One of the strangest is the idea that wholehearted devotion to parenthood is the same thing as completely sacrificing your own life in the process. This idea was reinforced for many years by the emphasis given to "child-centered" parenting, inviting us to address children's emotional needs with greater compassion and support. Many parents interpreted or used this as justification for indulging their children, even becoming so tied to them the only thing they could do was rescue them, smother, them, or even change places with them.

Another strange idea some people have about parenting is that power and control over children are identical.

Real power is not the same thing as control, manipulation, or other forms of coercion. The parents with real power tend to recognize at least one important element of parenthood. They view themselves as models and examples that children will imitate, and they create positive reasons that motivate children to do so. As a result children learn behavior that shows respect and regard for their parents. More than this, however, parents with real power have a fairly complete understanding of their children and how they develop and grow. This knowledge gives them power because it takes advantage of an obvious truth.

Parents are older and, for the time being, stronger and wiser. Parents with enough knowledge about each of their children are more likely to proactively promote their children's success. Parents who do not understand children and how they develop are more likely to react to their children and be more focused on problems and difficulties.

Knowing our own children and how they develop is a source of parental power.

It is fairly clear from many research efforts that knowing our own children and how they develop is a source of parental power. The evidence for this can be found in the anger, avoidance, and conflict that inevitably result when parents do not know what to do when faced with the need to do something. Feelings of responsibility, agonizingly tied to helplessness and misjudgment, lead to frustration and resentment. This is when we are most likely to be at our worst. For those who have done this, the solution is not self-recrimination. It is to find the real power of parenthood and use it successfully.

Find Your Power By Learning about Your Children

While we are caring for our newborns, we improve our abilities to take notice of them. We can see that they respond to the sounds we make. They look at us and hold our gaze while ripples of emotion generate wonder and awe toward this new life. They display their feelings through sounds and facial expressions. They are more responsive at one time than another. Shortly after birth they even have different purposes for crying and use these to tell us about pain, irritation, and fear. They can imitate our facial expressions and tell the difference between our voices and those of other adults. In all these ways, infants indicate their desire and ability to communicate. They are not passive, indifferent, and unresponsive. They are alert, aware, and involved. All this delights us, and as proud parents we are sure our babies are unusually intelligent and beautiful.

While watching to see each little change in them, we also recognize another significant thing. Children rapidly mature and develop. At first we may only appreciate the changes in their weight and length while understanding the other change with a growing awareness. Yet when we notice it happening in front of our eyes, this idea sobers us with its importance while it delights and amuses. In addition to pleasing us, our children's growth forces decisions upon us. Their development can be ignored if we choose, but if we have even a small appreciation for human life and a tenderness for the small life that is ours, then we must notice, respond, and do something about it. Questioning ourselves brings us to decide what we are actually going to do. When both the pleasure and the responsibility come together in the realization that what we do will influence our children, then suddenly we are greatly motivated to understand our own beliefs and practices about how we treat them.

Using and Overcoming Your Childhood Experiences

In our search to understand ourselves, one obvious source of information is our own childhood and what we learned about parenthood from our parents. We were reared by someone else, and these early experiences and the emotions linked to them are stored in our memories. These memories tend to surface and are expressed as actions when the feelings we have with our children match the feelings of our own childhood. If our parents were wise and skillful in using their power, then we are blessed with the foundation for similar positive abilities.

Like most people, however, our parents were less than perfect and many of us do not like some things they did. Yet, when we start our own parental careers we discover that childhood memories have a strong hold on us. Our family experiences happened with the people most important to us, at a time when we were most vulnerable to life's lessons. Though we may have promised ourselves that we would not do some things our parents did, we find that in many ways we react quite similarly, whether good or bad, and whether we want to or not.

There are at least four ways our childhood experiences influence us. One is the general attitude you have about being a parent. This may include the importance you attach to it, the amount of time and energy you are willing to give, the general notions you have about "good" and "bad" practices, and the judgments you make about what is acceptable and what is unacceptable. To find out what you have brought from your background, you can analyze yourself to see what your ideas are about parenting. You can also watch your reactions to other parents. "I would never do that," one mother said while observing a woman yank her child around the grocery store to signal her frustration at his crying. Her response tells her something about herself and her ideas about good or bad parenting.

Another way your childhood influences how you act as a parent is through specific memories of family experiences that you want to repeat or to avoid. Some of these memories are of traditions you may hope to perpetuate such as holiday celebrations or demonstrations of affection. Others are memories of parent-child events that stand out because of their negative and positive emotional significance. Most of us remember times of intense love or anger, for example. Other examples include memories of camping, fishing, and vacationing together.

A third type of influence your childhood exerts is through learned emotional reactions. Each person has individual emotional characteristics and in some ways is very different from his or her parents. Yet, it is often the case that the intensity of emotional behavior is tied to specific situations—like seeing a mouse in the kitchen, realizing a child is in danger, or witnessing a child spill the milk at dinner. The power of imitation is so great that parents repeat the same emotional intensity observed in their parents in the same situations. Angry parents, for example, often teach anger to their children, who in turn display it as parents. Passive, unemotional parents teach this lesson equally well. Loving parents, who tenderly comfort and support children even when they act unlovable may teach these same feelings to their children.

It is worth noting that sometimes, especially when emotions are harsh or negative, second generation parents are the opposite of what their parents were. Angry parents may help create passive, unexpressive children, for example. Though the emotional behavior is opposite, it may not be better. The opposite behavior may be even more negative. It is, therefore, important to have enough power to make choices about the emotional response you bring to your children from your childhood.

The fourth way our childhood experiences influence us is in our style of communication and thinking. We bring it with us and pass it on to our children as the standard mode of seeing and thinking about the world. This is how we perpetuate political, religious, occupational, and many other family and cultural attitudes. Our parents taught this to us when they taught us about language, and we pass our form of communication and thinking to our children by teaching them our language.

Although most of us are not fully aware of how much family and cultural knowledge we transmit to our children, we are usually aware that our parents transmitted such knowledge to us. When we, as parents, are called upon to do something about a situation with our children, our brains replay our memory tapes, and what we do can be heavily influenced by our childhood. As I suggested, we and our children are blessed if our parents were skillful. We and our children are challenged if they were not.

In either case, I propose that the real power of parenthood is more than simply doing or not doing what our parents did, whether it was useful or not. This power gives you the ability to understand what knowledge you bring with you into parenthood and adapt or fit it correctly to the children you bring into your family. This ability to adapt what we learn from our childhood comes from a deep understanding of our own children and the conditions in which we live while we rear them.

Successfully Using Current Social Conditions

We live in a social world and often find it necessary to be interested about events outside our families. We wish to know how they might affect our children. For example, many parents are coming to believe that the world "outside" the family is becoming more threatening to children. We read and hear about violence at school, episodes of child abuse and molestation, kidnappings, and assault. If these events occur close by, it is difficult to ignore them and we should not ignore them. We must decide how we are going to protect ourselves and our children. If the environment outside our families is more benevolent, we need to adjust to that and make a different set of decisions. All these matters, whether threatening or safe, make a difference in how we organize our families and subsequently influence how we act as parents.

Besides recognizing and adjusting to the environment, social conditions influence us in another way. They relate to the way we believe others perceive us. Parenting is both a personal, private experience and a social role where what we do can be observed by other people. Therefore, besides the influence of our childhood, we are affected by the belief that what we do as parents will be reflected to others in the actions of our children. How our children turn out becomes, in part, the measure of our own success. This belief exerts both positive and negative influences on us, depending on how we respond to it. The positive parts of this belief, for example, motivate increased responsibility by parents for children because we do not want our children to be poorly trained and prepared. When we are motivated in this positive way, we are more likely to help our children learn moral behavior, social skills, and many other things that will help.

When we are too anxious about what other people think, however, or wholly uncaring about it, our parenting practices can produce very unhappy consequences. In the first place, how children "turn out" is heavily influenced by genetics. In fact, genetics may account for as much as one-half of why children act the way they do. This does not mean that you are unimportant, it means only that you need to understand the significant role inheritance plays. Parents always have been, are, and will remain highly influential; but very good children emerge from very bad families, and the reverse is true as well.

> **Parents always have been, are, and will remain highly influential**

If your sole measure of success is the way your children turn out in a public perspective, you may improperly feel a sense of failure when they make mistakes, and you may therefore wallow in your guilt rather than being objective enough to help them. Or, you may be so anxious about them, you become like the overprotective gardener who pulled his plants out of the ground in order to check on their roots. Further, if your children turn out well, you may take more than your share of the credit instead of giving a fair share to them.

The more intensely parents believe that the way others view their children is the sole measure of their own success, the more likely they are to be excessively vulnerable to social influence. This leads us to adopt any current ideas about discipline and other forms of child care. Some of us, markedly influenced by the fads of the day, may try to adopt them simply because others are using them, rather than retain those practices that time has shown to be successful. More importantly, you may not develop parenting practices that are based on what you know about your children and better suited to them.

For example, the forms of disapproval parents show to children who make mistakes or misbehave are usually influenced by some "fad" currently in vogue in the social marketplace. As I have suggested these may include whether to spank, talk things out, ground a child for a time, restrict privileges, isolate, or scold. There are many, for example, who think children of this past generation have been reared too permissively. Therefore, we currently appear to be undergoing a revision and are now telling ourselves that we need to be more in control, more demanding, and more restrictive. Whether this is true or not is only one part of the question. The other is to consider where the idea comes from. If we apply an idea simply because someone else has presented it, we have neglected to measure its worth by the consequences for our children. This error should be carefully avoided because it takes power away from you. To have real power it is important to base what you do on the knowledge you have about your own children.

> **To have real power it is important to base what you do on the knowledge you have about your own children.**

Parents affected by current parenting "fads" often also adopt the goal of making certain their children will "fit in" and be acceptable to others. We should note this happens not because doing so helps the children, but because not doing so will reflect on the parents. Most behavioral scientists, and the parents who fall prey to this unhappy approach, identify some especially destructive side effects. Considerable anxiety is created when parents feel as if they do not have enough power. Yet, they have actually decided to let someone else be the measure of their own children's success. When this is the case, parental involvement is inconsistent, becoming important when their children's "social" behavior is in question and less important when other people are not involved. Children of these parents often react with distress and unhappiness. This is because their parents' exaggerated response to "social" expectations is at the expense of a balanced approach that more appropriately promotes their overall well-being. Well-known examples include parents of childhood stars, entertainers, or young athletes. These parents have not found the real power available to them, have lost it, or have given it away.

Let's examine why this is the case. I have proposed that what you learned from your childhood may or may not apply to your children. They are different and the times in which they live are different. If you attempt something you learned from the past and it is not a good match, then your children will quickly understand your parenting approach is not connected to them. Even if what you learned from your parents is useful, it still needs to be applied to your children based on what you know about them.

Using current social "fads" means that you are relying on someone else to determine what you should do. No idea, regardless of how good it is, will have the power to influence unless you measure and adapt what you learn to your own children. You cannot do this effectively unless you have great knowledge about them. Although the past and current information may have certain positive values, they are less reliable sources of information about successful parenting when they are not based on what you know about your own children.

To protect me and my siblings when we were young, for instance, my mother made our family take weekly doses of castor oil and wear long, ugly stockings in the winter. In the early years of my life, punishments included sitting for long periods on a chair and sometimes a belt or switch was used. We had to clean up our plates to save the starving people in distant lands, never talk back, immediately answer when called, perform many chores, always take a clean handkerchief when going out with someone, and communicate with respect even if our parents did not. Interestingly, we could eat some jelly beans just before going to bed, run free and wild for long periods of time, and bathe only once a week. There were few family rules because, as a farm family, we were usually too busy working to make, enforce, or disobey them.

If past experiences were wholly appropriate, then I should employ these same practices in my family even if I live in a different place, under different circumstances, and with children who are not biologically identical to my parents' children. No reasonable thinker would suggest that this should be the case. Like past experience, social influences are not totally reliable. Some of them change with the age, and what was fashionable ten years ago no longer is today.

With this perspective in mind we can see that the amount of control parents exert fluctuates from generation to generation just like forms of disapproval, both strict and permissive. Even if many customs, traditions, values, and parental practices remind us to do what appears to be good, they still may not be helpful in creating a positive parenting approach that makes parenting rewarding for us and successful for our children. This is because neither our childhood experiences nor current social "fads" are matched to our children.

No outside influence knows the uniqueness of each child the way a parent does. Rearing our children based on current trends or experience means evaluating our efforts and our children by someone else's standard of propriety. One need only think about that for a moment to realize the risks involved. General parenting methods advised by someone else may deserve consideration, may even be wise and thoughtful, but still may not suit you or your children. Good ideas become bad practices if you implement them without fully understanding how to connect them with any child. The following example will illustrate.

In the 1970s, one father heard someone he trusted state that there should be no generation gap between parents and children. The speaker was likely suggesting that parents should work to create positive communication, warmth, and affection with their children. This man, however, interpreted the advice differently. He went home and told his children that from this point on they would not be permitted to differ with him in any family decisions. The results created a wider generation gap than would have happened otherwise. He trusted the speaker, but he applied a principle he did not understand.

We cannot help but be influenced by values we learn from our parents. They are part of us. We can, however, decide what we value and how our values should be adjusted to our children.

Learn How Your Children Develop

I propose that you consider one principle of primary importance and use it as the central core of your attempts to find the real power of parenthood. This principle is nothing unusual, but for some reason many parents who know about it usually recognize its importance only after their children are grown. Others notice but do not know how to use it to good advantage, and it comes up mostly as a conversation topic rather than recognized with the true significance it deserves. This principle I am proposing is the fundamental and central truth of parenting.

The exercise of parental power should be founded on the premise that children develop and grow—they change over time, demonstrating more advanced behavior as they mature. Treating this concept as your central value will help you identify your children's growth potential and help you acquire the power to help them. All that we do, in my opinion, should reflect this idea.

In fact, the first principle of parenthood power can be defined as doing what will help—rather than interfere—with this process. Think about what this means. It is not the same thing as acquiring strategies to control your children, solve behavior problems, or help them be popular, smart, or athletic. It is not merely getting them to do their share of the chores and comply with family rules. However, these are often the measures parents use to decide if children are developing successfully.

Focusing on children and their development is very different from giving them the most up-to-date toys and clothes. It is very different from overindulging them or permissively allowing them to do all they wish to do. The real power of parenthood enables you to guide your children toward positive development so they become useful, healthy, and effective people.

Ample knowledge about how your children develop and grow will place you in a position to teach and reinforce the good things your children learn. It will lead to an enlightened parenting approach filled with positive methods that help you see the real effect of your efforts. It assumes you care enough to know your children, spend time with them, monitor their learning, and guide them through their good and bad times with an eye toward the goal of raising happy, well-adjusted adults. It implies the true responsibility we have to our children. Because we as parents move through life only a few yards ahead of our children, it is our responsibility to inform them about what we see and help them prepare for challenges, avoid mistakes, and find success. That is all that really matters. When you know your own children and how they develop, you will have the power to be more certain that your influence is constructive rather than harmful. You can better balance your efforts, fears, and concerns with an understanding that children have their portion of responsibility for their development. And, ironically, when you recognize this and no longer assume a total obligation, you will have more confidence in your abilities and discover that you are better at knowing when to be involved and when to stand aside.

Lastly, a parenting approach based on promoting your children's development requires genuine power. You will need it to pass through and succeed at those situations that most people find awkward, difficult, worrisome, or frustrating. You will need it when there are real crises and heartbreaking problems. You will need it on the day when a child wants to do something you do not believe is good.

Basing your parental role on the development of your children makes it clear what will help or harm them. It stimulates creative thought and gives you more alternatives from which to choose. Then, the choice is yours. You can contribute to or hinder their progress.

If you accept the importance of this type of power, you will find that parenthood contains both fulfillment and hardships. But, when you are experiencing difficulties, you can find ways to use these problems for positive purposes and you can look forward to results that make it all worthwhile.

You are probably familiar with the idea that parent-child conflict and children's misbehavior happen when we fail to understand our children, to supply effective care, or live an inadequate example. It should be fairly easy to conclude then that learning about them makes it easier for you.

The real power of parenthood enables us to focus on positive results and invites parents and children to be involved in the shared enterprise of family life.

If you accept and apply real power you can also understand how to help your children share in the enterprise of family life and collaborate with you in creating a strong family. Such a family is beneficial for them and a source of strength for everyone. Then, as they develop and grow and time passes, you can see your efforts better realized in the things which make you proud of what they are becoming.   ❀

Try Learning a Few Things

1. **Recognize and acknowledge your children's positive characteristics.** Make statements like, "I can see that you are becoming more organized," or "You are a very honest person." See if they accept what you tell them.

2. **Learn about your children's emotions, name them, and link them to their thoughts and actions.** Say, "I can see that you are _____" (unhappy, happy, cheerful, tired, excited, etc.). Link emotions to behavior by saying things like, "You feel happy because you were nice to that little boy." See if they accept your assessment of them.

3. **Learn how your children learn.** Teach relationship skills such as effective communication, empathy, kindness, honesty, love, caregiving, unselfishness, warmth, patience, tenderness, responsibility, and dependability. Observe your children and identify something they do not do well. For example, do they have trouble helping around the house? Tell a story that describes someone correctly applying the idea. Then role play or practice the behavior so your children know how and when to do it, and set a family goal to improve on it within the next week. As you do this, watch and see how your children learn: (1) by listening and talking, (2) by doing and participating, or (3) by watching and imitating.

Chapter Two

THE DEVELOPMENTAL PERSPECTIVE

Most of us love our children and find them fascinating. Sometimes we look at them and feel we cannot get enough to fill our eyes or our hearts. There seems to be no end to the remarkable things children say and do. For those who have more than one child, they discover that the first has taught them to be more observant of the second. I recall a friend telling me that he and his wife decided to place their new baby's crib at the foot of their bed so they could notice everything about him. "We learned," he said, "that we missed a lot of things with the other kids."

If you want the real power which allows you to take your children into a positive future, you must do more than watch them or pay attention just to see the new and enjoyable things they do. You must watch them to understand how they grow. Watching children to see their growth and progress is called a "developmental perspective." We can enjoy them all we can, but in addition, the developmental perspective means to have a view of childhood that stretches over time and to see it in one glimpse. It means that you try to understand where your children have come from, what they are doing now, and understand some things which are about to come.

Imagine that you are omniscient, and can see in one moment someone's past, present, and future. At any moment you could understand what a child has been like, what the child is now doing, and what would happen later. That knowledge and perspective would guide your thoughts and actions to help your children in a way your limited vision of the present and past cannot. This view, or perspective, helps you acquire increased power.

I remember watching one of my sons play basketball. As a former player, I watched him miss opportunities because he had not learned to play with his left hand. After that when we played together, I defended his right hand so he had to use his left. At first he was awkward, but gradually became better. Later, at one of his games, I watched as he turned to survey his options, hesitated just for a moment, and then used his left hand to score a basket. I felt a thrill of fulfillment although I never told him what I had been doing. I just saw how he needed to develop and helped him do it. I was older and understood what he would need. That experience was far more rewarding than his basketball successes.

Of course, we are not omniscient and can't see everything. As a result, our understanding is less than complete. Yet we can see much about a child's future if we are willing to pay attention. After all, we were once children, and we have developed and grown. Besides, watching one child go through several stages improves our abilities with those that come later. The point is, that focusing on the development of our children is simply the best perspective to help us formulate an effective child care and management plan. It is the best perspective because it is realistic. It is what really happens, whether we care to notice or not. By noticing, we can use our knowledge to make ourselves into the kind of parents we would like to be and find many rewards in the bargain.

Understanding some things about the way children develop gives us the real power of parenthood. We can monitor their development and help them, or get out of the way. In my experience this is the least used, but most valuable information available to parents. Yet, many do not understand this principle clearly until their children are grown. Then they recognize what they wish they had known and done while their children were young. This happens at the moment you think, "I wish I could start again," or "I wish I had known this earlier."

The Power of a Developmental Perspective

A developmental perspective is important for many reasons. First, it will improve your ability to understand your children. At any moment in time you can see what your children actually do and then link it to something you know or believe they will need in their future. Some parents, for example, give gifts to their children that will please them now and will be even more interesting to them in the next year.

Second, it gives us more ideas or options about what to do as parents. Suppose your three-year-old child won't go to bed when you want. Faced with that you might talk, threaten, or even spank. If you knew something about three year olds and how they are developing, you could also put the child in a routine so that going to bed was the last in a series of steps, or make the bed a friendly place where stories are read. In this case you have more options of how to help your child do want is best for both of you.

A developmental perspective also gives you more options when you have to respond to mistakes children make. Suppose you have a rule-oriented perspective and think your primary task is to make and enforce rules. Your perspective will focus attention on obedience and disobedience. If you think a child is breaking a rule, for instance, your obedience/disobedience orientation will create the decision to punish or not, and, if you punish, how to do it. This appears so logical that you might think of little else. It might not occur to you that misbehavior is a sign that the child is ignorant of something. Here, misbehavior can be an opportunity to teach an important lesson. However, instead of using the opportunity to teach, having no developmental perspective limits you to spend your energy punishing the child.

Third, a developmental perspective helps parents be more positive, effective, and constructive. Working toward some positive future leads to hope, encouragement, and satisfaction. Imagine the parents who discovered one day they could talk their children out of discouragement by getting them to pay attention to some positive future possibility. It not only helps the children, but gives hope to parents, too.

> **A Developmental Perspective:**
> • **Improves your ability to understand**
> • **Provides more ideas about how to respond**
> • **Helps you be more positive and constructive**

Let us suppose you watched your child jump out of the bathtub and run around happily and excitedly without any clothes. Imagine that he or she likes doing this and does it as often as possible. What would you think? Is something wrong and should you do something to stop this behavior? Or, is this natural behavior for a two year old that can be safely ignored since he or she will grow into a sense of modesty? If you understood child development, you would be patient and amused because most children "run naked," but soon learn modesty as a natural part of childhood. In contrast, suppose at an older age this child hits, bites, and pinches until another child is hurt and cries. This is not a natural part of development and some action likely needs to be taken so the child learns an improved method of behaving.

In the face of aggression it is hoped you would not be indifferent and unresponsive, but what would you do? You understand that something is wrong, but why is it? Again, if you simply see this behavior as incorrect you might devise a punishment designed to stop it. As some parents have, you might consider spanking or biting the child back if he or she bites you. That seems reasonable, doesn't it? It is *not* reasonable, and it is *not* effective since spanking and biting are acts of aggression. You will be rewarding the very actions you want to eliminate.

In contrast, if you have a developmental perspective, you will see beyond the misbehavior, recognize the signal that something is wrong, and correct it by promoting some growth or development. There are reasons for aggression that must be found and resolved. Your solution could be to find the causes of the aggressive behavior. Childhood aggression usually comes from imitating your example, experimentation, emotional stress, or the lack of affection and warmth. Then, if you have a developmental perspective you will recognize that knowing the causes is not enough. You will need to teach a better form of behavior because if uncorrected, your child will learn additional unhappy or unpleasant things. Your approach of recognizing the cause and teaching something new has more power to determine what the child does than merely punishing.

This example illustrates that a developmental perspective allows you to go beyond mere punishment and to actually correct misbehavior by creating some new, more successful behavior. You have more power as a parent to produce lasting results if you use your developmental perspective to see misbehavior as a signal that something is wrong and needs to be solved. A lasting solution will be to teach the child a correct form of behavior.

> **A developmental perspective will help you understand how children are maturing.**

In addition to this, a developmental perspective will also help you understand how children are maturing. It gives you goals that provide direction. A goal-oriented approach to life is generally a life of higher performance than a life lived without goals. It is possible to make goals for children that are too restrictive, but by using a developmental perspective you can help your children see in advance what they are going to develop to anyway. Then you can organize what you do, invite them to participate, and lay out a plan that helps them achieve what both you and they value. There is a great deal of evidence that children who have a sense of direction shared by their parents are less vulnerable to many forms of harmful behavior including drug use, early sex, alcohol abuse, and vandalism. In these cases, a developmental perspective gives parents a reasonable view of child development that includes what may be the best for the children instead of so many negative possibilities.

Every Child Is Working On Developmental Tasks

You can gain a developmental perspective of your children by realizing that all children are working on smaller forms of growth called developmental tasks. In fact, they and we do this as long as we are alive. This is the biological law for all living. Continuing development to achieve specific goals is the central purpose of life for children. Nearly everything they do is related to some form of growth. Learning about developmental tasks will allow you to know your children in more specific ways. You may think of child's play as a form of pleasurable fun. It is all that, but play for a child is also a way of learning social and emotional skills, moral lessons, and new mental abilities. If it involves physical activities, play is also a method of promoting physical development.

Developmental tasks are the new abilities children are working toward—the improved, more mature characteristics we see emerge in them as they grow. Imagine for a moment what this means. Children are around people who are more competent than they are, know more, can do more, and seem to function better in most ways. They understand that learning and developing is necessary. This "motivation" to grow is partly biological, too. Body and brain changes are a natural part of childhood. Change and development are central to every child's experience.

The idea about the existence of specific tasks has come from the research and countless hours of observations made by behavioral scientists. From this source, we learn that children are not passive individuals waiting for life to happen to them. They experiment, test, rehearse, and learn until they are successful. They adjust, adapt, repeat, and try again, and do so in at least five areas: mental, emotional, social, physical, and moral.

Children are not passive individuals waiting for life to happen to them.

Our true responsibility as parents is to teach, motivate, regulate, and exemplify healthy and worthwhile behavior in these areas. In fact, if you care a great deal about your children you would like to be powerful enough to ensure they grow in each of these areas. This can only happen if you focus on your children and how they learn and develop. Then what you do as a parent will have added power because it will be based on what your children are already working on and your effort will ensure it.

Knowing about these specific developmental tasks permits you to be a "behavioral coach" because you have the most intimate contact with your children. Your children will recognize this as well. They are more likely to accept what you want them to do because what you want them to do is related to their growth. Instead of trying to get them to do something else, I propose that you focus on helping them achieve their developmental tasks. No teacher, friend, sibling, or church leader shares in this expectation.

Let me give you an example. Some developmental tasks take many years to complete though we can see children begin them very early in life. Learning language is an example. Infants make vowel sounds when they coo and babble. They learn words, connect them to voice inflections, and use them in simple and then more complex sentences. Still, language development continues over many years and constantly improves if we continue to teach it.

Other tasks can be achieved in a shorter period and are specific to each stage of childhood. For example, infants are working to turn over, crawl, and walk. They do all these in a matter of months. Like language, however, achieving these and other similar skills is the work to which children give genuine effort and intent. The point is, you would have greater power to influence your children if you knew what your children were working on. In nearly every case, if you are interested enough and willing to learn, you can observe what your children are doing and help them be successful. You can, for example, match what you do with what your children are already motivated to do. This is possible if you understand that there are two general kinds of developmental tasks. Knowing both allows you to create situations which have lasting and profound influence.

Completing Biological or Inherited Tasks

Some developmental tasks are inherited. Everyone, for example, continues to grow until he or she completes or achieves a mature height and body shape. Other less obvious tasks might include development of certain types of intelligence such as mathematics and logic, music, and art.

Many people fail to fully appreciate the power of inherited developmental tasks. In fact, even to this day some parents continue to think that everything about a child is learned from experience. An abundance of scientific evidence suggests that much of what happens to children and influences how they act is carried in the genes, as the following story illustrates.

A student was walking on the campus of a midwestern university. A girl approached him, smiled, called him an unfamiliar name and attempted to kiss him. He stopped and backed away. Surprised, he asked her what she was trying to do. She chided him for refusing her affection and told him he wasn't being funny. He protested again that he didn't know anyone by the name she had called him and said that she must be mistaken. Just as she was getting angry, a young man walked up to both of them who looked identical to the first young man. He called the girl by name, but could not stop staring at this new look alike.

As the story unfolded, both men, who had been adopted, realized they were identical twins. Their story caught the attention of a newspaper reporter, and their picture was included as part of the story. Someone brought this article and picture to the attention of a third man living in a neighboring city. He was so similar to the other two in the picture that he called them. They all had the same haircut and shared many other interests. They were identical triplets, separated at birth, and placed in different adoptive homes.

This event sparked increased interest in the role our genetic background plays in our lives. Several attempts have been made to find others who share identical genetic backgrounds but did not share the same childhood environment. When twins were located, the similarity between these individuals was sometimes startling. In one case, two brothers first learned of each other at age thirty-nine. They had a strong desire to meet. Both sported beards, wore similar clothes, weighed about the same, had similar hobbies, worked in similar careers, married women with similar names, divorced, and remarried. They each had dogs with similar names. Not all cases are this dramatic. There are other cases where twins were not as similar

These accounts, and others like them, illustrate, however, that a significant part of human development is determined genetically by our biological parents. The older children grow, the more influence their genetic code has in determining personality traits, career interests, talents, and many other abilities. It may have as much as half the total influence on children.

Further, inherited traits are a powerful force in shaping the course that development takes. Medical researchers, for example, have now demonstrated that humans inherit an internal clock that determines the rate and timing of physical growth. This means that some children grow rapidly while others do so gradually over a period. Some children have early growth spurts during puberty and others grow more slowly.

We also inherit at least part of our emotional makeup because we know that at least five emotions are present at birth. Researchers have found surprise, disgust, anxiety, happiness/pleasure, and anger in every culture. This suggests that everyone inherits these emotions. We also inherit the ability to produce language sounds and interpret them into meaningful units. Brain researchers have found that we inherit our concepts of time, space, numbers, and the ability to classify or put ideas into categories. This shapes the way we think and learn and affects the emergence of our talents and abilities.

The fact that children have a "developmental code" built in when they are born—a genetic code that unfolds as they mature—should give parents considerable motivation to make sure that the code unfolds successfully and completely. The key word is "complete." We now better understand that if something is carried in the genetic makeup of a child, there is tremendous motivation to adjust, work, practice, and adapt until it is fully completed. This idea underlies the stories about very creative people who will work, sometimes under great opposition, to complete a project in order to satisfy the inner urge that motivates them. This same idea is the explanation for why bodies continue to grow and mature until full physical maturation is complete.

Let us examine several things that children work to complete that are clearly the result of what they inherit. By examining these, you can see that your children come loaded with possibilities. For example, children do not need to formally practice walking. We have little to do with changes in hair color, the start of puberty, or the type of play children find interesting. Boys are more likely to enjoy rough and tumble play while girls prefer other forms of relational play. Significant aspects of children's mental abilities and emotional style unfold naturally without much teaching or training from others. These are only a few examples.

In the last few years researchers have collected information that suggests the existence of more than one form of intelligence. Every individual may have some parts of all eight types but will obviously be more intelligent in some areas than in others. There is a strong biological factor that partly explains the origin and development of each person's intelligence. While reading the chart on page 40 about the types of intelligences described by Howard Gardner of Harvard University, think about yourself and your children. What forms of intelligence are prominent in each of your kids?

Some of each intelligence can be observed in every child and every child will be motivated to improve in each area. However, when someone is especially endowed with one or more of these abilities there is tremendous motivation to completely fulfill them. It is as if great writers have books inside them waiting to be written so they can complete

The Eight Intelligences

Musical/Rhythmic: The ability to understand combinations of blended sounds and to create or perform them. These sounds are used in composition, vocal, and instrumental performance.

Intrapersonal: Awareness of oneself including one's emotional life. This intelligence is usually demonstrated in helping professions and religious positions.

Social/Interpersonal: Understanding human relationships, social organizations, patterns of communication, and interaction. This intelligence may be observed in business, government, and other forms of social participation.

Logical/Mathematical: Understanding the rules of logic as applied to numbers and combinations of numbers. This intelligence is found in any task involving the manipulation of numbers and symbols.

Verbal/Linguistic: Understand words, what they mean, and how they are combined in order to communicate. This intelligence is applied in literature, poetry, and other forms of writing.

Visual/Spatial: Organizing objects in space. This intelligence is used in art and engineering.

Body/Kinesthetic: Ability in physical movement such as coordination and rhythm in dance or athletics.

Nature: Understands the environment, the outdoors, and living things.

their language abilities. Great dancers or athletes work to fully complete their physical abilities and are satisfied only when they sense or feel this completion. Individuals feel complete when they have fully and accurately described their own thoughts and feelings as part of personal intelligence and have been understood, or when they have made a satisfactory social contribution. Intelligences, and other inherited abilities, are part of children's developmental tasks.

Through them we see that all children have a similar goal—to fully and successfully complete what is within them. Their bodies and brains will not stop until they have finished their full biological measure.

Think about how you can contribute to rather than become obstacles to your children. If you recognize your children's abilities, you can provide additional opportunities for them. You can stimulate, encourage, and motivate them to continue until their inherited abilities are complete. If you fail to recognize what your children bring with them you cannot help them as much. Much worse, one accurate definition of poor parenting is to actively impede your children or to be an obstacle and prevent them from completing the improvement of a natural ability.

Achieving Competence

There is another category of developmental tasks. These are the tasks children work on to become competent. That is, they are trying to become competent at performing something required of them. Where we have biological tasks that children complete, this second type of task is presented by the environment which includes family, friends, religion, schools, etc. They are called environmental tasks which children learn.

Children in the Fiji Islands have remarkable auditory memory. Scientists were puzzled at the children's astonishing abilities until the scientists learned that all traditions, rules, ceremonies, and family histories are passed on orally by older people to their children. Thus, the Fiji children learned their histories, but also developed the sensory ability to be successful. This example, and many other situations like it, represents children's attempts to be competent in their own environment.

Polynesian navigators can observe natural signs and solve difficult and complex problems while navigating without instruments across thousands of miles of open ocean. Yet, they perform poorly on written intelligence tests that have a Western cultural bias. Clearly this represents another example of people becoming competent in their environment.

Becoming competent in the outside world is an area you can have real influence on. Whereas inherited tasks are

> **Competence is achieved in the specific situations of childhood.**

"built-in" and appear to have a motivation of their own to be completed, competence is achieved in the specific situations of childhood. Many of these you create.

As with the motivation to complete inherited tasks, there is an intense motivation to gain competency. There are many recorded cases, for example, in which children learn criminal behavior, laziness, some forms of mental illness, and character problems because these behaviors were the ways to become "competent" in their environment.

On a more positive note, if they are required to become competent in a healthy, supportive environment, children will learn many helpful things. They improve their natural language abilities to communicate with others. They learn how to properly display inherited emotions to adapt and successfully "fit in" with other people and in certain situations. They search for the opportunity to express their talents. They practice to improve inherited physical skills, practice to become competent at music, and talk and visit with people until they have positive social relationships. They will work unsupervised if their project is interesting and will demonstrate their competence in whatever way possible.

Like completion, achieving competence is the basis of much childhood motivation. Those who help children become competent, therefore, will be highly valued and will have lifelong significance. This is why any involved parent, mentor, teacher, or friend has lasting influence. It is important for you to distinguish between inherited abilities and the tasks at which children are learning to be competent. You might, for example, try to teach or require something children cannot do. You might fail to teach or provide expectations when you should. Further, unless you have a good understanding of the two types of tasks, you might confuse your children. For example, children are less likely to become competent if their environment requires them to do more than their inherited possibilities permit or if inherited qualities are denied. If your child cannot do a school task and prefers to do something else, you may need to work out some combination that allows the child to do more of the desired activity and use it as a motivator to improve in the one that is not easy.

In addition, when you are clear about both types of developmental tasks you will be less likely to create a condition called "learned helplessness." This is often fostered by a set of unpredictable or controlling conditions parents supply in a child's environment. An example is interrupting what children are doing without being aware of it and teaching them not to complete much of what they do. Or, you might do too much for your children and in the process teach them that they are not competent by themselves.

Yet, recognizing that children play a major role in their own development is important. They differ in their responses to the world. Some thrive when their families are a disaster of mistreatment, frustration, and discord. Others develop according to such dysfunctional conditions. In some families, children never match the expectations supplied by their family environment. They seem to lack the ability to do so. Others far exceed their conditions, defying the environment.

For us as parents, however, the best thing we can do is understand developmental tasks and know that we can positively influence how our children complete them by creating an environment that helps them. This idea is part of the real power you can have as a parent.

Using Your Power To Help Children Develop

An understanding of biological and environmental tasks helps us appreciate the real nature of childhood. Any observant parent can recognize and gain an appreciation for both. We admire and are sometimes in awe of the natural endowments our children bring with them. In other respects we are willing to work, teach, discipline, and train so that our children will become competent. In fact, we ourselves are still trying to complete inherited tasks and to gain competence in our world as we find it.

You will have greater power to be successful if you know and appreciate their inherited abilities and learn how to help them cultivate these abilities. Equally important, however, is that you create many of the early conditions children find in their environment. They will attempt to become competent in whatever environment you provide for them. This fact reaffirms your importance. We parents provide either a healthy family environment where children's development is encouraged or one where they find obstacles and difficulty.

As you begin to formulate a "parenting style" for yourself, consider what Lev Vygotsky, a Russian psychologist, thought. He acknowledged that children are born with their inherited abilities, which they seek to develop. He also recognized that parents offer the earliest and most instructive environment children ever know. He suggested that the two conditions create a "Zone of Proximal Development."

The range of development lies between what children bring with them and what conditions you supply. Consider the diagram on page 46. Think about this for a moment. Essentially, children will try to become competent at whatever conditions you create in your family environment. If you use high-quality language they will try to learn that type of language to communicate with you. If you use low-quality language, they will learn that. If you have excellent social skills, they will try to become competent in those areas, and so on.

Upper Level
Children's Environment
(What Parents Provide)

physical   mental   emotional

Zone of Proximal Development

language   social   moral

Lower Level
Biological Abilities
(What Children Inherit)

Further, we have learned that if a family environment matches the children's inherited abilities they are likely to be more successful than if the environment is a serious mismatch. In many cases, whether children complete their tasks and become as competent as possible depends on whether they can find appropriate opportunities—whether their experiences in learning match up with what they inherit. When this happy circumstance is realized, the results are usually remarkable.

Mozart's musical genius is legendary. His remarkable ability appeared early. At age four, he expressed irritation at and corrected other people's mistakes. These early abilities are evidence of inherited influences. Mozart's father and mother had strong music backgrounds and through their efforts created a fertile environment to match his inherited abilities. In him and others like him, we see the combination of inherited abilities matching up with opportunities to learn, producing extraordinary results. Even with different genetic possibilities, every child will benefit when natural abilities are matched with the right environment. Therefore, one skill we as parents will need is the ability to understand our children and organize a matching family environment.

Children do not work on all developmental tasks at the same time. They are trying to learn different qualities and abilities depending on their age. This means that part of your parenting style ought to include an understanding of children of different ages and stages so you can help them in each period of childhood. For example, children are born with the ability to look at, pay attention to, and respond to people. Language and emotional development give them improved social skills. Years later, going through puberty motivates them to become interested in heterosexual relationships. When it is time, they will leave to establish homes and families of their own. If they are successful, they will have completed their biological tasks and will have become competent during each of their life stages.

Understanding their tasks will help you identify their goals. Powerful parenting includes teaching, motivating, and preparing children for what is to come. This approach makes teaching and preparing much more important than trying to control. You will become your children's mentor—the person powerful enough to create lasting success. ❀

Chapter Three

THE POWER OF YOUR FAMILY ENVIRONMENT

Y our family environment is the sum of conditions supplied in the total mental, emotional, and physical family. All family members help create and live in this environment. Even though parents originate it and have a major role in deciding how it turns out, as children mature they have more influence in determining what happens. However, it is most useful to understand such an environment from the parental viewpoint because we are most interested in our own role.

The family is not simply a group of individuals who live together. This legal definition does little to help us understand the special role parents have in promoting child development. The family is the most powerful learning environment children ever participate in. Family environments are conditions set mainly by parents that affect children's growth. This is because the power of parenthood is in part derived by the fact that children are developing and growing. Parents want certain outcomes for their children and children want to become competent. These conditions emerge as you carry out hundreds of decisions while providing for financial survival, child care, living arrangements, community participation, education, and moral training.

It is possible to think about the family environment in a more simplified form. We can understand, for instance, that every family has five parts.

    1. Children who achieve developmental tasks

    2. Tasks or work requirements

    3. Relationships between parents and children

    4. Rule conditions

    5. Parents who provide leadership

The following diagram will help you remember the elements of the family environment.

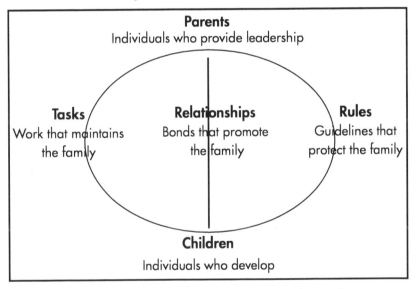

Parents
Individuals who provide leadership

Tasks
Work that maintains the family

Relationships
Bonds that promote the family

Rules
Guidelines that protect the family

Children
Individuals who develop

Earlier, I proposed that the power to help children to successful maturity begins with knowing about them. The best way to know about them is to understand each child from a developmental perspective. Once you have this knowledge and keep adding to it, you can begin to see how to organize your family to promote the types of developmental goals you want for your children so they can be happy and successful. This suggests something very practical for you. When faced with a problem to solve or a decision to make, it is generally a wise thing to begin by searching for information about your children. Further, if you wish to apply power successfully, frequently ask, watch, and communicate for the purpose of learning about them. Why? You may unintentionally create conditions that can harm your children. For instance, if you organize the work of your family in an unsuitable way, establish an inflexible or harsh rule system, or ignore your responsibilities to provide leadership, you risk your children's development. In any of these situations you will have failed to use your resources to give your children the greatest opportunities for success.

One reason most parents improve is because we have worked with our oldest child and increased our abilities to understand children and how they develop. But, if we knew beforehand what we learn from this child we could be successful with every child. If we had a set of practices designed to create a continuous learning program we would be able to refine what we do as our children develop, adapt it to changes we see in them, and use our power more constructively.

Your Developmental Perspective

Organizing a successful family requires that you learn about children, tasks, rules, relationships, and your leadership. Putting all these together well will add power to what you want for your children and give you better methods of influencing them. I have proposed that you acquire a developmental perspective which means that you understand the small tasks your children are working on. It is fairly easy to do this if you divide a child's life into the following five forms of development: (1) physical, (2) mental, (3) emotional, (4) social, and (5) moral. Let's review each of these types of development so you can become acquainted with them.

Physical development includes all things related to a child's body. Some of these are weight, height, walking, running, toilet training, health, sexual maturity, puberty, and gender characteristics. Most parents want their children to achieve all the physical skills and natural abilities they can. This will be one of your major areas of concern.

Social development is about friends, resolving problems together, talking and listening, membership in groups, and social skills such as cooperation and taking turns. You will spend considerable time and effort helping your children become socially competent.

Emotional development is about understanding our own feelings, recognizing what others feel, adapting how we show feelings to each situation, and developing more positive than negative feelings. If you have enough power, you can teach your children to love, to be happy, to be cheerful, warm, and affectionate.

Mental development involves intelligence, creativity, school achievement, memory, and the ability to make good decisions. It includes logic and imagination. You can learn how to promote the mental development of your children and see them enlarge their abilities as the result of what you do.

Moral development is about those important life lessons which help or harm people. It involves empathy, integrity, understanding what helps and hurts people, and regulating oneself to help others. As a parent you will face and make moral decisions about your children everyday.

When you understand some parts about each of these five types of development you will acquire a developmental perspective. This will help you organize your family environment in a way to help your children achieve success in each of these areas.

Family Work

The real power of parenthood is organized around what you understand about your children. After you develop abilities to do that and have acquired a certain amount of knowledge, the other parts of the family environment become the means by which you help them. For example, you have the family work that must be performed and which can be organized to promote or prevent children's growth. A family's work might include cleaning, cooking, repairing, landscaping, gardening, and outside employment.

Think about some of the family issues involving work. For instance, you can help children learn to work independently and be persistent until they are finished. You can develop a teaching method to help children learn to work, and in the process establish a mentor relationship with them. You can decide how much will be required, the standards of performance, how you reward or disapprove of their work, and how the work will be divided.

These factors will have a great effect on your children. Based on the way you approach the issue, children will—or will not—be influenced to be ambitious, learn to work independently, persist until they finish, have high standards, love to work, use work to build self-esteem, and develop a mature concept of work. Much of an adult's attitude toward performance and achievement was learned from the way work was created by his or her parents in his or her family.

Family Rules

In addition to the children whom we try to understand and the work of family life, most families usually have a set of rule conditions that can be applied to help or hinder children. There are two types of family rules. Formal rules are discussed and talked about openly, enforced by clear consequences, and applied to everyone. A curfew, putting toys away, and work before play are examples of formal rules.

On the other hand, informal rules are usually not talked about but emerge as part of family routines and are learned as "the way we do things around here." A family might learn informal rules because it develops a tradition for birthdays or holidays. Or, a parent might repeatedly remind children to be "efficient," thereby making efficiency an informal family rule.

Family rules exert great influence. There are properties about rules that deserve attention. Of course, as I have suggested they are used most constructively when they are applied to promote learning and development. Rules also become a basis for parents' judgment of children. You use rules to assess whether children are obedient or disobedient and measure them as "good" or "bad" kids. Using rules as a measure of judgment, however, has at least one potential problem. Rules may become the only or most prominent basis for judging someone else. For example, instead of understanding children from an emotional perspective or linking their behavior to their situation, it is possible for parents simply to create a rule and measure children by it.

On the surface this may seem like a good way to exert control over children. Quite often, just the opposite happens and parents lose the ability to influence. If rules are used extensively as the measure of performance, it is easy for children to learn they only have to appear to comply rather than "internalize" the underlying reasons for a rule's value. Many parents who use rules extensively, hoping children will be compliant, actually discover they have failed to help children develop the inner conditions necessary for moral behavior. In addition, suppose a child is "out of control," and the parental response is to increase the rules or the enforcement of them. Unless matched by equal concern for improving relationships, disobedient children become more disobedient, not less. We learn from this that rules are influential in children's lives, but they need to be used judiciously and combined with other forms of influence such as talking and teaching. All this needs to take place in the context of high-quality relationships where there is abundant love and communication.

Consider, for a moment, just a few alternatives available to us. For example, we can install rules ourselves without children's involvement or we can discuss them with children. We may have many rules or just a few. We can adapt the type and number of family rules to where we live. For example, we might have more rules if we live in a threatening environment than if we live in a place that is secure. We develop methods of teaching and enforcing rules. We must decide when to relax our emphasis on rules depending on our children's increasing maturity and ability to function on their

> **If used wisely, rules will be applied to promote some form of development in children.**

own. Some parents use rules to simply reinforce their authority over children, but if used wisely, rules will be applied to promote some form of development in children.

Family Relationships

Probably the most complex part of the family environment is the creation and management of relationships. This is because our communication, affection, and sense of attachment and belonging get caught up in our efforts to complete work, follow rules, and the time it takes to provide for our children. Like the other four parts of the family environment, however, we can participate with our children in relationships that create or prevent other growth opportunities. The possibilities are numerous and only a few alternatives are mentioned here to illustrate.

Relationships are about communication, emotional responses, attention and sensitivity, and the types of emotional attachments we form with the members of our family. There is a great deal of practical as well as scientific evidence, for instance, which indicates that parents and children form lasting emotional attachments. What is less well-known is that these attachments can be formed on positive as well as negative emotions. Mary Ainsworth, a researcher specializing in parent-child attachments, has demonstrated that parents and children can form an emotional tie on the basis of anxiety as easily as forming an attachment on the basis of security and love.

Consider a few other relationship possibilities. We can, for example, quickly react and judge children, or we can more patiently gather information and talk things through. We can communicate extensively or meagerly. We can display calm and confidence or panic and anger toward our children and teach them to respond to us in a like manner. We can show love and concern through verbal and physical attention or fail to show it because of indifference and neglect. Like many parents, we can also pay more attention to our children's work and rule compliance than to the importance of our relationships with them. Whatever we do will have lasting consequences for our children.

If we expect our children to leave home and establish lives for themselves, we should recognize that in the end all we have is the quality of the relationships we create while they are with us. We will find that "relational" experiences are those most vividly remembered by children.

Your Leadership

I have described five forms of development you may want for your children. I have described examples of work, rules, and relationships. Now, how it comes together, if it does, depends on the type of leadership you supply. This is not a neutral question or one that any parent should be passive about. You can create a family environment to stimulate or retard the development of your children.

Suppose you organize it by combining your powers to regulate children with great emphasis on teaching and nurturing them, providing positive work opportunities while warmly and consistently drawing them into positive communication and many forms of affection. This combination emerges when you know about children, acquire a developmental perspective, and then use it to organize work, rules, and family relationships.

Some or all of the five elements are involved in nearly everything you do. The five parts are present in any family activity or event. For example, eating a meal or going on a vacation involves performing some tasks, following rule conditions, understanding children, and participating in relationships among family members. It is easy to see that nearly every activity involves more than one element. When children make a mistake and something must be done, you will involve children, leadership, and your relationship with them. When you try to get children to perform their family tasks and use strategies to get chores completed, more than work is involved. It is important for you to recognize how the five elements are or may be integrated.

The point to remember here is that more than one thing is involved. The real power of parenthood depends on your understanding of how to put rules, relationships, and tasks together with what you know about your children. You may have several rules in your family, for example, or just a few. You will have your own method of forming and enforcing them. You might be strict or flexible. Your children might be obedient or disobedient and you will have some methods of approving when they comply and disapproving when they do not. As with family work, you spend a good portion of your time addressing specific rules and their application to your family. You will learn more about your children, apply parental leadership, and develop a positive or negative relationship depending on the way you apply rules in your family.

Consider a few other examples. All the parts of the family environment can and ought to be involved when you are solving conflict between two children, correcting misbehavior, teaching a child some new skill, and participating in recreation. These situations require that you adjust or vary the emphasis you give to each (e.g., we might emphasize rules more in one situation than in another), but they are all involved to some degree.

It is also important to note that the type of rules and work might change and diminish in importance as children mature, but the significance and the importance of family relationships actually increase. Because of this, family relationships should not be thought of as similar in importance to getting work done and getting compliance with the rules. The quality of your relationship takes on a much bigger and more important role. Family work and rules, therefore, could be organized to promote the quality of family relationships.

This idea suggests to us that we cannot use certain means to get children to work or to obey if it will excessively damage the relationship. These may include beating children, sexually or emotionally abusing them, lying to them, or rejecting them. All these justifiably create suspicion instead of trust, fear instead of love. If you do any of these you lose the power to influence your children toward a positive outcome. We can only use those means that promote healthy and positive family relationships. We cannot use undue force, coercion, or harshness to ensure that children get their work done without risking the quality of the relationship. We cannot ignore or be indifferent to their work or family rules either. We cannot be verbally or emotionally abusive to our children while hoping to communicate that our relationship with them is important to us. We are foolish to expect that mistreatment or neglect of children will influence them to comply with our rules or motivate them to work effectively.

While we are thinking about the family environment, it is also important to remember that these elements (rules, work, your leadership, understanding children, and parent-child relationships) create security for your children. They will attempt to become competent at what they find in your family environment. This idea has far reaching possibilities for you and for them. Your standards of language, emotional behavior, effective work, regard to rules, and social and relationship skills are the models children will pursue. It is not a secret that they are developing and growing toward some destination. It is also clear, as I have proposed, that at least one part of that growth is to become competent in the environment that parents supply.

Let's consider an example where parents have lost much of their power to influence their children. There is considerable research, for example, that suggests children are more likely to experiment with drugs and other controlled substances under two conditions: (1) when families overemphasize rules, which means parents have too many or enforce them too harshly and ignore the importance of quality family relationships; or (2) when parents fail to care enough to apply any rules.

You can imagine the rigidity in an environment where parents are excessively demanding about work and chores. It is easy to see how children may become "competent" at laziness or disorganization when parents do too much and make it unnecessary for them to achieve anything. Or, you can consider how parents may form relationships with their children which promote dependency and helplessness rather than self-efficacy and self-reliance.

All this supports the conclusion that much of parenthood involves interplay between work, rules, and relationships. How you sustain it over a period of years can significantly influence the personality development of your children. It can and does have both immediate and lasting consequences for them. The quality of their lives and achievement is significantly influenced by what happens in their family and often what happens moment to moment or day to day. This influence can be illustrated in the story of a friend who taught school. Every morning at school he asked his students to rate how happy their family was when they left that morning. He was able to establish a strong correlation between children's high performance and their families' happiness when they left home in the morning. Low performance was tied to the absence of affection or with family arguments.

To illustrate the positive power of how you organize your family, I am going to describe some examples of how the family environment can influence children in a negative way. This will serve to help you understand that the family never does nothing. It either moves children toward something positive or toward something negative. Children are, after all, trying to become competent at whatever their environment requires.

"The Hardworking Family"

A successful farmer said his childhood experiences consisted of a lot of hard work. He told how his father was "totally committed" to making their family farm a success. "We didn't have a lot of time to play," he said. Every day was filled with new assignments and each evening consisted of giving reports of what had been done and plans of what to do the following day. "When I was eleven years old," he said, "I remember trying to show my dad a puzzle I had finished putting together. He was talking on the phone at the time and I tugged on his arm to get his attention. He shook me off, but I tugged again because I real-

ly wanted him to see it. It was interrupting him. My dad shoved me and I fell backward to the floor. I remember looking up at him and realizing that whatever was important to me would never be important to him."

Eventually, what was important to the father became important to the son, who carried this same tradition into his marriage and family life. As an adult he knew little about creating positive relationships with his children. He did not understand the importance of his children's emotions, the need to play with them, or the quality of stopping work to spend time in other family activities. As he took over his father's farm it was soon clear that he too was "totally committed" to the work. He worked long hours and when his sons were old enough he taught them to do the same. They seldom took family vacations and he felt guilty if he went out for dinner or took time out to do something fun. After an argument with his wife over his treatment of his sons, she counted the number of times he became angry with them or with other family members. She counted seventy-seven times in one six-day period.

He was and is a good-hearted man who loves his wife and his children. His attempt to change, however, came too late to avoid a family tragedy. One day, he tearfully described working in the field on the tractor with his little daughter. He told how she grew tired and asked, "Daddy, I am tired. Would you please take me home?" He looked out at the field and estimated that he could finish it by working another forty-five minutes. He answered his daughter by saying, "In a few minutes, honey." A few minutes went by and she pleaded with him again, "Please, Daddy, take *me home. I am really tired." Shortly after, when the tractor made a sudden turn, she fell off and was killed.*

We can learn from this man's experience. In his own childhood, feelings and desires were considered less important than the work that was required. Work may sometimes be a valid priority but it is not usually so when children's needs are concerned. It might be that the indifference shown him when he was a child prevented him from considering his daughter's desire to be important. Had this accident not happened, he may never have thought twice about what he valued the most. Had she lived, however, the chance is still good she would have learned the same thing he learned during his childhood.

The ability to work and achieve is an important part of any successful person's life. However, where children and their development are concerned, work is not the most important thing. As I have proposed, achievement and the ability to accomplish goals is most useful when it serves to improve or maintain the quality of important family relationships.

"The Perfectionistic Woman"

In the previous example, the man's parents taught him to be a hard worker. This was a positive condition only if he had been taught to also value the importance of relationships. Other parents organize a family environment that strongly emphasizes family rules. They talk a great deal about rules, often to the exclusion of other things. They create many rules, perhaps too many, and occupy a lot of family time with their methods of enforcement. Sometimes they are overly critical or harsh. Their children attempt to become competent at understanding rules and complying with them. Sometimes children rebel against the rules, while others become overly submissive. In either case, rules occupy a great deal of attention. It was possible to see how this type of childhood experience influenced one woman.

She sat firmly upright. Her voice was clear, precise, and articulate. Every hair on her head was perfectly coifed and every article of clothing was immaculate. Her makeup was expertly applied—lipstick and eye shadow matched perfectly. She had matched her clothes with an elegant vengeance. To the casual observer, she had no flaws.

For years she had pretended well. Most people would not have guessed the feelings she had for her husband. Nor would anyone know that she made life miserable for them both and for their children by being demanding and exacting. As her husband said, "It wouldn't be so bad if there ever was some warmth or kindness." When pressed, he acknowledged that she was nice sometimes, but only after he had done something exactly as she required.

She was very unhappy with herself. Nothing ever seemed to be good enough, no matter how hard she tried and no matter how much her family members tried to please her. She had grown up in a family with numerous family rules. Her mother was a demanding, critical, and exacting authority figure. Whenever they went out in public she had to face her mother's inspection. On occasions when rules were not followed, her mother would not speak to her or display any type of affection for several days. She learned that identifying rules and complying with them was in her best interest. Her mother seemed to pay great attention to rules and measured her by her degree of compliance.

This woman brought a tradition of valuing rules more than anything else into her family because she had become competent at it. There are many good purposes for family rules, of course, but instead of focusing on promoting the healthy development of her children, she had focused on her anxiety about creating rules and insisting they be obeyed.

A Faulty Relationship Ideal

What happens when parents help create a family environment where work and rules are ignored? Sometimes this happens because parents have little energy or because they simply want to please their children by not requiring anything of them. Such an approach seems to reduce the pressure and stress of family life. The following example illustrates what happens when children become competent in a family where "relational" things are emphasized without giving enough consideration to work and rules.

He was a well-liked person. He got along with his neighbors and friends. He was pleasant and kind and would 'give you the shirt off his back.' He had a warm manner and all who met him were impressed. He was charming and could relate to people of any age.

He grew up as one of two children. His parents were in their mid-thirties when they married and were in their early forties when he was born. His older sister was six years older and, as the last child, he was considered the "favorite." His mother cared for him in the usual way by cleaning his room, cooking, and washing and ironing his clothes. He discovered early that she would do things for him if he complained of tiredness and said he "didn't want to do anything." His mother and dad attempted to get him to perform on occasion, but he argued and fought back. He was not generally a disobedient child, but there were so few rules or demands that there was little opportunity to be disobedient.

He married when he was twenty-three years old. He had completed high school and had some technical training which he had not completed. His work experience was sporadic. After trying several different jobs he told his questioning wife, "I am not able to find just the right job." There had been many marriage conflicts about his inability or unwillingness to find work, but despite these he had not worked in a good-paying job for fourteen years. Instead, he spent his time visiting with friends and "looking" for the right thing. He had tried making a few investments and had lost some money his wife had earned. He had gone into partnerships with other men who eventually quit on him. He said it wasn't his fault, of course. "Besides," he suggested, "I can find other people." A careful examination of his business ethics revealed a pattern of dishonesty and deception. He had never been caught, however, and said, "After all, it's no big deal."

In this man's world, a work ethic and a respect for rules were absent as he went about pleasing, placating, and exploiting other people. Apparently, his goal was only to avoid disapproval from others. He had a poor view of himself as a "worker," and he felt little value in complying with any rule condition that got in his way.

In this man's case, work and rules were not employed to achieve high-quality relationships with others. He did not feel compelled to provide for his wife and children but only to act as if he were trying. Like the previous examples, however, he had become competent in his family environment.

A Positive Family Environment

It is possible to learn several things from the foregoing examples. First, there are numerous types of families, each with its own unique environment. Second, regardless of what it is made up of, the family environment usually exerts tremendous influence on the way children develop. Third, we should remind ourselves that the influence is greater in positive or negative ways when children's inherited characteristics are matched by opportunities in their families.

For example, in recent years researchers have learned that infants demonstrate one of three temperaments. Some children are considered "easy" children because they soon develop a rhythm in sleeping and eating, enjoy affection, are mild in their emotional displays, and are fairly easy to comfort. Some children are labeled "slow to warm up" because they demonstrate fewer of these positive characteristics. Approximately ten to fifteen percent of all children are considered "difficult" because they demonstrate few if any of these positive characteristics.

Because these characteristics are demonstrated early, researchers believe they are inherited. The characteristics offer us an additional way to understand children and permit us to speculate what might happen if certain family environments are matched with certain types of children.

For example, think about what might happen to difficult children and their development if their family environment has exaggerated emphasis on compliance to rules or work and not enough attention is given to relationship conditions such as acceptance and patience. While we might not be too exact in our speculations, we still might be able to recognize this as a problematic combination. Where an "easy" child might be able to adapt to these conditions, a "difficult" child might feel harassed and frustrated. The combination of family environment and the child's inherited temperament might create difficulty for both the child and the family.

In our enlightened time of history, one would think that we would be able to recognize the combination of what children bring with them and the type of family environment we create. Many families do. Yet, sadly, many children have even worse experiences than those described previously. They live in family environments that present obstacles to their growth. These dysfunctional conditions can have lasting impact.

The organization of the family environment should create conditions that will positively influence children and help them succeed. A positive family environment is best for every type of child, whether "easy," "slow to warm up," or "difficult." These positive conditions can be created if parents are effective with rules, tasks, and relationships. If you have not come from traditions where this is the case, it is still possible to learn.

We recognize that we will face misbehavior, inadequate learning, and slow development. Nevertheless, we are committed to the idea that our central tasks are to provide experiences, actively teach and nurture children, and supply attractive examples of what children could and should become. This parental approach is also positive because it gives greater emphasis to pleasant and positive emotions. There is more love than anger or fear, more cheerfulness than despair, and more encouragement and support than criticism.

This parental approach is based on the idea that we as parents acquire authority and the power to exert leadership, not by our larger size or our ability to impose control, but by virtue of our skills and the fact that we apply them to promote the development of our children. This does not mean that to be a "good" parent we must be totally skillful or do everything perfectly. Families are imperfect environments where people are growing, learning, and trying to become better. In that sense, we undergo a great deal of development and growth along with our children.

The evidence is clear and abundant, however, that the families that are best at promoting children's growth and development are those with strong and powerful parental leadership. Among the first things these parents do is recognize their family as a source of learning unequaled by any other place or situation. They organize the family to provide survival, support, and opportunities to learn. Then, they skillfully promote the growth of their children by using available work, rule conditions, and relational experiences.

Read the following examples. They illustrate how parents use their power to organize a family environment that helps children grow. These examples include social, emotional, moral, mental, and physical development.

Social Development

Mary was worried about beginning preschool. She was excited about it, but didn't want to go when it was time. Instead of getting mad at her, Mary's mother talked with her and reminded her of the times they had played school. The mother explained that Mary was a smart, friendly girl and that the other children would like her. She knew how to share, cooperate, and help others.

Social success depends on the ability to share, cooperate, negotiate differences, and understand others. Positive parenting means focusing on and teaching these skills and helping children to achieve them.

The Jarveks developed a family practice of shutting off the television at least two nights every week. During these evenings they talked together, played games, and tried to make the evenings enjoyable. Sometimes they used these times to have conversations and make decisions. As their children grew older the parents requested their children to "talk it over" as a method of solving problems or correcting misbehavior.

Social development includes the ability to talk with different types of people in many different situations. Family conversations invite children to learn conversation and other social skills.

Emotional Development

A six-year-old boy named Todd often became "hyper" when confronted by new situations such as meeting strangers. Also, he demonstrated rapid mood changes from happy to angry. His mother decided to help him get in control of himself by showing him what control meant. She had him practice getting "in control," and rewarded him for being able to regulate himself. While doing this she explained that if he could not control himself he would have to sit in the "quiet chair" until he could. Later, whenever Todd was "out of control," she told him to get "in control" and placed him on the chair if he could not. He gradually improved his ability to do so.

Mature individuals regulate their emotional behavior. Parents need to know which displays of emotion are acceptable and which displays are not. They can then teach and enforce emotional limits where children learn to regulate themselves. To do this, parents can set an example, create a rule, or simply pay attention and encourage positive displays and discourage the negative.

Robbie often came to breakfast in a bad mood. He complained about the food and about other family members. In addition, he would sometimes show sadness and unhappiness without a good reason for these feelings. Then he would spend long periods in his room without talking with anyone. His mother met him before breakfast and talked cheerfully and showed affection. His dad recognized his sad feelings and talked encouragingly with him and sometimes "horseplayed" with him to change his feelings. It took a while, but Robbie learned more positive feelings.

Positive parenting is to develop a set of transforming activities designed to alter negative emotions into positively-toned emotions. Instead of showing frustration and anger at children and their moods, positive parents ruffle their children's hair, talk cheerfully and encourage them, show real empathy toward them and their situation, whisper love and sweet nothings, and invite children to talk about what they feel.

Moral Development

Jenny planned her birthday party and wanted to invite all but one neighbor to it. Jenny's mother talked with her and asked why she didn't want to invite Gail. Jenny explained that Gail was not liked by some of the other girls. Jenny's mother asked her to think about how Gail would feel if she were the only one not invited. She also asked her to think about how Gail would feel if she were included. Then, she asked Jenny to explain how her choice would help or harm Gail.

Parents use children's decisions to teach about what helps or harms other people. In this way, children learn their actions have consequences for themselves and others. Plus, parents can show equal concern for what children do, the rules which may apply, and the relationships children have with other people. This is the essence of moral development.

Jed came home long past curfew. James, Jed's dad, asked him to talk about his reasons for being late. During the conversation, James asked Jed to explain the consequences for other people (i.e., Jed's girlfriend, her parents, and Jed's parents) and about the benefits of the family rule. Jed had a chance to talk about his belief that the family rule no longer applied to him. James asked if Jed was willing to demonstrate his ability to be responsible if he were willing to change the rule. They worked out an agreement which included Jed having to describe his plans and tell the time he intended to come home. If he responsibly did what he said, James agreed to eliminate the rule for most nights.

Parents help children understand the value of rules as they apply to helping or harming themselves and other people. In addition, parents adjust rules to fit children's level of maturity and responsibility. Both events promote moral development.

A sixteen-year-old girl named Heather worked after school at a bakery. Sometimes, especially during holidays, she was required to work late. One night, while working late, a thick fog enveloped their town and her neighborhood. Since all the customers were talking about how dangerous the fog was, Heather grew increasingly worried that she would have difficulty driving home. Her boss let her leave a little early because of her concern. As she went outside to get into her car, she noticed her father's pickup truck was parked right behind her car. He smiled and waved. She drove home with her father's bright fog light guiding the way.

Because of our intimate knowledge about our children, we can provide them with "emotional validation." This ability to give correct, matching responses is one of the most valuable parental skills. Validation recognizes children and lets them know of our care, concern, love, and understanding. Appropriate responses to what we know about them and their situations create lasting, emotional memories.

Mental Development

Jerry Henderson, a single parent, made a practice of being with his children during their evening meal. He brought up topics to discuss that included ideas about government, social issues, and their beliefs and values. He questioned their ideas and challenged them to evaluate what they said. They soon learned to challenge his ideas, too. The family had many interesting and stimulating discussions.

Questioning strategies are first learned in family communication. By teaching children to question, to challenge themselves, and to learn, this parent promoted their mental development in school, at work, and during creative and innovative time. He was promoting mental development and building better relationships with his children.

The Westerbergs started reading to their children shortly after they were born. They knew their children could not understand their words, but knew their voices would be stimulating, even to newborns. As their children grew, these parents continued to read to them and continued their own personal reading activities. Eventually, they took their children to libraries, museums, and on small "field trips."

Mental development is enhanced when parents take an active role in teaching about ideas. This may include reading or any other school subject. Mostly, parent companionship and involvement lets children know of the great value parents place on learning and developing their mental abilities.

Physical Development

After their oldest child was twelve, Jim and Sue Johnson were more confident about being parents. They had watched their oldest child's growth from year to year and had learned to look forward to each new event. They used what they had learned with him and applied it to their other children. They recognized the signs of their son's impending puberty in enlarged feet, acne, and a voice change. They encouraged him to be patient because he was growing into something really neat.

Helping children become strong, get exercise, and develop their physical abilities is a familiar family theme. It is positive when parents help their children understand their own growth and what to expect. This gives children positive attitudes about the changes they have made and will make.

Alex was four-and-a-half years old. His birthday was in the middle of September. His parents decided to delay sending him to kindergarten because he was somewhat smaller than other boys in preschool. Even though they thought him mentally able to perform well, he was not able to run or throw as well as the other boys.

Physical development is tied to all other forms of development. If it is slow, other forms of development will be slow, too. Further, during childhood social and emotional opportunities are especially linked to physical abilities. These parents made a good decision allowing Alex time to grow so that he would receive the most benefit from school opportunities.

The foregoing examples are likely to be found in any family. They are used here to show how one or more parts of the family environment are involved in every parent-child incident. Further, their purpose is to show how parents can exert their leadership to teach, organize, and otherwise promote their children's development. These five areas of growth and learning are basic to any child's life. Promoting them for children is the real and most significant purpose for a family. Lastly, there are many different good ways to respond to each situation. You have a great deal of flexibility in how you do it. If you act with skill to provide positive leadership, however, you can create a fun, loving, and enjoyable family at the same time you are helping your children learn and develop.

Adapting the Family Environment

We have identified two types of developmental tasks. One is the biological motivation to fully and successfully complete inherited abilities. To help, we can recognize what is inherited and create conditions that allow completion to take place. The other type of task is for children to become competent within an environment. We can help by recognizing the power of example, imitation, nurturing, teaching, and the very conditions we create as part of family life. Both completion and competence are fueled by tremendous motivation.

We have also learned about the five parts of the family environment that make up the first and most influential environment to which children are exposed. In some respects, this environment may be unique for each family. There may also be similarities in every family. This is because of the type of leadership we supply as parents. Our style of leadership emerges by the way we understand our children, organize and participate in the family work, rules, and relationships. How we organize the family environment will determine how well we help or harm the growth of our children.

Now it is time to put the two ideas together. Obviously, we begin by understanding our children. If we want to promote their development, we need to understand what they are working on. In other words, we need to know our children's developmental goals at each stage of their lives. Quite often, when we are faced with a problem or difficult decision we will do almost anything else before we recognize that the solution might come from the children themselves if we are willing to focus on them and deepen our understanding of them. There are at least five types of information we need to know about them. We must understand their emotional, mental, social, physical, and moral characteristics. When we can get an accurate view of a child's current situation and the development we hope they make, we will find solutions to problems and answers to difficult questions.

Suppose, for example, one of our children will not share with his friends and has difficulty taking turns during playtime. We recognize this is common for many young children but that positive social development requires these forms of behavior. We will be more likely to find some way to teach and encourage sharing than simply punishing children for misbehaving.

What would be a useful solution to the situation where a child hits other children or is otherwise physically hurtful? The most common responses include scolding, restricting a privilege, spanking, criticizing, or isolating the child for a "time out." These methods focus on misbehavior but by themselves do not promote any positive learning, which is necessary for social, emotional, and moral development. We may disapprove of a child's behavior, but a lasting solution to this situation will consist of something more than punishment. It will include some form of teaching experience where the child improves his emotional control and realizes the positive consequences for learning not to hit when he is frustrated. Positive parenting usually includes an active teaching and nurturing response to help children learn.

The foregoing solutions are possible because we combine what we know about children with what we want them to learn or develop. Then we use our parental leadership to organize the family to ensure that a child develops improved abilities. We can, for example, organize our family for the long term and respond effectively to specific situations as they arise.

In this effort, scientific research and common sense have come together to propose a method of adapting the family environment to the ages and abilities of our children. This method is based on the following four adaptation principles: (1) the maturity principle, (2) the preparation principle, (3) the "goodness of fit" principle, and (4) the balance principle.

It is worth noting that a new measure of parental success is being identified. It is not how well you control
children or how much you give them. It
is not the amount of affection you have
for each other, the amount of hard work
they do, or the level of their achievement. It is none of these by itself. Parental

Adaptation Principles:
1. Maturity
2. Preparation
3. "Goodness of Fit"
4. Balance

success requires these considerations to be tied closely with
helping children develop and learn. Successful parental
leadership is measured by our ability to adapt our family
with these four principles in mind. As you read further,
you will see that these principles are familiar and fairly
easy to understand. They have typically not been given the
credit they deserve.

When parents and children are successful by any responsible measure, it is usually because parents have applied
these principles successfully. However, because they seem
such a natural part of family life many of us fail to recognize
their true importance. Instead, we need to pay full attention to them because they allow us to adjust and adapt our
family to the developmental needs of individual children.

In an earlier chapter, I described the enhanced results
for Mozart when his natural abilities were matched by a
family environment that helped or fostered them. This, of
course, can be contrasted with a situation where the conditions in the family do not match a child's abilities and

may frustrate the child instead. If growth does occur it will be in spite of rather than because of the family.

The adaptation principles are guidelines that help us do a better job of linking what we know about our children at various stages with the family conditions that will help them the most. The following idea can be confirmed in virtually all conditions where the survival and success of living creatures and people are involved. Development and growth are enhanced when an individual's natural abilities find an appropriate opportunity for stimulation and expression in the environment.

1. The Maturity Principle

Our children benefit when our family environment matches and contributes to accomplishing their current developmental tasks. They will have opportunities to learn from people who recognize and respond to their needs in situations organized in their interests. Sometimes this is difficult because children work on different tasks at different stages of their lives. This requires us to keep up with and recognize their changing level of maturity.

In contrast, more conflict and difficulty occur when there is a sizable mismatch between our family environment and a given child. Most family conflicts simply signal the need to make adjustments. It would be a useful thing if all parents understood conflict in this way. Where there is a mismatch between individual and the conditions in the environment, there is conflict. If there is no change, the conflict will continue and growth will be limited. It is important therefore, for us to prepare for and expect the need to adapt our family as children mature.

The first adaptation principle, which will be familiar to all but the newest parents, is to adapt our family according to the age and maturity of our children. This is the maturity principle. It simply suggests that we adapt our family environment based on our children's increased maturity. This means that we have focused on the children and recognized added maturity. Then we use our parental leadership to adapt the work, relationships, and rules in the family. We will see, for example, that families go through developmental cycles much like individuals do. In each of these family stages, we can see children at different levels of maturity.

Family Beginnings

This stage begins when our first child is born and lasts through the fifth year. Children have many developmental tasks during this period, including gaining control of physical movement (e.g., crawling, walking, and running), identifying gender concepts, mastering language, and learning social and emotional skills. Parents provide basic care, experiment to develop a discipline plan, and implement family chores and rules. Parent leadership emerges as parents try to balance work, rules, and relationships.

Conditions in the family are designed to match the abilities of children five years old or younger. This means we will have work, rules, and relationships that are appropriate to the emotional, social, physical, mental, and moral abilities of our children at this time of their lives. We can, if we choose, organize our family to ensure that children achieve some developmental goals in each of these areas.

Family Consolidation

This stage begins when the oldest child approaches six years of age and continues through his or her eleventh year. Developmental tasks include improving physical abilities, social and emotional skills, abilities to reason and think, and moral reasoning and judgment. At this stage, parents organize family traditions and develop plans to consolidate the family so everyone has a sense of belonging.

This requires that we make some adjustments in the way we participate in family work, relationships, and rules. We adapt to promote and take advantage of improved abilities. For example, children are capable of more work, increased responsibilities, and more adult communication. Adapting the family environment enhances these abilities.

Family Flexibility

During this period, parents must cope with great variation. The oldest child is between twelve and eighteen, which means that the other children will be in their various developmental stages. The family needs an elastic organization in order to adjust to new demands. Children in this period have developmental tasks which include becoming reproductively mature, learning about emotionally intimate relationships, making decisions, and acquiring a personal concept of morality. We can adjust our family environment to give added emphasis to relationships. Work and rules may be adjusted to promote the children's development as well.

Family Launching

The first child prepares to leave home. This begins a process in which children go and return. Their developmental tasks include increasing personal competence, selecting a mate, choosing a career, and forming new networks of friends and acquaintances. We can adapt the environment to encourage going and coming by making use of each opportunity to solidify the family and emphasize love and warmth.

Most of us understand the need to make adjustments as our children mature and try to do so even if it is difficult. The importance of making adjustments is often better illustrated by negative examples. One young man, for instance, reported that his father was displeased with something he had done and grounded him from his car. This is a strategy appropriate for someone fairly young. It was not very useful for this son who was twenty-four years old and married!

Adjusting is not easy for many of us, and is clouded by the fact that it is easy to be emotionally blinded when our children take on new and more mature characteristics. We invest deeply felt emotions in our children and often watch their growth with mixed feelings of delight, pride, and apprehension. This may be the case with youngest children (or with an only child) where we might hope to keep children as young as possible for as long as possible.

There are other examples of the difficulty some parents have in adjusting to their children's increased maturity. It is more important, however, that we have examples of how to be successful so we can be successful ourselves. Examples of successful adaptation fill the remainder of this book.

2. The Preparation Principle

Knowing that you have to adapt your family as your children mature brings another adaptation principle to mind. This is the preparation principle. Like the others, this principle is highly significant and can add many new parental options. In one sense, it means that part of a parent's task is to prepare children for each subsequent stage of life. That is, to help them successfully make the transition from "Family Beginnings" to "Family Consolidation," and so forth. If children are prepared they will be more successful at learning and developing a new set of developmental tasks for each age and stage. We can help by preparing them for what is to come.

The preparation principle has another, more practical meaning. It can become the basis for our discipline and child management because preparing and teaching children how to do something well is more important than controlling or punishing them for misbehavior. We can apply this idea to parental leadership in two ways:

(1) Organize an active teaching and training program in which we nurture and prepare children, helping

them succeed. Numerous possibilities range from teaching social skills, work habits, and rule compliance, to teaching about sex, morality, academics, and so forth.

(2) **Use children's misbehavior as evidence that they have something to learn and require them to learn it as part of the consequence for misbehavior.** Doing this means that we do something in addition to (or in place of) traditional punishments such as spanking, scolding, lecturing, restricting privileges, or sending the children to their rooms. The preparation principle suggests that the best form of punishment is to require children to learn to do the correct thing (instead of what they did).

Applying these forms of preparation creates a family climate that focuses on development. It is a positive discipline approach that prepares children for success and helps them make smooth and safe transitions from one stage to the next. When children display the characteristics of advanced maturity, we feel that we have helped with this effort and take a reasonable amount of pride in what they (and we) have accomplished.

Over and over again, many successful adults attribute their success to time and teaching given by caring parents who prepared them. It may have been in an area like sports, music, or academic achievement. We can also prepare our children emotionally, socially, morally, and mentally for what is to come and help them be successful in these areas, too.

3. The "Goodness of Fit" Principle

We are usually surprised when we learn how different our children are from one another. Sometimes we can hardly believe that two siblings have the same parents. These differences usually appear early in infancy. Just how unique and different each child is from the others, however, usually emerges over a period of years. Physical characteristics like height, weight, hair color, and eye color are easy to recognize, as are some of the more obvious emotional styles and mental abilities.

The fact that children are unique and thus different from one another places an added burden on us. In order to promote our children's development, we need to adapt our leadership and other parts of the family environment to achieve a "good fit" with the individual characteristics of each child.

Many think that parents become more flexible as we gain experience. This is especially true for older children. Rather than being lax with family rules, however, this usually means that parents are better at adapting because we have learned from our experiences. This flexibility is useful, but not entirely effective unless we focus on the children and learn how to constructively fit what we do individually for each of our children.

Applying the "goodness of fit" principle means that we pay attention to and understand how each child is unique. It means that we know about the family environment and how to make adjustments in it. When a "good fit" exists, it will be easier for children to accept and respect our leadership and feel comfortable as members of the family. Children immediately sense and understand that what we do is (or is not) related to them. Therefore, their compliance and participation is often related to whether they think family conditions are applied to them.

Many children accuse their parents of "not being fair" when parents treat them differently. Sometimes, we feel guilty as a result of this accusation and try to give and do the same things for every child. Because of all the differing and competing needs among our children, it is generally better for us to respond to this accusation by telling our children we do not intend to be fair. At least not if fairness means that we treat all children alike. Where there might be the need to give material goods on some equal basis, it is a fairly foolish thing to expect to treat all children the same. One child needs more control while another needs less. One needs more social time while another benefits from time alone. The differences are so many it is not possible to catalogue them all. Therefore, we can make only one conclusion. The most effective thing is to find some way to communicate to each child that we recognize his or her uniqueness and are willing to adapt if we can.

The Smith family made a successful adjustment to make a good fit with one of their children. She was a bright, creative girl. She displayed this early when at four years of age she began tinkering with the piano. She would use two hands and make up her own little tunes. When she was seven years old, she started piano lessons just as her older siblings had. She learned rapidly, progressing in a climate of encouragement and firm expectations. She often created her own music.

As time passed, her music began to take shape, and at eleven years of age she submitted an original composition to a contest supported by the public schools. She performed this music in public and was a state finalist in the contest. However, she began to spend more and more time composing and less and less time practicing. She claimed she hated to practice, and she had to be reminded and pushed to do it.

What should her parents do? All the children in the family took lessons and practiced until they were seventeen or older. Her parents decided to make an adjustment. Having some musical background, they understood the difference between performing music and composing it. They were more interested in their daughter's growth than anything else, so they contacted someone who was willing to teach composition and would help their daughter improve her skills. For a while, she increased the amount of time she spent playing, but it was because she was composing, not practicing. Eventually, she discontinued playing the piano except for personal pleasure.

4. The Balance Principle

Successful people know how to work and how to enjoy what they do. They are able to establish and maintain high-quality relationships. They obey appropriate rules or laws. These three conditions are an important part of life and deserve emphasis in our families from the time children are young to the time they depart.

When all three of the above conditions have their rightful place, our children will become competent at them.

They will learn to work and achieve independently. They will learn about communication, affection, problem solving, empathy, and love. They will also learn about good and bad rules and will decide to obey those rules that help themselves and other people.

Our family work, rules, and relationships are the conditions we use to promote development in our children. They are the tools that help children learn moral concepts, emotional skills, social behavior, and mental abilities. None of the three, therefore, is unimportant. It is useful, however, for us to vary the amount of emphasis we give to ensure that we adapt successfully.

If we do not provide our children with a balanced environment, they may learn negative lessons. Due to unbalanced environments, some children do not learn about organization and achievement. Some are lacking in social and relationship skills. Some have conflict and frustration with rules and the people who enforce them. The choices that they make later in life will reflect their competence in some areas as well as their lack of development in others. Some children work long and hard and ignore their relationships, while some ignore the rules or their work. Some enter every situation and participate by making certain they know the rules and insist that other people do, too.

Successfully modifying your family environment means that you ensure a balanced emphasis on work or achievement, relationships, and rule conditions. Organizing and solving the interplay between these three conditions will occupy much of your parenting efforts. As I have suggested, parental leadership emerges as we address these parts of family life. The balance principle suggests that all are important and deserve their place in what we do.

When we use a balanced approach we avoid being too extreme in any one area. Most of us want children who are successful in all three areas. Since we teach them to our children it is important that we examine ourselves to ensure our leadership includes each area equally.   ❀

Family Environment

The family environment is made up of the conditions parents create for their children within the family unit. A family is a group of people who live together for extended periods of time and depend on each other for survival, emotional well-being, growth, and development. Because these important things take place within the family environment, families exert great influence on both parents and children.

Your family is the environment to which your children bring their inherited abilities and where they seek to develop them. You can be more effective as parents if you skillfully organize your family and provide an environment that both supports and gives opportunities to your children.

In some respects, every family is the same. In other respects, every family is unique. First, we will consider the similarities every family shares with all others. Later, we'll discuss how and why they are unique. Every family environment consists of five parts :

1. Tasks or Work: These include family chores, parents' jobs or careers, and how the work is planned, organized, and performed.

2. Rule Conditions: These are formal or informal guidelines that regulate children and parents as they perform work and participate in family and social relationships.

3. Family Relationships: These include actions family members display toward each other such as displays of feelings, communication, and support and sacrifice.

4. Children Who Develop: Children develop competence and complete developmental tasks.

5. Parents Who Exert Leadership: Parental leadership includes the way parents choose to get the work done, establish and enforce rules, and participate in relationships.

Family Environment Case Studies

The following case studies describe situations that any parent might face. While reading them, notice that work, rules, and relationships are all involved. How parents respond will indicate to the children what part or parts of the family environment they should pay attention to.

Case 1: The Curfew

Susan and Bill Arnold were parents of a sixteen-year-old girl. Most of the time their daughter was like other kids her age. She was doing average or above in school, had good friends, and generally cooperated around the house. When she started dating Randy, her behavior changed a little. She seemed quite caught up with him and excitedly talked about him in glowing terms. Susan and Bill were happy for her and enjoyed watching her learn about feelings, boys, and relationships. Soon, however, she started to violate the family curfew time of 10 p.m. on school nights, 1 a.m. on Fridays, and midnight on Saturday nights. Both parents talked with her and she agreed to do a better job of coming in on time. For a few days she was better, but one Wednesday night she came home at 11:45 p.m., nearly two hours late. Bill was up waiting for her, and, as most fathers would, felt both concern and frustration because she was not keeping her promise.

Consider his options. What is Bill emphasizing if he:
  a. Tells her she is grounded for a week?
  b. Explains that she will be too tired to do well in school tomorrow?
  c. Shows his relief that she if safe and hugs her?

What could he do to ensure that rules, work, and relationships are all involved?

Case 2: The Angry Twins

Bobby and Sam are twins. Bobby is taller and is a better athlete than Sam, but Sam does better in school. They argue quite a bit, and for ten year olds, their arguing sometimes gets quite heated.In the past when this has happened they have gotten mad, called each other names, hit each other, and broken things of value to the other.

What should their parents do?
  a. Form a rule against fighting and if the rule is broken impose a major consequence?
  b. Assume the twins are not busy enough and impose more work for them to do?
  c. Stop the fighting whenever it begins and make the twins learn new relationship skills before they have any privilege?
  d. What else is possible?

Explain: How does your decision incorporate work, relationships, and rules?

Chapter Four

CLEAR AND CONSISTENT
LEADERSHIP

There are many names for what parents do. You might think of yourself as a disciplinarian, a child manager, a teacher, a coach, an errand service, a friend, a mentor, a servant, and/or an audience. You might be all of these from time to time. The success of your children, however, may depend on how well you are able to understand that you can and should be something else. To acquire the real power of parenthood and use it successfully it is necessary for you to think of yourself as a person who supplies family leadership. I am not certain why this role has been given less attention than the others. Perhaps it is because as a freedom-loving people we are not fully comfortable with the idea that parents do and should have power where their children are concerned. Maybe it is because we are busy reacting and responding to what our children do and often feel much more like a follower or handmaiden instead of someone who provides leadership. Where growing and developing children are concerned, however, it is the idea of leadership that stands out as the preeminent need.

An effective leader has a vision of where to go and how to achieve it. Rather than stand on the sidelines, through his or her example, such a person is involved in working along side those who follow in the enterprise of living. A successful leader motivates others to accept this vision, believe in it, and organize plans to achieve it. Such leadership also monitors progress and keeps everyone focused on what is the most important, encouraging, correcting course, and on recognizing real achievement. It has the power to salve life's wounds, restore belief and hope when there is discouragement, and enable others to find and fully develop their talents and abilities. True leadership inspires commitment from others because it supplies a unique blend of freedom to make decisions while expecting responsibility. When all these are done in the name of love and care, parental leadership has as much, if not more, power than any other situation including government and business.

Leadership, especially parental leadership, is a form of behavior so important that both those who lead and those who follow pay close attention to it. It is so influential that we often describe it in moral overtones evaluating when it is good or bad. When it is good, more is done for families than would be the case if there were no leadership. But when it is bad, more harm is done for longer periods of time than most of us imagine. In most cases the consequences of bad parental leadership last for several generations. This is because the outcomes and objectives of parental leadership are found in the personal characteristics of human beings.

This is why it deserves a thoughtful and thorough examination. It is generally accepted that parents have the first and most profound influence on their children. This does not mean that children do not exert their share of influence on us or that they are not influenced by their genetic make-up. Both of these are the case. It is still true, however, that parents exert enormous influence even if you cannot determine exactly how your children turn out. It is often the case that many of us do not fully understand leadership. If you are a parent it is not possible to *not* exert influence on your child.

Birth parents who may never actually see a child before it is adopted often think and wonder about the child for years. Then to end the wonder, a child who has become an adult will spend time and resources to find a person he or she has no memory of. Those of us who have the opportunity of rearing our children to adulthood soon learn there are two levels of influence we have on our children. One is the positive things—like love and discipline—they gain from our association with them, our example, and our teachings. The other is the negative things—like fear, anger, and mistrust—they learn from our mistreatment of them. When you are committed and skillful you can fill your children's lives with many more positive and constructive things than what is negative. When you are not, their lives may have the pain and suffering or emptiness inflicted on them through mistreatment. Like leadership in other situations, the application of parental power is a moral issue. There is very little that is neutral. That is why you need to examine the quality of your leadership and learn how to earn the right to apply authority through responsible behavior designed to help instead of harm your children.

I was reminded of this when I visited with a father, mother, and their adult daughter. The daughter had not seen her father for seven years. At seventeen she told a school counselor that he had been abusing her since she was eight years old. The authorities were called in, the father was imprisoned, and the courts placed an injunction on him which prevented him from contacting her. This meeting was held at her request as an attempt to put past pain behind her.

Everyone was nervous. I asked him about his expectations. He began by telling he hoped to have a relationship with her in the future. As he spoke I listened to him focus again on what he wanted without much concern for her. I respectfully interrupted him and asked if he would like to start over. Humbly, he asked to know what he could do differently. I proposed that he think of her and what she needed most at this important moment. This, I suggested was an acknowledgment of all he had done, a true apology from him, and a plea for her forgiveness. He began again acknowledging that he was at fault for all that he had done. He mentioned briefly that he had himself been abused when a child but, to his credit, he did not attribute what he had done to the mistreatment of others. He continued on in his statements that he had "robbed her of her childhood," that he had been a person who "took pleasure in the suffering of others," that he was excessively controlling. He acknowledged that he had learned that because of what he had done, she had been unable all her life to go swimming without worrying about him, have a sleep-over with friends without worrying about him, go to bed without worrying about him. Then with tears streaming down his face he told how sorry he was and pled for her forgiveness.

While he was describing what he had done to hurt his daughter, he was also stating what he had not done to teach her all the good and wonderful things a father could bring into his child's life. He did not remind her of happy memories they had shared, positive lessons they had learned, or warm moments that had filled both of their lives. Apparently there were not many to mention. He did not tell of the times when he had loved her, listened to her, or encouraged her when she was lonely or disappointed. There did not seem to be many of these moments. As he talked she sat stone faced, unable or unwilling to know how to respond. She was not angry, nor was she warm and interested. She was coldly indifferent. Their initial conversation did little to shrink the chasm between them. He discovered that much, much more would be required to achieve the greatest outcome he could think of: her simple warmth and her peaceful acceptance of him as her father.

Parental Leadership Is More Than Discipline or Communication

Parental leadership is much more than a disciplinary plan or a program of communication. Sometimes parents get caught up in whether to spank a child or not, whether to use a certain form of punishment, or how to talk or listen. A form of punishment or communication is an important decision, but very limited. How you discipline or communicate is only a part of a leadership plan and probably should not be thought of as all you do or need to do. The value of any disciplinary or parental practice is measured by its ability to contribute to a child's development and growth. That is the true essence of parental leadership.

The outcomes or results you probably want are numerous pleasant family activities, personal fulfillment from the experience, and children who mature well and when they leave your home are ready to live successful lives of their own. To achieve these you may be willing to do the cleaning, organizing, errand running, teaching, and so forth that comes with the territory. In all you do, however, as a leader you will never be entirely free from thinking about the need to focus on your children and promote their development. If it is successful, your leadership will result in advancing and enhancing their growth.

There are not many other examples of leadership which can be used as valid comparisons with what parents do. A business executive, for instance, works toward revenue and implements practices designed to maximize efficiency. Parents often allow inefficiency so children have opportunities to learn. Our goals are internal characteristics rather than some external reward. The leadership of school administrators is aimed at test scores and proper conduct which reflect a certain type of learning. Parental leadership is focused on both natural experience and the type of learning desired by schools. Government and political leaders implement programs and activities with an eye toward public opinion and public welfare. Parents are often required to do things which are not popular but which they believe their children need. Clearly, parental leadership is linked to children and to families, and the purpose of it is growth, learning, development, opportunity, and

> **Parental leadership is focused on both natural experience and the type of learning desired by schools.**

the elaboration of talents and abilities. I have proposed that this type of parental leadership begins when the parents find the power of it to acquire a developmental perspective for their children and combine this with skill in organizing and adapting their family environment to promote moral, physical, mental, social, and emotional development.

The Importance of Being Clear

Being clear about your leadership means that you have an understanding of what you, as parents, want your children to become. They will have their opinions and desires which may or may not be the same. You will need to accommodate their desires for themselves. When you are clear about what you want, however, it helps you be more consistent with what you do. This means that whenever you have a problem with a child or are organizing some family program or activity, you can begin by thinking through and deciding what you "want" for your children and what you think they need. In order for leadership to be "clear" it is focused on desirable development you are promoting or working toward. Having a very clear idea about the growth and development you want for a child will provide direction for you as you try to solve problems, when you correct misbehavior, when you teach, and when you organize the rules, relationships, and work of your family.

Being clear about what you want provides the second necessary form of parental knowledge. The first is to know your own children and how they develop. The second is knowing what you want for your children. Knowing what you want and knowing about child development can prevent you from making common parental mistakes. These mistakes include making decisions or acting toward your children in ways harmful to them. When you are not clear about what you want for them or fail to understand how to promote their development you are more likely to be too harsh, get upset, or fail to do what helps them. You may be uninvolved when you need to be, or over-involved when they need more space. These errors of judgment or undesirable behavior usually result when the powerful emotions few of us are prepared for meet our lack of knowledge about children and our lack of clarity about what we want. Most of us regret these mistakes and wish we could avoid them and do something better. But until you know about children and are clear about what you want for them you may often repeat what you don't want to. Your mistakes may demoralize and make you think you are incompetent. Sometimes rather than feel the guilt and apprehension which accompany these thoughts, like other parents, you may withdraw, thinking maybe it would be better if someone else raised your children. It is better that you solve these feelings by learning about children and identifying what you want for them.

Clarity about what you want for your children helps produce feelings of self control because you will know what you are working toward instead of feeling powerless because you do not know. Plus, being clear about what you want for your children will help you find a good balance between what you want and what your children want for themselves. You will be able to talk more openly and clearly with them when it is time to make important life decisions. This will make you less reactive to what children do and other events which you cannot control. Many of our negative emotions and frustrations come from not knowing where we are going or from being annoyed and feeling powerless to do anything about it. If you have a bad past, the old behavior emerges and you do something you wish you wouldn't. Knowing what you want and hope for in your children helps prevent a return to something less desirable and will give rise to ideas and methods which are more constructive.

Forming a clear idea of what you want for your children provides another benefit. This benefit is found in the fact that it is easier for parents to agree about what to do if they focus on the development they want for their children. It will be no surprise to learn that parents often disagree about how to rear their children. They often disagree about whether a disciplinary method is appropriate such as spanking or "grounding." One may be more strict and think the other too lenient. The other parent may see the partner's strictness and wish to soften it by more warmth and allowance. Sometimes this conflict burns along at low heat throughout the child-rearing years, but even at a low level it can have harmful consequences for the children.

One of the most common consequences is that children soon learn how to approach each parent and if the gap between the two is fairly large, the child will learn to manipulate both to his or her advantage. In extreme cases this is how a child learns that a family rule is not a rule which must be followed or that chores do not have to be done. Further, some children join with one parent against the other and add to the conflict.

The more extreme this disagreement becomes the more likely it is for one parent to "withdraw" from the conflict in the name of peace. When this happens there might be fewer arguments but one person, important to the child, is removed from having positive influence. This reduces the potential benefit to the children and diminishes the fulfillment parents feel about their family.

In contrast, knowing about children and being clear about what you want creates the foundation to become more unified as parents. Unity is easier to achieve about desirable goals than it is about the methods to achieve them. If you disagree about discipline methods, delay that conversation until you are focused on what you want for your children. One lady asked during a parenting class, "How can I stop my child from throwing his toys all over the house?" I responded by asking, "How do you want him to care for his toys?" She didn't hear my question and went on saying, "I am so tired of the mess I don't know what to do." Again I asked, "How do you want him to care for his toys?" This time she heard. "What do you mean?" she asked. I replied, "I believe you can correct your child's behavior if you will decide what you want and then create a program for him to learn."

Suppose you and your partner have a child who made a mistake or has a conduct problem. As a way of making a decision about what to do, ask each other, "What do you want for our child?" If you ask and listen carefully you may be able to reach agreement because you discover you both want the same things. If you don't want the same things at first, continue to discuss it asking questions and listening, recognizing that anything you do needs to begin with shared understanding of what you both want. Otherwise, you may contradict each other as you apply any solution. Talk until you are very clear about how you want the child to act, feel, and think. Then, if you can reach agreement about what you both want you will find that it is easier to see what could and should be done to achieve it. Methods of teaching or strategies of discipline often logically flow out of the decision about what parents want for their children.

Suppose that periodically you take the time to reflect or think about what you want for each of your children for the next few months or so. Then, if there are two parents in the family discuss what both of you "want" for your children during this period of time. By discussing and informing each other about your ideas you will be laying the foundation for what you do as leaders in your family. If you are a single parent you will find that reflecting about what you want for each child and making it clear to yourself also helps provide ideas about what to do to help them. Knowing what you want helps you decide what to do. Clarity about development and growth makes it easier for parents to be consistent in their efforts to promote them.

Being Clear Leads To Being Consistent

For years people have argued about whether it is best to be strict or provide a more lenient disciplinary approach. I have suggested earlier that these attitudes provide the current fashion of the day. All this happens in public attitudes without regard to what child and family scientists report from their research. They suggest that either method can be useful if it matches the right situation. If the environment outside the home is more risky, then a more strict approach may be useful. When living conditions are less risky and more stable and positive, strictness may be less reasonable and a lenient method more appropriate. Each approach has strengths and weaknesses with neither showing a clear superiority over the other. What does emerge as important is how consistent parents are in rearing their children. To most, consistency has been interpreted to mean that parents treat their children without surprises whether they are strict or lenient.

Parental leadership has more power when it is based on a different meaning for the term "consistency." Here, consistency is used to mean that whatever you choose to implement in your family is consistent with what you desire or want for your children. Suppose, for example, that you want your children to be socially skillful. This means you want them to be good friends, be at ease with meeting people, and understand how to communicate well while applying fairness and justice. Consistency, as I am proposing it, means that you introduce activities and practices into your family designed to help your children learn these skills.

The manner in which you communicate, apply fairness and justice, for example, will influence whether your children learn the social skills you desire. Some of your methods may be on the strict side, some may be more on the lenient side. Either are likely to be useful if they are consistent with the development you wish to see in the lives of your children. Equally important is the fact that your methods will be more acceptable to your children if they can see a link between what you are doing, what you want for them, and what they want for themselves. Being consistent in this manner has one very strong and positive advantage. Children are more likely to accept whatever you do instead of resenting or rebelling against it. When parental activities are consistent with parental objectives for their children, the children are more likely to believe in and accept them.

They have a much more difficult time accepting what you will do when they cannot see a connection between your actual practices and what they believe you want for them. They also will have more difficulty accepting what you do if they do not know what you want for them. Adding clarity to consistency adds real power to your efforts to promote the growth and development of your children.

Furthermore, you can achieve greater consistency if you adapt your family environment based on the time of your children's lives and the developmental tasks your children are trying to achieve. Young children may not know or fully appreciate what you are doing and in most cases they may never need to. Older children benefit when they can see how you are adapting the family based on your goals and what they are working on. But, adjusting your family to promote desired development will help your children feel and believe as if your parenting plans match what you are teaching them and hoping they will learn.

Fathers and Mothers

It has not been a very easy thing for researchers to identify the separate contributions of fathers and mothers. When both parents are at home and involved both have influence on their children. When one parent is out of the home we can measure what the negative consequences might be but not what the positive possibilities are. The many individual approaches of men and women, who have their own personal methods, also seem to suggest it would never be possible. In recent years, however, scientists have had the opportunity made available to them to finally get a better understanding of the effect each parent may have on children. Unfortunately, this happened because in recent years we have seen more children being reared without one parent or the other and many others being reared where both parents spent less time with their children. Based on national surveys, for example, nearly forty percent of the children in the United States by the year 2000 will grow to adulthood without access to their fathers. Approximately seventy percent of the children between the ages of six and seventeen live in homes where both parents work outside the home thus reducing parent-child time together.

These two conditions, and more advanced research methods, appear to now be providing better information about fathers and mothers. The findings which are emerging are interesting and somewhat surprising because they do not coincide entirely with our traditional expectations. They do confirm that both parents are very important to children. What is surprising is that each parent has more impact in some areas where the other has less. For example, contrary to what many people expect, fathers appear to have more influence in helping children develop empathy for other people, more influence in helping children control their impulses, more effect in promoting academic achievement, and more influence in the development of gender adequacy and satisfaction.

When a father is not available to children, mothers appear capable of promoting these attributes, but apparently at some sacrifice of what mothers traditionally provide. Mothers appear to have more influence in the nurturing and comforting role, development of talents and abilities, learning communication abilities, and the development of social-emotional skills. Like the fathers' contributions, when mothers are absent, fathers tend to pick these up but not as well as when a mother is present, if she is competent.

If we are concerned about the development of children, it is apparent that the skillful involvement of both parents is what is best for them. This means, however, that parents must work out a unified approach where each recognizes the importance of the other and both work comfortably together without much conflict. Otherwise, it is like the situation where one parent is a Democrat and the other is a Republican. They may cancel each other's vote. Where children are concerned, the influence of father and mother is accumulative. It is, therefore, not a trifling matter when parents have sharp disagreements and fail to resolve them.

In the field tests with this parenting program I have learned that parents are more likely to achieve agreement after both understand the idea of developmental tasks and have a developmental perspective. Then, when they were asked to learn how they might adapt their family environment, they worked together in order to under-stand how to do that successfully. These two steps appeared to take them away from the traditional sore spots of con-flict about disciplinary methods where most disagree. In others words, when they were able to focus on the children and understand where children are growing to they were more willing to cooperate with each other. They were also helped by knowing that each has an important part to play in promoting their children's growth. One father said, "I have often felt useless at home, but now I feel like I have something important to do." Many mothers indi-cated they felt alone in rearing their children and were frustrated with their husbands' apparent indifference. Many in this situation reported excitement about the pos-sibility of having their husbands join with them and assume their share of the responsibility.

I think it is a very worthy ideal for both parents to enjoy teaching and promoting the suc-cess of their children. All parents deserve to find fulfillment and challenge in help-ing their children mature into people who represent their parents and family well. At first it may seem a much small-er thing, as compared to what else we might value, to help children grow and learn. The longer we live, however, most

> **It is a very worthy ideal for both parents to enjoy teaching and promoting the success of their children.**

of us come to realize that our effort to achieve this is the best thing we have ever done.

Six Leadership Principles

After thinking about what you want and seeing your family environment as a place to implement plans to achieve it, what remains is the actual application of your leadership. Suppose that you want to know the most effective, successful, powerful, and competent things you can do to promote the development of your children. Hundreds of separate studies have been conducted addressing this question.

The professional literature is quite clear about parental practices which contribute most to successful children. For instance, researchers might interview, survey, and test a hundred families where children did not become involved in drugs or crime and compare them with a hundred families where children did. Researchers have conducted "intervention" studies where parents were asked to change their behavior in order to alter their children's undesirable behavior. For example, parents have been asked to apply "talking" strategies and cooperation strategies in order to influence children's aggressive behavior.

Families have also been studied to see what produces academic achievement, social and emotional skills, and moral behavior. I believe that if we were to summarize the results of these studies, disregarding research that was poorly designed or conducted, we could conclude that the most successful parents apply leadership based on six general leadership principles. I believe that any parent can learn them and apply them to achieve the real power of parenthood.

(1) Prepare More Than You Punish

As growing and developing human beings, children deserve to have help in becoming prepared for new and interesting things their new growth brings to them. If you only have time for one, which would you rather provide your children: the ideas and experiences which lead to their success or your response when they have made a mistake or failed? Organizing your family to prepare your children probably is much better than letting them go throughout life without any. Parents who actively try to prepare and teach their children resort to punishment less often because less is needed.

In families where children are successful, parents employ some form of active teaching program. This program may include teaching children school subjects such as reading and arithmetic. Other teaching efforts or preparation may include helping children learn a specialized talent or ability like sports, music, or dance. Further, some parents also spend time teaching children about important values they hope will be adopted and other social and emotional skills like respect, courtesy, and moral behavior like integrity. What you attempt to teach, however, is only part of the benefits from applying this principle.

Apparently preparing your children more than you punish them creates a "teaching relationship," a special type of link between you and your children. Children become convinced that parents love them and have their interests in mind so that when parents do make rules or establish some practice that children may not appreciate, they are more willing to accept what is done.

In addition, parents as mentors or teachers create a reward condition for them and their children that entices them again and again to be with each other for that purpose. Actively preparing your children to learn what you want and what they need can save hours and hours of problems and difficulties you will not have to experience.

Punishment, as we know it, may always be required when it is necessary to demonstrate that some behavior is wholly inappropriate and should not be repeated. But if punishing is all you do, even if you are trying to correct a child, you are forgetting that at least one reason why children misbehave is because they do not know what else to do or what else to do that is better. This may seem strange to you because you think you have told them, sometimes over and over again. The problem is that telling is not the same thing as teaching or preparing them to act as you would like them to.

Children learn through a combination of experience and what they hear and see. If they hear or see something without experience they may not know what to do or how to do it. The solution for misbehavior, therefore, needs to include an opportunity for children to learn something better. Punishment needs to be combined with teaching something that is better for them and for you.

In this book I propose that one consequence you apply for misbehavior is for your children to learn about and practice what they did not do when they misbehaved but which would have been the right or better thing. Suppose two of your children are arguing and hitting each other. To apply this idea you would only need to stop the fight, listen a little about each child's point of view, and then require them to learn how to talk and solve problems by creating a joint solution. If you applied this suggestion you would be requiring them to learn something from their mistakes.

Preparing your children more than you punish them is also an indication that it is important to you that your children learn about important things. As you apply this principle over time you will acquire several methods of teaching both as a positive means of helping your children be successful and as a response to their misbehavior. In either case, you will be sending a subtle but powerful message to your children: learn and become better.

(2) Communicate More Than You Control

It may be a bit surprising that communication and control are considered together because logically the opposite of control is the absence of it. The two are closely linked in family life, however, because when you communicate enough and do it effectively it is less necessary to exert control. When a child seems disruptive or disobedient, for example, this same child often has less access to family communication. Further, when family members spend time communicating they are more likely to have shared values and goals because they transmit these through the process of communicating. Therefore, when you communicate more you are more likely to bring your children along without having to use as much pressure.

To understand, remember that real power comes from promoting your children's growth and development. In order for them to make progress and learn they need to communicate. In order for them to move toward goals and achieve their developmental tasks they need to keep focused. Parents with real power are more likely to keep their children on desirable paths by communicating to teach them, communicating about the world and all it offers, communicating to form positive emotional ties with family members, and communicating to understand and solve problems. They do this more often so they can be involved with control and control problems less of the time.

The traditional view of parenthood includes control of some type. Consider four examples. One is permissiveness where parents are lax and exert few routine controls. Another is a democratic approach where parents invite children to participate in forming family rules. A third is authoritarian behavior where parents establish themselves by virtue of their ability to exert control without the participation of the children. Lastly, is authoritative parents where influence is exerted through their expectations of competence and high performance in their own lives and in the lives of their children. Many family scientists believe there are different consequences for your children depending on which of these parenting methods you use.

What these four methods do not explain to us, however, is the connection between communication and control within each type of parenting. High-quality communication through one-on-one talks, family councils, family meals, talking to correct behavior and solve problems, and other family activities appear to apply an information form of control which makes parental control less necessary. That is, communication invites children to develop internal methods of control so they are not so dependent on the parents to apply external control to their lives. Apparently this is because through communication they are more informed, they have better emotional ties, and they find a place for their ideas and feelings. More communication means that everyone can be understood, can be a part of important decisions, and can gain an understanding about the world as a place they can succeed in. More communication helps parents communicate their desires and goals, transmit values, and teach morality and important social skills. Control generally reminds children about parental authority and the rules parents establish. Therefore, where both may have their uses the principle suggests that children will be more successful if parents communicate more than they control.

In addition to an overall plan for talking and listening to each other that might include bedtime talks, after school talks, family decision making, and so forth, one of the most important times to talk is when children are faced with a problem or have done something you don't like. "Let's talk about this," probably is a statement that would benefit both parents and children. When tempers flare, when there is sorrow over a mistake, and when children lie and misbehave are all appropriate times to talk. When you make mistakes, when you aren't quite feeling as you would like to and say and do something you regret, knowing there is a place to talk things over with a sympathetic listener gives you and your children a chance to stabilize an unstable family boat and get things going right again.

Contrast this with imposing more control than communication. It is easy to do if you have a difficult child or if you are not aware of the need to correctly apply this leadership principle. When you control it means that you exert your authority by criticism, control by applying reward and reinforcement, make rules, enforce them, and/or physically manage the children. These are the more mild forms of control and all may be useful from time to time. If you control more than you communicate, however, you might notice that you are spending more and more of your time applying one or more of these methods and feeling like that is all you do. Then, you may also be able to notice that the more you control the more you have to do, and this requires that you apply the mild forms of control more often or resort to tougher and more extreme measures. Hitting, yelling, swearing, name calling to humiliate, withholding love and affection, or taking away something important from your children are the next level of control. They are not as mild nor as positive. If your children get into your game, they will oppose, over-conform, become bullies, show disrespect, or become more aggressive. Control struggles between you and your children are on the horizon and may, unless something else happens, become the nature of your relationship with them.

Instead of permitting this to happen you can apply this principle from the time your children are very young. You can communicate, as I have proposed, in a variety of settings. This will increase the likelihood that you will be rewarded one day in the future by your children coming to you and talking about many things including something they have been shown or read which disturbs them, by coming to you and talking about something they have done wrong, by coming and talking to you about their successes. After they have left home they will come and talk just to see how you are doing and reestablish the bonds of family love. All these are possible if you communicate more than you control.

(3) Encourage More Than You Criticize

The desirability of encouraging children is probably familiar to you. It may be an ideal that you are hoping to reach, especially after you regret pointing out what a child has done wrong. While it may be necessary from time to time to correct something and clearly describe or criticize what children are doing inappropriately, it is important to encourage them more of the time. Both encouragement and criticism tend to be habits. They are learned as a result of what you choose to pay attention to. Your attention is a powerful influence on children. If you choose to pay attention to what they are doing wrong you will likely have the habit where criticism is more frequent than encouragement. If you pay more attention to what children are doing well and what you would like them to do, you will develop the habit of encouraging.

Unhappily, your habits of paying attention may become linked to a specific child where one gets more encouragement and the other more criticism. Or, like many parents, you may get busy and fall into the trap of saying little when children do well but comment when they do something you do not like. There are many of us who have this habit as reflected by research showing that criticism of children is ten times more common in American families than praise. This means that we are more likely to pay attention to what our children are doing wrong or what we do not want them to do. This is troubling. If you are committed to promote the growth and development of your children, part of the power of your attention will come from your willingness to pay attention to their efforts and improvements. I will explain.

Children are knowing, growing, learning, and facing new situations all the time. Their efforts to succeed will in part depend on the amount of encouragement they feel for even trying. When you say, "I know you can do it," or "You might think you cannot do this, but I know you can," you will be telling your children they can be successful if they try. Hope and faith are powerful motivators and the overall quality of your children's lives depend on them.

Criticism has its place of course because not all children do everything right or excellently the first time. But where child development is concerned it needs to be well placed and timed so that you use it to point out something less successful and point out what they need to do differently and better. When your criticism becomes a regular form of behavior it is then potentially very damaging to children.

By itself, without a positive alternative, criticism is fairly ineffective and useless as a tool to change how a child acts. Rather it acts as a reinforcer for the very behavior you would like to get rid of. It is your attention that wins the day and if you are criticizing your children very much you are paying attention to what you do not want. In abundance it communicates to children they are not ever finished, their work is never done well enough, their ideas are flawed, their social behavior is inappropriate, and their manner of dress and speech inadequate. All these are possible because the power of comments made by parents is greater than comments made by other people.

One teenage daughter and her mother had serious and intense conflict about the mother's criticism. The girl told how her mother criticized the way she dressed, the boys she dated, how late she came in, her language, and what her mother thought was excessive flirting. This happened often. Instead of realizing she was in real danger and her mother was trying to help her, or that there were hidden reasons why her mother was afraid and showed it through criticism, the daughter simply was hurt and angry. The girl said that one day she concluded her mother did not trust her and was afraid she would make a sexual mistake. She then said this very revealing statement, "If my mother worried that I might do something bad, instead of having confidence in me, I might as well go and do it." And, she did.

In its best sense, parental leadership directs children toward positive possibilities and then encourages them along the way. When more encouragement exists then appropriate criticism is muted enough so that the focus is on what is positive rather than what is wrong. Children are more likely to improve when they look at themselves, honestly believing they can succeed rather than being angrily or fearfully concerned about their parents.

Therein is the secret of encouragement. It, too, has power. It is powerful enough to help your children have the courage to try, the fortitude to face difficult challenges, and the ability to withstand pressure they receive from others to do wrong. It can motivate and inspire. Encouragement is not praising when it is not deserved. It is a symbol of your attention suggesting that children can do something, can succeed if they work, and they are significant whether they succeed or fail.

One family I know spends time at the evening meal to identify ten good things they did or positive things which happened to them that day. Another father and mother have the practice of sitting at their children's bedside and while saying good night, tell them reasons why they are loved. They believe that children will more easily believe what is wrong about them than about what is right and good. Therefore it is necessary to tell their children dozens of times they are loved before they believe it and believe they are loveable. When you are able to convince your children, you are applying the real power of parental leadership.

(4) Involve and Individualize

Of the six leadership principles this is often the most difficult for parents to apply successfully. This principle suggests that to be the most successful, your leadership involves your children so they belong and feel included. It also means that it is important to treat each child on an individual basis which might include allowing one to not do what everyone else is doing.

Depending on the way your children came to your family you might find it easy to refer to the "little girls," "the twins," the "big boys," and so forth. These labels signal that you are thinking of your children in groups much like a school teacher thinks of her students as "people," or "students," or "children."

If this type of thought is excessive you run the risk of being less aware of individual children and organizing your family in ways which do not satisfy their unique needs. This increases the likelihood of hurting them by making the wrong decision, establishing an inappropriate rule, or ignoring some important need they hope to have fulfilled. On the other hand, if you do not require that your children involve themselves with you and family activities, you risk fragmenting your family so much that children are removed from care, comfort, and concern.

This leadership principle suggests that you need both types of activities as part of your parental plan. Learn about each child and have some idea about how each is unique from the others. Find ways to recognize how children differ from one another, pay attention to each child's abilities, and provide for unique experiences which match a child's interests and desires. While you are doing this, however, it is also possible to involve them with you and what the rest of your family is doing. These can be family meals, family conversations, family vacations, or holiday traditions and rituals. When both of these exist it is more likely you can find a balance between the two important parts of family life and a child's growing up. The parents of one "individualized" teenage daughter faced this dilemma when she did not want to go on a family vacation. They told her, "We will try to let you do what you want as often as possible, but sometimes you will need to join with the rest of the family. This is one of those times." This method worked because at other times they had created opportunities for her to do what she wanted.

The satisfactory application of this principle helps parents achieve that fine balance between keeping themselves separate from each child and becoming over-involved. As children mature this is one of the most difficult challenges we face. The strength of the emotional tie between us and our children varies in intensity. For some children and some periods of time it can be very intense and for other children and other times it is less so. The fact that it is not constant makes it a real challenge to know what to do. If you over-involve a child you may create a tie that binds so tight that you prevent growth.

When the tie is too tight children and parents may actually participate unconsciously in efforts to maintain it. It is well-known that children in this situation can develop behavior problems, spurious illnesses, and other forms of emotional difficulty to which parents respond by perpetuating their involvement. One mother told of her eighteen-year-old daughter who she described as unwilling to go on a high school choir tour. She described her daughter as dependent and fearful of social participation. As I investigated further I found that this daughter was quite willing, in fact wanted, to go on the three-week tour. I inquired further about their situation and learned that the daughter had a rare developmental disorder which required numerous life-threatening surgical operations. Over the years her mother had cared for her, wakened her in the morning, laid out her clothing, driven her to her appointments, and satisfied many of her social and emotional needs. It was quite reasonable to conclude that it was the mother who did not want the daughter to go on the tour. When I presented this possibility to the mother she paused for a moment and then tearfully told of what it was like to wait in the waiting room at the hospital worrying that she might lose her daughter. Her admission, however, did not solve the problem. We had to involve the husband to help her stop over-involving herself in her daughter's life. He adjusted his time and companionship with his wife to help compensate and together all three made a good adjustment in the balance between involving and individualizing.

That is one side of the question. The other is when to separate to allow individual preference. If you under-involve a child you may risk feelings of loneliness and discouragement. You may communicate through your efforts that you are indifferent or unloving. If the child becomes afraid or sufficiently distressed he or she may compensate by forming attachments to people less positive than you are. Generally, this question can be answered by making certain that you do both things. If you have both sets of activities where you involve your children so they belong and feel included and also act to provide individual opportunity, you can create self-reliance without a lot of dependency. Involving and individualizing are the twin methods that permit parents to help children be strong individuals still in need of belonging, successful with other people but able to function on their own.

(5) Love More Than You Isolate

It is a very common practice for parents to send their children away from them when they are angry at or unhappy with them. "Go to your room," is a common response to the time when a young child has disobeyed. This practice probably comes from the idea that separating someone from the society of others is a punishment which someone hopes will reduce the possibility the same mistake will be made. Yet, while this practice is probably widespread there are several things wrong with it. For one thing, when it comes to helping children learn, sending them away takes them from the people who are best able to teach them. It also helps children learn that when they err, it is best to separate themselves from the people they disappoint. Later in life when mistakes are made a pattern has been set and children avoid others and isolate themselves. Frequently, isolation angers children who, instead of accepting responsibility for what they have done, focus their frustration on you. In many instances, especially when parents do not talk to their children after the isolation, children form some mistaken conclusions about themselves and their parents which can last a lifetime. In contrast, as parents we are interested in development, learning, and growth. Mistakes and misbehavior are part of a child's life and in spite of their negative impact, they are opportunities to teach.

It is important to distinguish between two types of difficulty. You may send a child to his or her room as a cooling off technique when there are intense emotions difficult to control. You may also isolate a child when a mistake has been made or there has been some form of disobedience. This principle applies differently to each. If you send a child away for a cooling off period, then follow up by teaching and communicating afterward. When a child makes a mistake or disobeys, what if, instead of separating and isolating your children, you brought them to you to talk, to work together, to help them overcome their mistake and learn something from it?

We do not stop loving a child because a mistake has been made. That is, unless you want to create such intense anxiety for the child it can emotionally cripple him or her. Some children view isolation as withdrawal of love and that is the most frightening thing to them. Love means that when children are young it is wise to seldom leave them alone for any significant amount of time, but communicate to them that you are there for them and especially you are there when they fail or have some difficulty. When children are older it is equally wise to communicate that your love is unfailing and that you love them regardless of what they do: good or bad.

You could expect that by doing this during a child's life he or she will learn to turn to you for many different things.

When your children succeed you will be close by. When they are disappointed in themselves they know you are available. By loving more than you isolate you will have prevented patterns of isolation from turning into habits of rejection.

It is also plain, in my opinion, that promoting the development of children requires attention, involvement, communication, and varieties of companionship. By any measure these are forms of love. Some parents busy themselves with other things justifying what they do with the idea that they will make up their absence later. Some of us think about "quality" time hoping to invest more if we can just find time later on. None of this is true for children. They need enough involvement to grow. No one seems to know how much is required but we know one thing for certain: Unless time with children means controlling or smothering them, no child with severe problems ever blamed it on parents who spent too much time with him or her.

Love for a child cannot be measured in minutes or quality versus quantity time. Love in this case is having fun together, conversation, attention, shared activities, belonging, and responsiveness. It is affection, warmth, delight in each other, and longing to see each other. None of these are possible if we isolate our children.

Some parents and children benefit from "time out" times when children are especially upset or troublesome. A brief "time out" may be very useful if it is followed by attempts to help the child improve how he or she responds to some situation. It too, however, can move from a small useful technique to the idea that it is a positive thing to isolate children when we do not like what they do. We can easily teach them, "Come to me," "I will help you calm down," or "Let's work on this together." And require that they do it.

Resolving things between child and parent, in my opinion, is so important that children should be taught the necessity of doing this from early on. More than most other things, this is where children will learn they are loved when they do well and loved when they do not. It is this that motivates their own desire to do well as much as they can.

One set of parents I know carries this idea a step farther than most. They calmly require their children to talk to them, especially after an argument, mistake, or emotional discharge. Sometimes their children resist this. They wait until the child wants to do something and then they say, "Okay, you can do it as soon as we have a talk." Through this the parents have used their power to solidify their children's ideas that they are loved and cared for.

(6) Love Enough To Limit

One of the greatest challenges in parental leadership is helping children gain control over themselves and not be fully vulnerable to influence from external sources. This is necessary for children to develop moral behavior, social skills, emotional health, and any other reasonable concept for living with others. There are, for instance, emotional limits where children are helped to understand that anger is not to be focused on others; they must regulate themselves so they do not harm themselves or others.

There are limits to family resources, limits to talking, limits to time, limits to several different forms of emotional behavior. Establishing limits on any of these is essentially the same thing as preparing your children to adapt successfully to many different situations. This ability to self-regulate is a hallmark trait of someone who is mature. It is involved in the development of integrity and it is also involved in learning how to handle social situations with skill.

When their children lose emotional control, one mother and father invite them to sit in the calm chair. This chair is in the presence of the parents and the children must sit there until the parents believe the children can "control themselves." Another family applies this principle another way. When their children get too upset after being refused something they want, the parents suggest to them they may need to practice handling a "no" more often. Faced with the possibilities of more refusals, the children usually learn to adapt.

It takes one of the best forms of love for parents to apply this idea. It seems much easier, at least in the short term, to give children what they want and let them do what they want to do. It is more difficult and more loving to establish limits for children that benefit them. Children are more successful when they have internalized limits to anger, to spending, to telling untruths, and to time. These limits enable them to find success where children without limits do not.

Like the other five, this principle of leadership enables you to promote the development of your children in very real terms. It allows you to use your power to bring to your children one of the most important ingredients to their happiness. When balanced with freedom and opportunity, these limits are sources of power to your children because they are less likely to be adversely affected by friends or other peers and instead maintain control over their own lives. Saving them from being adversely affected is a real act of love.

The Real Power of Leadership

Whatever leaders propose and followers accept eventually merges and they become a reflection of each other. If your leadership is based on the six principles I have proposed, you can expect your children will be interested in learning, communicating, encouraging, being involved and being an individual, confident in other people's love, and demonstrate the ability to regulate themselves.

I believe these are the underpinnings of all other life success. They permit children to achieve, to form positive and close relationships with others, and to live a life of integrity. The application of these principles help children be happy and optimistic. These are the basic building blocks which allow you to influence children as they grow mentally, physically, emotionally, morally, and socially. They allow you a mixture of intimacy and closeness with your children without getting too close and getting in their road. They allow you to instill a vision of things which are possible and the hope that what is dreamed about can be achieved. That is real power.   ❀

Adaptation Principles

The remaining portion of this chapter describes four adaptation principles. When these principles are correctly applied, they are the conditions which effectively contribute to children's development. When they are not correctly applied, they can interfere with children's lives and delay or sometimes prevent positive development.

The principles are familiar and sensible. We usually think about their importance, however, after our children are grown and we wish we had done some things differently. The objective here is to help you know about and skillfully apply these principles right now. Please read the description of each principle and then think of an example of how you could apply it in your family.

1. The Maturity Principle: Relationships, family work, and rules are adapted according to children's level of maturity. Maturity may be measured by watching five kinds of development: physical, social, mental, emotional, and moral.

2. The "Goodness of Fit" Principle: The family environment can be adapted in very individual ways to reaffirm that parents understand each child as a unique person. A child's uniqueness is measured by watching physical, social, mental, emotional, and moral behavior.

3. The Teaching and Preparation Principle: Every family environment includes teaching and preparation to help children learn and grow. Parents prepare children for future developmental tasks.

4. The Balance Principle: Adapt the family environment to ensure balanced emphasis on work, relationships, and rules. Balance is achieved by clear and unified parental leadership.

Observing Yourself

For those who care, being a good parent is very important. Sometimes it is useful to examine carefully what we do in order to gain information about what we do successfully and what we need to improve. The purpose of this activity is to help you acquire information about yourself.

By observing what you do and completing this form you will add to what you know about yourself. Do not be overly excited about what you do well or overly dismayed about what you do not do well. Concentrate instead on getting accurate information.

1. **Record how you displayed the following forms of emotional behavior:**
   - anger
   - frustration
   - affection
   - enthusiasm
   - love

2. **Circle one of the answers below to estimate the amount of affectionate touching you participated in with your children.**

   None   A little   Some   Quite a bit   Very much

3. **Estimate the time you spent communicating during the following family situations:**
   - As an entire family
   - As a married couple (if married)
   - One-on-one with a child
   - About positive things your children did
   - About negative things your children did

Chapter Five

FAMILY BEGINNINGS

Pregnancies, births, and the subsequent care children need set the stage for parents to discover how much life changes when the first child is born. You relinquish time you would ordinarily spend elsewhere, and the attention you must give is fairly constant because the child's needs are never far from your thoughts or feelings. Emotions are deep and lasting. For most of us there is tenderness and love mingled with a little annoyance at the new demands. There is apprehension and a sense of responsibility. There is exhaustion, too. We are amazed by this new life and grateful for being a part of something so wonderful. One mother described these feelings when she said, "The first time I gave birth I knew I had done the most significant thing I would ever do."

Parenthood is a personal and intimate enterprise. Many of us are shocked at the depth of our feelings and find ourselves responding to every sound the child makes. These feelings are amplified by recognizing the almost total dependence infants have on parents. Yet, it is this dependence and need that forces us to recognize that we have a major role in determining our child's success or failure. We want to be good parents and we want our children to be successful, yet at first glance there seems to be so much to learn. We feel a bit helpless, and, as time passes, it appears that parenthood will be more complicated than we thought it would be.

The first five years of parenthood are filled with an astonishing variety of parenting tasks. By the end of five years, you will know how demanding parenting is. You will also have learned that parenthood requires continual adjustment and refinement. You are faced with much that is new, so you draw upon the examples of your parents and the concepts of parenting provided from your cultural heritage. These two sources of information exert great influence on how you organize your family and treat your children.

In the first family stage, parents encounter many new experiences. Becoming a father or a mother is a new personal and social role. To adjust to the tasks and emotions of parenthood on a personal basis, you must establish routines of practical care, develop discipline strategies, and find some way to balance personal time with your parental obligations. You begin to see that the journey is long and wonder if you are up to it, but you recognize the rewards among the other demands.

Parenthood is a very social activity. Grandparents have an interest in your children, as do uncles and aunts. Neighbors have influence over and are affected by your children. Other children are affected by what your children do; your children want friends and must learn successful friendship skills. You begin to expose your children to the world outside the privacy of your home and, with new sensitivity, try to understand what may be good or bad for them. Your efforts as parents are put on public display in church, at nursery, at preschool, and in kindergarten. There is an ever-widening circle of social involvements.

What you do as a parent is influenced by a collection of personal experiences and desires and by the perception you have of your place in the social world. You might read baby care books, learn about discipline strategies, search for the secrets of self-esteem, and find out how to prepare your children for school. It is hoped that you will also sharpen your ability to observe each child and acquire a more refined understanding of how each develops and grows so that what you do can contribute to that process. Promoting development is the most essential task you undertake.

During the first family stage most parents realize that development is not always easy. Some of it is not "natural" and children often do not like to do what they need to do. Sometimes, adjusting to the world is neither convenient nor comfortable; parents must insist that children learn and adapt, often requiring repeated trials. This kind of commitment extends our love from the warmth and affection we idealize to the practical love shown by the tough work and real investment that child rearing requires. Parenthood is often demanding and difficult. Some days the rewards are few and seemingly nonexistent, but the effort is worth it if, at the end of a family stage, our children are ready to progress.

> **The effort is worth it if, at the end of a family stage, our children are ready to progress.**

Children's Developmental Tasks

In the first family stage, you need to understand how children develop during the first five years of life. Once you have acquired knowledge about their developmental tasks, you can organize your family environment to promote development. You will be able to teach and prepare your children, adapt to their growing maturity, establish a good fit between your parenting techniques and the unique characteristics of each child, and balance your efforts among tasks, rules, and relationships.

There are numerous developmental tasks—so many, in fact, that it is too complex to catalog all of them specifically. It is wise, therefore, to focus on the major types of development. Doing so will increase your sensitivity to those tasks and will help you make the best adjustments for each child.

Physical Development

Children grow rapidly, but after the first two years this growth gradually slows. It is enjoyable to watch children improve their physical abilities, beginning with the small fluttering movements at birth to lifting themselves, turning over, crawling, walking, and running. These milestones are used to gauge other forms of development, so it is important to know about them. In addition, children have other physical developmental tasks including:

1. Toilet training
2. Wellness and good health
3. Naming body parts and learning their functions

4. Positive body image

5. Rhythm and coordination

6. Small motor skills (tying shoelaces, coloring, cutting, drawing, and printing)

7. Accurate gender information

8. Growth in height and weight

Mental Development

Children inherit more mental abilities than we have previously imagined. They have a biological plan to acquire cognitive control over their bodies so they can think and intentionally act as they desire. They inherit abilities to reason about time, space, and numbers. They also inherit the ability to evaluate things they encounter as good or bad. Some of the major forms of mental development during the first five years include:

1. Use of senses (vision, hearing, smell, taste, and touch)

2. Language, numbers, time, and space

3. Ability to reason, remember, and solve problems

4. Strategies to work with objects and people

5. Creative intelligence shown by their preferences (music, reading, sports, art)

6. Active learning

Social Development

Children are born prepared to communicate with other human beings. They enjoy watching the human face at three days of age, and they move their arms and legs in synchrony with their parents' speech by three to four months of age. They gaze for long periods of time and learn to respond in synchrony (peek-a-boo) with other people. They develop the ability to play, and through play acquire ideas about social rules, conversations, how to display emotions, and how to adapt to many different social situations. The major forms of social development during the first five years include:

1. Involvement and active participation with parents
2. Movement from solitary to cooperative play
3. Development of patterns of cooperation
4. Appropriate adaption of behavior in several different situations
5. Knowledge of conversation skills
6. Awareness of their own unique thoughts and feelings

Emotional Development

Emotions play a major role in life, especially during early childhood when they first appear. Children inherit at least five emotions: surprise, anxiety, anger, disgust, and a happy or pleasurable feeling.

Very young children are either mild-tempered and easy, slow to "warm up," or emotionally challenged. Children develop a variety of emotions (positive and negative), become aware of these emotions, regulate, and adapt them.

The major emotional tasks during the first family stage include:

1. Displaying a variety of positive emotions
2. Regulating emotions within appropriate limits
3. Adapting the display of emotions to the situation
4. Talking about positive emotions (e.g., "I am happy")
5. Accurately recognizing other people's feelings

Moral Development

Children are born prepared to learn about moral concepts of good and bad, right and wrong, and they have a primitive concept of empathy. More importantly, they can, during the first years of life, understand what helps and harms people—the true basis for morality. During the first five years, children develop the following moral abilities:

1. Demonstrating rule-governed behavior (i.e., knowing about rules and how to act upon this knowledge)
2. Learning about and developing love and trust for Deity
3. Learning the first level of self-control (behavioral limits of what to and what not to do)
4. Making judgments about right and wrong
5. Understanding that their actions have consequences
6. Learning what helps and hurts people
7. Feeling empathy and concern for other people's distress

Organizing and Adapting Your Family Environment

You have read previously that the family environment consists of tasks that need to be performed, rule conditions, children who develop, parental leadership, and relationships. In the first stage of family life, your parental leadership will involve trying out and establishing the tasks you want performed, the rule conditions you think appropriate, and the nature of your relationships with your children. In other words, you are organizing your family.

Involvement with your children as you establish these three conditions forces you to develop a style of leadership. You will continue to experiment because you will find that some of what you do will not be quite as you would like it, but as time passes you will develop increased confidence and assurance as you find what works. When you understand your children's developmental tasks, you can use your leadership to organize an adaptable family environment to help them. Review the following four adaptation principles.

---

1. **Matching your family life to children's level of maturity**
2. **Adapting to fit each child**
3. **Using teaching and preparation**
4. **Ensuring that you have a balanced emphasis on work, rules, and positive relationships**

"Family Beginnings" is the stage of family life when your oldest child is younger than five years of age. These years have unique requirements, and successful adjustment can be accomplished by doing those things appropriate for children's current needs and future growth.

We need to know some things about children from birth to five years of age. We have already reviewed some developmental tasks and can use them to understand their level of maturity and what we can reasonably expect.

Children reveal some parts of their personalities very early in life. Other parts will be demonstrated later. It is a good practice, however, for us to find what makes each child unique as soon as possible. To do this we need some words which describe emotional, social, and mental behavior. Describe what each child is like. For example, is the child intense, warm, and loving? Is the child outgoing, friendly, and comfortable with others? Is the child inquisitive? Is the child hot-tempered? Is the child a fast or slow learner? Can the child concentrate and spend time on one task or is he or she distractable?

Having described the child, we can identify how he or she is unique and adjust our level of communication. Our expectations for chores and rules should reflect what we know about each individual. For example, children under three years old typically do not understand the concept of rules. We have to remove them from danger and remove fragile things from them. As their language skills improve, however, we can make rules and use verbal instructions to get them to obey, while remembering to achieve a "good fit."

We also want to develop active teaching or preparation programs because teaching creates more success and prevents more problems. The choice is ours. Teaching can be a part of regular family life. With young children we can enjoy teaching them about life's basics.

Lastly, we need to balance our emphasis on rules, work, and relationships. We form parental habits early and if we want the best balance later on, we need to establish all three during the first period of family life.

The following suggestions portray how to apply the four adaptation principles in your family leadership. Further, they indicate how to help children achieve their developmental tasks. Besides loving them, having fun with them, and enjoying them, applying the four principles is the most important thing we can do for our children.

Provide High-Quality Basic Care

Newborns are intelligent, yet dependent. They need care that provides for survival, but, obviously, they need more than food and sleep. The patterns of involvement you establish early in your relationship tend to continue thereafter. High-quality basic care includes following these guidelines:

1. Establish predictable routines of feeding, clothing, bathing, and sleeping. This calms and creates the security that permits the child to develop trust for the caretakers.

2. Pay close attention to the child's reactions. Look at the child's eyes and face. Examine the child's response to temperature change. Try to understand the meaning of crying, cooing, and moving.

3. Touch and caress often. Speak and laugh in soft voice tones. Display warmth and affection.

4. Provide stimulation through sight, sound, touch, smell, and taste.

5. Converse and play to demonstrate language sounds and create exchanges of parent-child actions (e.g., peek-a-boo).

Encourage Movement/Teach Physical Skills

Good physical development promotes all other forms of development and, in the early years, is a natural process that can be encouraged by parents who play with, touch, and help children practice rhythm and coordination. After basic skills are acquired, children relate to the world through their bodies. They learn about themselves and others through physical activities that involve running, jumping, and other forms of physical play.

Positive social and personal concepts about themselves are linked to their appearance, size, weight, and physical abilities that they can display to other people. Their bodies are of interest to them, especially gender differences, because they want to understand the difference between boys and girls. The following are ways you can promote physical development:

1. Teach children physical skills that improve their rhythm and coordination.

2. Teach children the names of their body parts and display a positive view of their bodies. For example, say, "Look how nice your arms and legs are." "That is your penis. Boys have a penis and girls have a vagina."

3. Begin a positive program of toilet training when children are between two and three years old (typically girls can begin earlier than boys).

   a. Label bowel and bladder functions (e.g., "Go potty").
   b. Have the same-sex parent demonstrate the desired behavior, using the word.
   c. Have the child sit on a potty chair or toilet at appropriate and regular times using the words you have selected to describe bowel and bladder functions.
   d. Express praise and warmth for success; ignore failures.
   e. Gradually move from diapers to training pants.

4. Point out positive abilities associated with "being a boy" and "being a girl." The words you use will become labels children remember. For example, the words "pretty" and "handsome" are passive words. Also use words like "strong," "happy," and "fun."

5. Praise children's physical appearance and point out their positive features.

6. Engage in physical play with them such as racing, wrestling, skipping, dancing, and playing sports.

7. Teach children to complete tasks. This can be done by (a) showing them how to do a simple task, (b) having them practice, (c) praising them, (d) starting them on a task and then leaving briefly so that they work alone, (e) praising them if they are working on

their own when you return, or (f) focusing them on the task if they are not.

Promote Mental Abilities

Children's mental abilities improve because their brains grow naturally from the stimulation of exploring their world and communicating with their parents. During the first five years children learn an amazing amount of information on their own and will benefit from active and frequent parental involvement. Improved mental abilities are closely tied to the development of language and communication skills.

1. Encourage children to explore new situations and learn about new places, people, objects, and situations. Discuss what they are going to see and ask them to talk about their experiences.

2. Talk and communicate often to promote children's language skills. Use distinct words and complete sentences. Teach new words by naming things and letting children imitate your sounds.

3. Get children to talk while they are using objects such as toys or tools. Saying what they are doing enhances language as well as thinking skills.

4. Read to your children. It teaches thinking and language abilities. Tell stories and talk about your experiences.

5. Teach children about numbers and spatial ideas (i.e., up, down, over, between, behind, far, and close).

6. Ask questions and invite children to solve minor thought problems and make decisions. (For example, "What would you do if a mouse ran into the room?")

Encourage Emotional Development

Through positive involvement with each other, children and parents gradually build a lasting emotional attachment. Since attachment is the foundation of emotional development, relationships should be secure, warm, and consistent. This type of relationship is usually established by the time children are two years old. Even before that, however, they will have started to imitate the way you display your emotions through facial expressions, in language, and through body language.

Once language improves children will be able to use words to name feelings, and will be able to listen to you while you tell about yours. Even before age five, children should be able to talk about their own feelings. Children also need to learn to regulate their emotional behavior by recognizing and keeping within certain limits. In addition, they will need to know how to adapt their feelings from one situation to another.

1. Show children a variety of emotions (mostly positive) and tell them what you feel (i.e., love, kindness, happiness, surprise, calmness, and cheerfulness). Ask children to display these feelings at mealtimes and other family activities.

2. Organize a plan of discipline that establishes limits to emotional behavior.

3. Teach children to adapt their emotions to many different situations.

   a. Use the word control to help children understand when they are "in" or "out" of control.

   b. When children are "out of control," they can be helped to go to a specified place (a chair, a bedroom) where they must gain control of themselves before they can do anything else.

   c. Focus on the emotion before the action (e.g., say, "You must be angry" before saying, "Why did you hit him?" or "Why did you break that?").

   d. Include conversations about your feelings and the child's feelings (and the feelings of other people involved) while correcting misbehavior.

4. Explain any new situation and show children how to express themselves appropriately (e.g., demonstrate how to answer the telephone, how to act when a neighbor visits, how to act in a restaurant, how to act at church). Then, ask them to practice.

   a. Practice or rehearse desirable emotional behavior before participating in the new situation.

   b. Praise children when they are able to adapt themselves correctly.

   c. When children cannot adapt, remove them from the situation and calm them. Then, return to the situation prepared to praise them for success.

5. Help children recognize other people's emotions (e.g., "That little girl is crying, she must be sad").

6. Teach children about new emotions (as part of helping them understand themselves and other people). This can be done by helping them acquire new words. To a four or five year old, say, "I am going to show you a feeling. Watch my face." Show the child what each emotion looks like. Then, ask the child to show you what each emotion looks like. There are many emotions that are easily shown by facial expressions. The following list contains some suggestions:

love	guilt
cheerfulness	excitement
pride	happiness
calmness	discouragement
sadness	confusion
surprise	anxiety
anger	concern
disgust	fear

Promote Moral Development

Moral development is the ability to appraise or interpret situations. A moral person has the integrity to help rather than harm anyone involved. Moral development requires children to understand themselves and their relationships with other people. They need to develop a strong sense of responsibility for how they act and develop the self-control to govern their actions. Moral development begins when children are young. The following suggestions are guidelines to help promote moral development.

1. After your children are three years old, implement one or two family rules and enforce them firmly, consistently, and kindly. Accompany enforcement with conversations that explain the consequences for following and not following rules.

   a. Make certain that the rule is clear and relates to important behavior. (Good example: "Brush your teeth after breakfast." Bad example: "Always walk to the bathroom.")

   b. Explain what you are doing while you show the correct actions to the child. Explain when the child is to follow the rule.

   c. Help children by reminding them that the rule needs to be followed. Ask, "What is the rule?"

   d. If children are slow to comply, encourage them by saying "I know you can do it."

   e. Use abundant praise of their inner qualities (e.g., "I think you are a helpful boy," or "You are a very kind girl").

   f. Make very few rules and eliminate any you do not have time or energy to enforce.

2. Teach children to be helpful to you and to others. This enables them to understand what helps or hurts people, including themselves.

   a. Demonstrate helping by using the word "help," and by telling children you enjoy "helping" them.

> b. Ask children to "help" you and let them do something within their abilities. Respond with affection and warmth.
>
> c. With your children, perform helpful acts for other people.
>
> d. When children hurt someone, talk with them about what hurts people and why.

3. Teach children to describe their behavior accurately. Describing themselves accurately in an event or situation is the basis for integrity. Use both positive experiences (when children have done well) and negative experiences (of conflict or misbehavior) as opportunities for evaluation.

> a. Calm everyone by stopping the misbehavior or conflict. Then say, "I want to learn something."
>
> b. Ask for information.
>
> c. After children have given the first answer, ask "What did you do?" and follow this by saying, "And then what?"
>
> d. Repeat what you hear and ask them if your summary is correct.
>
> e. After getting an accurate description, you will be able to decide what to do.

Remember: If you excessively accuse or blame young children, they will protect themselves by intentionally or unintentionally hiding information.

4. Teach children about consequences.

> a. Use praise to tell them of your happiness when they are obedient or do something well.

   b. Tell of your positive feelings for them so they will know of your love, warmth and concern.

   c. Help them understand what happens when they do something that is "right" or something that is "wrong." Clear and objective explanations are much more effective than attempts to shame children by excessive criticism or scolding.

5. Use family opportunities to teach children to take turns, to cooperate, and to be fair.

Other Features of High-Quality Parental Leadership

In its truest sense, leadership means to form a vision of future possibilities, and to motivate and inspire others to achieve it. This definition may seem a bit out of place when thinking about children younger than five, but this type of leadership is never more applicable. Young children only have a future, and whether they move toward it successfully is usually determined by the type of parental leadership that guides them. The first five years are important for the rest of their lives, and because of that, we as parents are essential to our children.

The most effective parental leadership is clear and consistent. Clear means that as you get to know your children you identify what you want them to develop to become. What goals do you have for them physically, mentally, emotionally, socially, and morally? You must struggle with the idea that parents should have goals for their children rather than letting children grow up as individuals who make their own decisions.

I am not proposing that you plan on controlling them excessively or predetermining what their lives should become. I am proposing, however, that based on your knowledge of what children are developing, you can identify some things you want for them. These goals can and probably should be based on what you know they are working on during this period and any period of their childhood.

Next, it is important that you organize a set of family activities that contribute consistently to what you want for your children. For instance, if you want socially developed children it might be useful for you to organize your family environment so your children learn positive social skills.

Lastly, clear and consistent leadership includes the application of six principles which hundreds of research studies have shown to be the most effective. The six principles are as follows.

(1) Prepare More Than You Punish

While punishment might sometimes be necessary to help children learn an important lesson, children's successful development occurs as a result of your willingness to spend more time teaching and preparing them than you do thinking of ways to punish. This can be done in two ways.

First, organize little teaching programs to help your children learn what you want them to know about school, social skills, etiquette, language, numbers, and so forth.

Second, when they misbehave, instead of simply applying a punishment of some kind, use this as an opportunity to re-teach something so they will learn what successful behavior is rather than simply learn what they did wrong.

(2) Communicate More Than You Control

Begin little communication routines to "talk things over" when you make decisions or try to solve a problem. Develop family times, such as meals, so everyone can communicate. Taking the time to communicate reduces the amount of emphasis you give to controlling them.

(3) Encourage More Than You Criticize

Developing children benefit from a lot of hopefulness because of all the new things they face. They are learning so much about life they need someone to tell them fairly often that they "can do it," that they only have to "try something out" to find excitement and achievement. Encouragement suggests that you focus more on what you want your children to do than what you don't want them to do.

(4) Involve and Individualize

This leadership principle suggests that you do things which ensure your children belong and participate with family members and work to individualize each child. Family activities, family communication, ceremonies, traditions, and customs make for a great belonging experience. At the same time children need acknowledgement that they are unique, different in some respects, and parents recognize their needs and desires. This requires that you find ways to communicate these characteristics of each child.

(5) Love More Than You Isolate

Instead of sending your children away from you when they make a mistake or misbehave, bring them to you and find solutions. A cooling-off period might be necessary but loving your children through difficulty and showing commitment and loyalty instead of rejection and neglect are those conditions which enable them to grow comfortably and positively toward good goals. Love is a constant.

(6) Love Enough To Limit

Part of loving our children means that we help them establish a variety of limits, especially limits on the way they express emotional behavior. Rather than allow them to express any emotion as they choose, we help them limit extreme negative emotions like tantrums by setting limits on what they say and do, and expect them to be "in control" of themselves.

These six principles might be a bit new to you but you can see them applied in forms of parental behavior which may be more family. Read these next sections and see how each of the six are involved.

Nurturing

We give children a good start if we organize our family environment with a balanced approach. This means we introduce our children to positive rule conditions and an appropriate amount of work or chores, but do not let either of these prevent us from embracing them in a relationship filled with warmth and love. For children under five, a nurturing relationship is more significant than anything else. They start out in an unusual world filled with strangers; they benefit from your tenderness and alertness to their needs. They are stimulated by your touch, affection, and voice. They will trust and have confidence in you if you try to be consistent and if your care is satisfactory.

Then, if your relationship is filled with warmth, companionship, and communication, children will learn autonomy and will display a desire to do things on their own. This, as famed psychologist Erik Erikson proposed, is followed by initiative, the willingness to start and create new things.

Predictability

For young children, parental leadership must be consistent. They are made more secure by regularity because they can predict what is to come. You can establish dressing and eating routines made up of a series of steps. When each step is followed in sequence, children quickly learn what to expect and derive security from the routine. Children demonstrate the need for predictability by wanting the same blanket, repeatedly wearing the same shirt, and favoring familiar toys.

Besides predictability, routines contribute to effective child management. Experienced parents learn not to ask a two-year-old if he wants to go to bed. He will say, "No," and an unhappy discussion might follow. Instead, effective parents form a routine made up of a sequence such as: (1) "Put your pajamas on," (2) "Brush your teeth carefully," (3) "Now we can say our prayers," (4) "Climb into bed," and (5) "Now we can read a story." Children enjoy routines like these; they are proud to go from step to step to show that they have mastered them. If the last step is something enjoyable (such as reading a story), they are even more likely to participate in the sequence with little fuss.

Positive Conversations

Part of leadership is communication. The type of communication you create while children are young typically becomes part of a recurring pattern. Use your leadership to create a positive conversational relationship with each child.

This will require that you understand the forms of communication and use some more often than others. For example, family communication has several uses:

1. *Regulatory:* "Please move the chair."
2. *Informative:* "A cat has furry hair."
3. *Instrumental:* "Let's do the dishes and then sweep the floor."
4. *Personal:* "I am happy."
5. *Interpersonal:* "You and I are friends."
6. *Discovering:* "Why do cows have tails?"
7. *Imaginative:* "Once upon a time..."

When children improve their language skills it is natural for us to use communication to regulate their behavior. Most children under three, however, do not have sufficient language skills to understand all that we mean.

Parents often use words children do not understand and we try to communicate our meanings with our voice tones (e.g., sounding stern), which they may fail to pick up.

Therefore, children often do not comply with our attempts to regulate them. We might say, "Clean up your toys," assuming they understand that "clean" refers to picking up the toys and putting them away. We, however, have probably used this word in reference to bathing or washing. Using it in reference to the toys can be confusing and often fails to produce action.

There is a poignant little story about a mother who told her three-year-old that he could play outside if he stayed in the back-yard and didn't go past the corner of the house. He soon wandered off. She was patient as she brought him back and restated her rule. He left again. After the third time she assumed he was deliberately breaking the rule and spanked him, saying, "I told you not to go past the corner!" In tears, he asked, "Mommy, what's a corner?"

If a second child is born to us, the new baby requires attention and increases our motivation to regulate the older child by spoken commands. We say, "Stop it!" "Come here," and "Go and get me a blanket." Soon, children discover that parents are busy and that by progressively delaying for longer periods of time they might not have to do what is asked of them. Repeated asking, commanding, telling, and nagging will be ineffective. Instead of falling into this pattern, set a rule for yourself to ask or remind no more than twice. If there is no compliance, get up and take the child by the hand without saying anything, point to the task, and whisper, "Hurry." Then, praise the child's effort.

As part of creating positive communication, do more than regulate and organize (*instrumental*). Tell lots of stories (*imaginative*), tell about your feelings and experiences (*personal*), ask questions and listen carefully (*discovery*), and tell your thoughts and feelings about your children (*interpersonal*). Using all forms of communication will ensure that good conversation habits are balanced.

Communicate To Solve Misbehavior and Teach What You Want Them To Do

It is easy to have a quick reaction when children misbehave. Especially if we think we have "told them" and they should know better. Many parents are quick to scold, spank, or send children to a room to isolate them. These disciplinary methods may all be useful at one time or another, but each will have limited effects unless accompanied by conversation. When children are young, they deserve to be spoken to and given explanations until they understand. They can be asked to describe their own actions and what they thought or felt. The habit of explaining and listening to their opinions when misbehavior takes place will reduce the number of times children repeat the misbehavior.

Parental Teamwork

If there are two parents, it is wise for them to show support for each other. This might include telling children you agree with the other parent, stopping the children from showing disrespect, and complimenting the other parent when something was done well.

If differences between spouses exist, these differences will appear as soon as you start disciplining the children. For example, one parent might make a rule and then give in to be compassionate while the other parent continues to hold to the rule in order to be consistent. Even when parents are generally in agreement, each will be compassionate at one time and consistent at another.

During the "Family Beginnings" stage it is important for parents to clarify with each child what is wanted in a specific situation (e.g., when she will not eat, when he throws a toy, when she bites). Obviously stopping misbehavior is desirable, but this is only half the solution. What actions do you want as replacements for the misbehavior? For instance, instead of the child throwing a toy, you might want him to slowly place it on the floor in a certain place.

Next, it is important to identify the methods used to get the desired behavior. To continue the example with the toy, you might demonstrate what to do with the toy, have the child practice doing it, and ask the child to place it on the floor when he is about to throw it. If he throws it anyway, have him practice placing it on the floor as a consequence.

If you are a single parent, you can receive support and encouragement from your children if you are willing to give compliments and praise for good behavior. It is stressful to rear children alone and it is easy to communicate the

stress to your children. Giving extra effort to build positive emotions in children will produce more compliance
than will venting your anger and frustration.

Summary and Transition

If all this seems like too much for you to do, remember
that you have five years. If you start early, you will be able
to accomplish all of these tasks during "Family Beginnings,"
and much more. Even if you and your children have not completed everything, life affords some flexibility. Keep in mind
that children have their own developmental rates. Some
will develop quickly and others more slowly. Except for
extremes, a wide range of variation is considered normal
and healthy.

Children need to develop new abilities, but they
need not be pressured to do so by a certain deadline.
Some special cases will require extra effort. You may have
a child with poor health, a learning or cognitive disorder,
a physical handicap, or an injury. Such conditions cause
"developmental delays."

Still, by trying to apply the four adaptation principles
(see the box from the beginning of this chapter), you will
have created a foundation for your children's success. You
will be ready to make the transition with your family from
"Family Beginnings" to "Family Consolidation." It is time
to organize and strengthen your family in new ways. It is
a time of new skills and fulfillment.   ✿

Summary of Developmental Tasks
(Children 0-5)

Physical Development

1. Toilet training
2. Wellness and good health
3. Naming body parts and understanding what each part does
4. A positive body image
5. Rhythm and coordination
6. Small motor skills (tying shoelaces, coloring, cutting, drawing, printing)
7. Accurate gender information
8. Large motor skills (crawling, walking, running, jumping, throwing)

Mental Development

1. Language
2. Using senses to learn (vision, hearing, smell, taste, touch)
3. Ability to reason, remember, and form plans to solve problems
4. Strategies of working with objects and people (how to get a bottle from mother)
5. Creative intelligence shown by enjoyment of most activities
6. Active experiential learning

Social Development

1. Active participant in social games with parents
2. Move from solitary to cooperative play with peers
3. Patterns of cooperation (taking turns)
4. Appropriately adapting behavior to several situations
5. Conversation skills (talking, listening, humor)
6. Awareness of self and own thoughts and feelings

Emotional Development

1. Displaying a variety of positive emotions (love, affection, cheerfulness, enjoyment, surprise)
2. Regulating emotional behavior by reducing extreme displays and preventing displays that harm other people or self
3. Adapting how emotions are displayed to fit several situations
4. Talking about emotions ("I am sad")
5. Accurately recognizing other people's emotions

Moral Development

1. Demonstrating understanding of rule-governed behavior
2. Showing empathy for others
3. Learning about what helps and harms people
4. Understanding concepts of "right," "wrong," "good," and "bad."
5. Knowing that actions have consequences

Summary of Adapting Your Family Environment

(Children 0-5)

Prepare Children At Their Level of Maturity

1. Provide High-Quality Basic Care

    a. Routines
    b. Attention
    c. Physical affection
    d. Stimulation
    e. Conversation and play

2. Encourage Movement and Teach Physical Skills

    a. Practice rhythm, coordination, running, and throwing
    b. Name body parts in a positive way
    c. Develop positive concepts of "boy" and "girl"
    d. Praise physical appearance
    e. Play with children
    f. Provide toilet training
    g. Teach children to complete tasks.

3. Promote Mental Abilities: Explore, Talk, and Teach

    a. Explore new experiences that involve children's senses
    b. Talk and listen, expanding children's words to improve their language development
    c. Get children to talk while they are using objects
    d. Read to children
    e. Teach about numbers and letters
    f. Ask questions about minor problems

Create a Balanced Family & Achieve a Good Fit with Each Child

1. Promote Emotional Development

    a. Show a variety of emotions (mostly positive)

    b. Organize a plan of discipline that establishes limits to children's behavior

    c. Teach children to adapt themselves to social situations

    d. Teach about new emotions

2. Promote Moral Development

    a. Establish rules

    b. Teach children to be helpful to you and to others

    c. Teach children to describe themselves accurately

    d. Teach about fairness and equality

    e. Teach children to identify what helps and harms people

    f. Help children understand the consequences they create

Chapter Six

FAMILY
CONSOLIDATION

T aking your first child to preschool or kindergarten is one of those milestones that jolts the routine of life enough to create an appreciation that time is passing. The transition is often met with tears, reflecting the sadness that some cherished moments have passed. Such times tell us that family members are getting more involved outside the home. Like other things, this reminds us that the exclusiveness and security of family life will not last forever. To be full and complete it must be shared and enjoyed before much time has passed.

Your family is in the period of "Family Consolidation," which lasts from the time your first child turns six to when he is about eleven years of age. It is so named because during this time we organize and strengthen our sense of "familiness." We consolidate ourselves because growing children become more involved with things outside the family. Things become more complicated for us, requiring increased organization. Plus, there is greater competition for each family member's time.

Employment, for example, is an outside influence that affects families. While work provides resources, it decreases our availability to each other. It also affects the emotional quality of the family because it takes energy that we otherwise could have used for something or someone else. Friends, hobbies, school, church, and civic involvement all take place outside the home. When we or our children add these things to our lives it becomes even more imperative to consolidate.

Children benefit from parent-child stimulation. It is important for them to have enough time with you. The level of involvement you establish with them from pregnancy, through birth, and for the next five years sets a tradition that lasts a long time. There is abundant evidence that high parental involvement early in a child's life stimulates increased achievement, intellect, and social success. Thereafter, time together, at any period of family life, is the glue that bonds parents and children together.

As children mature, however, we see more clearly how external involvements affect the family. Also, you might have more children. So, in addition to the new things you do outside the home, you will be stretched further by new and increasingly complex demands. Rearing one child is an involved process. Bringing another into the family confirms the principle that the whole (family) is greater than the sum of the parts. In addition to a new child we have new relationships, new leadership tasks, and much more detail to notice.

During the next six years you and your children may be involved in many things. School has its PTA meetings, volunteer programs, and parent-teacher conferences. You may become active in civic or religious organizations. Your children will start sports programs and a variety of lessons, develop their own interests, and cultivate their own friendships. Your work may require more time. All these things seem worthwhile and so we encourage them, often without realizing their combined impact on us and our family. It does not take long for us to discover, however, that helping widen their exposure to the world will take both them and us away from home and each other.

Each parent responds in an individual way to increasing competition for time. Most of us accelerate our efforts to become more organized and efficient so that we can keep up. Eventually there is no choice but to simply ignore some demands in order to satisfy the others. Hopefully, we will choose to consolidate our family into a positive unit.

While adjusting to ever-changing demands, most people realize that even positive outside involvements can prevent family members from forming a cohesive unit, knitted together in enduring bonds of affection. Possibly because of your own memories, you may sense the importance of building strong family ties and decide to take

> **Take steps to consolidate all family members into one unit.**

steps to consolidate all family members into one unit. There is ample motivation: If you miss the chance now, you may miss it permanently.

During the crucial bonding period most families establish their own traditions and customs. Your family may develop unique communication rituals like nicknames, chants, "high fives," sounds, and statements, all of which have meaning only for those who share them. We plan holidays and other special occasions with the idea of making them unique to us. We begin "family" vacations and start family activities based on the requirement that all participate.

Creating such "familiness" may also include the practice of telling personal experiences. These shared memories become part of a common family history which for years thereafter members review with each other and build upon. The retelling of stories and experiences becomes a principal method of connecting ourselves to one another. These ties of shared history, once firmly formed, are maintained. Children become adults and pass them on to their own children.

While you are consolidating your family, your children continue to develop and grow. They build on what they have already developed. In addition, they work toward the developmental tasks for this period of life, maturing physically and finding greater fascination with new-found abilities. Typically, children rely on physical acts such as running, throwing, jumping rope, and other new-found feats of coordination to know themselves; they also begin to pay attention to their physical appearance as they seek to achieve status with others. The most popular children are usually those who best match up with any cultural ideal.

Physical development is crucial because on its solid foundation rests the equally important but less tangible aspects of social and emotional development. In addition to their physical development, children acquire improved and more complex social and emotional skills as their social situations require more from them. Increased social involvement, along with improved mental abilities, enables them to develop more complex moral thought and judgment. They now can see consequences and responsibilities and understand how they might contribute to what is good and bad.

Their new and improved mental competence allows them to make remarkable leaps in how they are able to think and reason. As they become more proficient in reading, thinking, and remembering, their ability to understand symbols (e.g., arithmetic and language) grows. Every child's mental growth is highly unique, making individual talents and abilities easier to understand and foster.

If you focus on your children, the developmental tasks during this period will become a set of goals to guide you in adapting your parental leadership. The tasks will help you create a family environment that will enhance their growth most effectively. When you lack an understanding of how your individual children are developing, your adjustments may not take into account their increased maturity and their unique abilities; they may reach the next family stage inadequately prepared. Further, your family environment may not be a balanced representation of rule conditions, tasks, and relationships. You may instead be a chaotic family, so intruded upon by external influence that you feel yourself chasing after things that are less meaningful and worthwhile instead of leading your family to a good destination.

Children's Developmental Tasks

Infants start out with wonderful abilities and their continued growth becomes even more varied and complex over time. In this stage of childhood as in all others, there are new and more difficult requirements to master, and for us there are new adjustments. If they are physically healthy and without other serious impairment, their biological abilities and their abilities to learn are equal to the challenge. Those who have been ill, injured, or have some other challenge deserve compassionate and appropriate attention.

Development may be delayed for some children and accelerated for others, and individual rates of development remind us that we need to understand each child's situation rather than making comparisons or thinking of all children as the same. Each child has a name, an emerging personality, and a unique way of thinking. In order to respect and affirm each child's individuality, we may need to avoid lumping children together by calling them "the twins," the "older girls," or the "little boys."

As you read the following descriptions of various developmental tasks, keep in mind that as children mature, the rates at which they achieve these tasks becomes more varied or individualized with age. The older children become, the more different they are from one another. Further, for those who develop extremely slowly or extremely quickly, there are many forms of "normal" development. Therefore, instead of comparing one child with another to measure what is "good," or "not so good," we need only to have separate categories for each. This means that we watch what a child has been during the last period of time and compare this new phase with that. It is easier than comparing any child with another.

Physical Development

The period of middle childhood sees many physical changes. Children typically double their weight and height, simultaneously improving their coordination and rhythm. Those baby teeth that took so long to come in now leave in the same order in which they appeared. Children can perform more complex physical skills such as sports, dance, and running. Physical dexterity is the basis of many social and emotional opportunities such as popularity, leadership, and acceptance. Children generally develop and display the following physical abilities:

1. Children show fascination with *specific physical skills* such as whistling, spitting, acrobatics, skating, bicycling, facial contortions, sound effects, writing on arms and hands, and making false tattoos.

2. They display increased *gender interest* around the age of five or six and try out "boyfriends" or "girlfriends." This "false courtship," as it is called, gradually changes and children lose this interest in favor of same-gender friends and interests.

3. Physical growth is accompanied by growing *awareness of gender* and refined concepts of male and female. They have increased interest in knowing about sex and reproduction.

4. Children typically experience one or more *growth surges;* rapid growth is usually preceded by weight gain, which naturally becomes integrated with new body size.

Mental Development

The human brain continues developing as its cells become more connected and integrated. As a result, children are capable of learning more complex things. During the years of middle childhood, for example, children are faced with the necessity of increasing the speed of learning. They learn faster by using symbols (words) that represent other things (objects). The crucial ability to use symbols can be applied to speaking, arithmetic, reading, music, and many other fields.

The use of symbols generates a rapid improvement in language use; in addition, a child's ability to reason naturally deepens into greater complexity. In earlier years, their senses might trick them into mental mistakes. When mental abilities improve, they begin to use their minds more effectively and are less likely to make the mental mistakes of early childhood. They might, for example, make a judgment or decision based on one small aspect of a situation instead of considering many factors. "Centering" on one small part of a situation is like looking at a painting and focusing on one part such as the fence around the house or a tree in an orchard of trees.

As children develop new mental abilities, however, they can reason and think and become more aware of their own thought processes. They recognize the need to remember, to check out their reasoning, and evaluate what they do. As children gain an understanding of time and the real properties of the world (such as shape, size, weight, depth, and numbers), they can project hypothetical outcomes and predict consequences of their actions.

Because they participate in many forms of individual thought they (and we) become more aware of how their thought processes work. Children have an enhanced ability to "think about how they think," and can make adjustments to improve themselves. Loving parents can help children in their refining process, allowing them to understand how their thoughts may be different than the thoughts of others.

This new mental ability creates a sizeable jump in increased social understanding and acceptance. Specifically, they learn that other people may have different opinions than they do. This *perspective taking* permits children to develop an increased awareness of themselves while improving their empathy and understanding of others.

Children are vulnerable to the opinions of others and benefit greatly when parents encourage them to discover and expand their new abilities. This is why we focus on the children first and learn about their developmental tasks. By learning what the tasks are, we can help children achieve them. When they are about six to eleven years old, children typically work at developing the following mental abilities:

1. Becoming aware of specific thought processes such as strategies for remembering, solving problems, and creating new ideas
2. Increasing vocabulary and learning how to use new words and sentences and apply them correctly in new social situations
3. Discovering they are naturally more interested in (and better at) learning some subjects than others and learning more about physical movement, personal relationships, math, music, language, and art
4. Organizing thought processes to become effective thinkers and taking more information into account while they are solving problems

Social Development

During ages six through eleven, children are faced with many complex social situations that require them to use more sophisticated abilities to think about themselves and other people. This is necessary so they can adapt to a variety of social situations without embarrassment or disapproval.

They must know more about how to adapt to the requirements of going to a grocery store, eating at a restaurant, behaving at church, adjusting to numerous situations at school, and generally learning how to communicate more effectively with others as their world expands. In order to become competent at these requirements, children work to achieve the following developmental tasks:

1. Communicating with and adjusting to authority figures
2. Talking and listening as part of communication
3. Participating in the give-and-take of friendship relationships (including negotiating differences and finding solutions to problems)
4. Developing accurate person perception (understanding what other people think and feel)
5. Learning how to act and adapt appropriately in a broad range of social situations
6. Learning and practicing fairness, cooperation, and loyalty

Emotional Development

Living a more complex life places greater emotional requirements and increased pressure on children. They are evaluated by others and participate in numerous social situations that require better emotional skills. To become competent they work at achieving improved abilities. These can become our goals, too, if we understand. The tasks for emotional development include:

1. Understanding positive and negative emotions and learning to express the positive more frequently than the negative (avoiding complaining)
2. Regulating and controlling anger, frustration, and aggression toward others (assuming responsibility for their own feelings instead of blaming others)

3. Talking about their own emotions and what their feelings mean to them

4. Accurately seeing and understanding what others feel (identifying and understanding others' feelings with empathy and concern)

5. Adapting emotional responses to fit many situations by learning to regulate intense emotions and fit their emotional displays to what a situation demands

Moral Development

Increased exposure to situations both in and outside the family brings children into full-fledged participation where they are required to understand more complex moral circumstances. These are situations where they can help or harm themselves or other people. If we teach them, they will refine their ideas about what helps and harms people during this period. They will better understand that their actions have consequences for themselves and others.

They learn more about the value of moral rules as applied to themselves and others, as well as improve their ability to understand concepts of right and wrong. We can help them if we understand these developmental tasks. Review the following list.

To become morally competent children must learn to—
1. *improve* their knowledge of what helps and harms themselves and other people,

2. *understand* their own intentions or motives and those of other people,

3. *develop* an increased sense of personal responsibility for their own actions,

4. *learn* an increased sense of caring, acceptance, and empathy for other people,

5. *learn* how to apply rules and perform tasks that will help people, and modify potentially harmful rules or deeds,

6. *participate* in communication with people who can teach them moral concepts,

7. *understand* that good or bad consequences inevitably follow their actions, for themselves (and sometimes others), and

8. *describe* their own thoughts, feelings, and actions accurately and fully.

Keep in mind there is great variation in each child's development. This means that some children may reach certain developmental tasks before they reach eleven years of age while others may take longer. Rarely making progress indicates a problem, of course, but most children will demonstrate at least some achievement of developmental tasks by the time they are eleven or twelve. The importance of the tasks is not that children reach developmental milestones at a specific time, but that you include them in what you do to help your children grow. You can also use them to expand your thinking about how successful your children really are.

Adapting Your Family Environment

In the first family stage, you are busy experimenting to establish a family. The amount of communication, affection, attention, and so forth lays the foundation for your relationship with your children. The type of work ethic you teach your children as they mature and what you do yourself reveals the emphasis you place on tasks and work. If you count the number of rules and understand how you enforce them, you can get an idea about the rule conditions you have created.

By now you have some impression about what is successful and what you would like to change and improve. Some of what you are doing will "feel" right and other parts will not. You might, for example, be too intense about some things or want to get more involved in something else. Part of what you do will not fit a child the way you would like; it may be so inconvenient that you want to rid yourself of having to do it. How do you decide how well you are doing?

For one thing it is important to measure the amount of fun, enjoyment, fulfillment, and satisfaction you are getting from your family and from being a parent. This is the first measure of your success. Then ask yourself how your children have benefitted from the family environment you have created. If they approach achieving the developmental tasks suggested for their first five years, they are doing quite well. Ordinarily, the amount of benefit your children have received as they pursue their developmental tasks plus the amount of fulfillment you feel are the best ways to measure whether you are organizing an effective family environment.

Happily, being imperfect parents in an imperfect world, we can still find one perfect possibility. It is represented in the idea that life affords opportunities to make adjustments. With our children growing older, now is a good time to renew our efforts to continue the process of forming a family environment that we like and one that contributes to our children during this important period of time. While we are thinking about the changes or improvements we would like to make, we can remind ourselves of the four adaptation principles: maturity, goodness of fit, balance, and preparation. Also, remember that each stage of family life invites us to make adaptations to best promote the developmental tasks our children are currently trying to achieve. When we exercise leadership to satisfy the four adaptation principles, we will more likely see healthy, thriving, and competent children.

In the previous chapter, I suggested it was possible to observe the four adaptation principles applied while we promote the five types of child development. I did that to emphasize the importance of understanding children from a developmental perspective and focusing our efforts as parents on helping them succeed. Please note that this chapter includes a description of some developmental tasks children try to achieve during the second family stage.

These descriptions are placed early in the chapter to emphasize again the idea that our family environment, including our leadership, needs to be linked to what we know about and want for our children (*The Real Power of Parenthood*). Children are one part of the family environment, and positive parenting is based on what we know about them and what we can do to promote their growth. In this chapter, I am attempting to show how the four adaptation principles can be applied directly into the way we organize and adapt the other parts of the family environment. We can organize work, rule conditions, and relationships to promote our children's success. The quality of our leadership is found in how effectively we do this.

Using Work and Activity To Promote Development

You can promote physical development and help children learn other social, mental, and emotional qualities by helping them organize work and participate in physical activities.

Family Chores

As children mature, add chores to their responsibilities so they are able to make greater contributions to the family. Ask children to spend about thirty minutes each school day and more on Saturday. Another suggestion is to rotate the chores (except for personal care of rooms) with other children on a weekly basis. Remember to ask or remind a young child only two or three times to perform a given task. After that, you are paying attention to noncompliance (reinforcing the very thing you do not want). Instead, lead the child by the hand to his work and point to it, saying, "I will come back and check to see how you are doing." Children are as consistent at doing chores as we are at providing supervision. The following suggestions will help you ensure children will follow through with their chores.

1. Make the chores specific ("Get the vacuum from the closet, plug in the cord, and then clean the living room").

2. Link completion of the chores to a specific time ("Vacuum the living room each day before five o' clock").

3. Set an achievable standard of performance ("Vacuum so that each part of the carpet is cleaned").

4. Use encouragement rather than nagging ("You vacuum very well, and I am happy when it gets done").

5. Put low probability chores, such as vacuuming, ahead of high probability behavior ("When you are finished vacuuming, then you can watch TV").

6. Use appreciation and recognition when the chores get done. After a child completes the tasks regularly, expand your attention by suggesting that doing the chores means a child is organized, clean, dependable, and efficient. Parental reinforcement helps children develop an "identity" or "self-concept" as a positive worker.

Physical Activity

Physical activities such as dance, sports, and games are essential to physical development. They provide great health benefits, self-esteem opportunities, social advantages, and moral education pertaining to fairness and rule compliance. Participation in physical activities is best when the following conditions are met:

1. Parents and children participate in the same activities.
2. When the condition above is not possible, then parents give attention to children's participation and help children develop physical skills.
3. Positive, "sportsmanlike" participation is regarded as more important than the outcome (winning or losing) of any event.
4. Parents and children discuss how well the child is participating and use activities to teach important lessons such as fairness, self-discipline, and goal setting.
5. Children participate in a variety of activities, but no more than one or two at a time.
6. Performance and participation should seldom be accompanied by parental criticism or pressure.
7. Children will pursue various activities because they find them satisfying and fulfilling, not because parents provide rewards or incentives.

Achievement Motivation

Achieving at school, at home, and on the job is based on children's motivation (which is linked to their experiences with family work). Some children appear more inclined than others to organize and achieve high standards. A desire to achieve is learned at home. You can use homework, family chores, or physical activity to teach achievement motivation.

1. Discuss with children the positive possibilities of achievement. (e.g., "You are a success if you are trying hard" or "You can become a great scientist").

2. Ask children to predict how long it will take to perform a task and what the outcome will be (e.g., the number of math problems they can figure correctly in a certain time).

3. Start the work and then follow up consistently. Express abundant praise and give affection for achievement. Criticism may motivate temporarily, but it creates fear of failure rather than incentive to achieve.

Improving and Adapting Family Relationships

Family relationships are the principal means of promoting children's social, emotional, mental, and moral development. A relationship is made up of two or more people; it involves communication, companionship, and emotional exchanges. Healthy and successful relationships include trust, loyalty, cooperation, unity, affection, and caring.

Your familial relationships are influential models that build lasting impressions. Wise parents recognize the importance of relationships with children and spend whatever time and energy is necessary to help their children become nurturing, loving, and respectful. The consequence for doing so will help children succeed in virtually every walk of life. There is little (other than time isolated from others) that does not include relationship skills. If relationship skills are learned in families they can be applied elsewhere. If not learned in our families they may not be learned at all.

Conversation Skills

Establish patterns of talking and listening so that your conversations are not one-sided. Taking time to talk with children about their needs not only helps them perceive their immediate situation more clearly, but also gives them an abundance of memories they can cherish as adults.

1. Ask open-ended questions that invite children to tell about their activities, their feelings, and any other personal impressions. Express genuine interest; ask follow-up questions that show your depth of concern. You listen—let them talk.

2. Listen attentively without being critical, becoming defensive, or passing judgment. Suppose, for example, you and your children participated in the same activity or they returned from doing something in school or with friends.

Practice Initiating:

> "Can you tell me about..."
>
> "What do you think about..."

Practice Listening:

> "Let me see if I understand..."
>
> "So, you are saying that..."

Practice Disclosing:

> "I had an experience like that."
>
> "I thought of something I'd like to tell you."

Use conversations to stay acquainted with each other, to solve problems, to handle misbehavior, and to prepare children for new experiences.

Examples:

- "Let's talk about this."
- "We need to sit down and talk."

Recognizing Emotions

Recognize the importance of emotions and address children's feelings in family situations. There are many ways to understand and interpret children. The most useful way is to view children from an emotional perspective. Emotions supply more information. They tell us about the children and what we can do to be the most successful with them. Emotions are tied to everything we do in our families. Having emotional skills enables us to use them in varieties of helpful ways when the need arises. Recognizing and using emotions to lead children is the one set of skills parents should not be without.

1. Notice and comment on what your children feel. (*"You seem to be happy about something."*)

2. Help them describe their feelings when they have misbehaved, when they have made a mistake, or when they are involved in an experience with friends or other adults. (*"How do you feel about what you did?"*)

3. Ask children to pay attention to the feelings of other people, including their parents, siblings, friends, and acquaintances. (*"How do you think she feels?"*)

4. Disclose your feelings about yourself and situations, especially those that are positive.

Examples:
- *"I am pretty sad that happened."*
- *"I love you."*
- *"I feel close to your mother/dad."*

---

5. Create an environment where children feel comfortable expressing their feelings and where they can articulate both negative and positive emotions clearly.

Play a pantomime game where everyone "mimes" five different emotions to be guessed by others. Rotate until everyone learns the names of new emotions and how each is displayed.

Teach Relationship Concepts

Family life affords numerous opportunities to teach children important concepts such as empathy, acceptance of others, loyalty, fairness, justice, warmth, cooperation, taking turns, sharing, and caring for others. All of these involve two or more persons. That is why they are called, "relationship concepts."

These concepts can be actively taught in family settings. Some families organize one night a week to teach such ideals to their children and to help them develop practical social and emotional skills. Further, relationships concepts are part of moral development. Parents who ensure their children have knowledge about high-quality relationships are more likely to see their children develop refined concepts of moral reasoning and judgment.

1. Learn and use the definitions for the foregoing concepts (empathy, loyalty, fairness, etc.) and make them part of the household vocabulary.
2. Use the concepts in stories you tell. Use them when helping children play. Knowledge of relationship concepts can help children adjust to each other and solve problems.
3. Demonstrate these relationship concepts and explain to your children what each one means as applied in your relationships with your children.

Show Warmth and Affection

Warmth and affection are basic ingredients to any good family relationship. If you show affection in a variety of ways, your children will likely learn and display it in return.

Demonstrations of parental warmth and affection help meet many emotional needs. In addition, they serve other developmental purposes.

For example, fathers who display warmth are typically viewed as more positive masculine examples for both male and female children. Mothers who display warmth and affection are more likely to be respected and obeyed. The following are suggested ways to improve our abilities in demonstrating warmth and affection:

1. Find the humor in family situations and make use of laughter and fun.

   Jennifer was discouraged when she didn't make the school basketball team. After talking about that and recognizing her feelings, her mother reminded her of the time when she first played as a third-grader. Her suit was too big, she insisted on wearing earrings to her first practice, and she was so small that she could not get the ball to the basket. They laughed at their memories.

2. Use displays of affectionate touch, such as caressing, holding, hugging, patting, squeezing, wrestling, dancing together, and kissing.

   At night before bedtime, Lynn made a habit of stroking and caressing his children while telling them of his love for them. Then, just as his children were drifting off to sleep he explained why he loved them. He told his friend one day, "You only need to tell a child one time that you don't love him and he will believe you. You have to tell a child many times that you love him before he will believe that."

3. Use holidays and special occasions such as birthdays and anniversaries to show warmth and affection as measures of recognition and admiration. In addition, spontaneously creating special occasions—a surprise picnic or pizza night—teaches children to celebrate everyday life.

Sixteen-year-old Laura Martin had been in the hospital recovering from a serious car accident. She had sustained some deep scars on her face that would require later surgery. She came home late one evening with her parents. As they turned onto her street, every house had yellow ribbons tied to trees and bushes. When she reached her home the neighbors were waiting. They lined up and applauded her when she was helped from the car. "We love you," they shouted. "Get well soon," came another cry. "We're with you," came still another. Her tears soaked the bandages on her face while she thanked them for letting her know she was loved.

Create an Adaptive Rule System

In the foregoing section, I described some methods of promoting development by organizing and creating positive family relationships. Hopefully, we will be able to use these and others with our children. Positive family relationships are the principal means by which children learn social, emotional, and moral skills.

In addition, the relational experiences we create with our children are often imitated and used by them with people outside the family. The quality of family relationships is a positive outcome by itself. When we are close enough, happy enough, and loving enough we consider ourselves fortunate and blessed.

High-quality relationships make all the other parts of family life better and more workable. Positive relationships, for example, better motivate children to work and to learn. They also make family rules more acceptable and the degree of compliance is greater.

This section is devoted to describing how to organize an adaptive rule system during the stage of "Family Consolidation.". The rules you establish in your family create a unique system unlike any other family's. It is also one of the areas where we face some of our biggest decisions.

There are two types of rules. There are formal rules that are talked about, consistently enforced, and applied to everyone in much the same way. There are informal rules that consist simply of what we learn as part of family routines. For example, families conduct mealtimes, bedtimes, or car travel in a routine fashion. This promotes the emergence of repetitive behavior that, by its nature, is like a rule.

Families consolidate in part because we organize some type of rule system that affects every family member. The rules are influential as guides for behavior. Our family will also be affected by how we use time and attention in teaching, discussing, and enforcing family rules. The most successful families have a few basic, formal rules.

After helping a child comply on a regular basis while he is young, parents begin to enforce the rules more flexibly. This will be based on an understanding of the child and the child's situation. Usually, these same successful families have several informal rules which emerge as part of routine activities such as mealtime, bedtime, driving in the car together, and other every day situations.

A rule is more than a guideline however. A rule establishes the basis for how we judge our children. We can be harsh and rigid about rules or we can use them more kindly to teach consequences and provide children with a sense of right and wrong and what helps or harms people. So, in addition to creating an orderly family organization, family rules can have a significant role in promoting children's concepts of morality.

> **A rule establishes the basis for how we judge our children.**

You may view rules and the power to enforce them as the chief means of maintaining parental authority. In many parent-child contests it often seems as if "the children are testing us," and "we must force them to obey." There may, in fact, be a few obvious cases when children should comply simply because we ask or require it.

Most often, however, children fail to obey because they do not have sufficient knowledge about the rule and need to be taught more about how a rule applies to them. Or, young children often do not know how a certain rule applies in a given situation and need to be taught. If you have frequent conflict over your authority, however, the problem usually is not just the rule or children's failure to obey. If your child is non-compliant, your relationship lacks something.

Try resolving authority conflict by examining the rules. Perhaps you reinforce rules too harshly or autocratically. Combine your evaluation of your behavior with increased attention and companionship to shore up the warmth, communication, and affection in your relationship.

The following suggestions will help you organize a rule system and adapt it to promote the development of your children.

Organize One Rule at a Time

- Select any formal rule with care to ensure it can be enforced and the enforcement does not create undue inconvenience to you. You can create rules for completing family work (i.e., "Make your bed before you go to school"), rules for relationships (i.e., "Be respectful to adults"), rules for social events (i.e., answering the telephone), and rules for personal conduct (i.e., bedtime, allowances, etc.).

- Present the rule to children and discuss what successful compliance is and what the positive consequences will be for complying as well as what the consequences will be if it is not followed (e.g., "Your mother and I think everyone should be home for dinner between 6 and 6:30 p.m. If you make it on time with your hands washed, we will be happy, you will be happy and we will be together as a family. Unless you have a good reason, if you are not here, you will have to fix your own or miss dinner").

- Adapt personal conduct rules to children's personalities and levels of maturity (i.e., different bedtimes for older and younger children). Some of your children will claim you are "unfair." They do this because they believe you are favoring one over another.

In fact, you are unfair in a sense, but you are applying a higher principle of parenting. You are communicating that rules exist for the welfare of the individual person (e.g., "You're right. I am not being fair. I don't intend to be. You will have to learn to trust that I care about each of you and what you need at the time you need it. I do not intend to treat all of you the same way").

> **Rules exist for the welfare of the individual person.**

Be Prepared To Change Formal Rules

When children are young they benefit from having a clear understanding of rules and how to comply with them. As they mature, however, too much emphasis on explicit rules often makes it difficult for children to assume responsibility for themselves.

As you think it appropriate, remove a rule from the formal condition by simply watching to see if a child complies, or by asking a child to follow it rather than making it into a "rule" that implies your authority and a child's submission. Then, point out times when the child follows the rule without being reminded about it.

Competent Parental Leadership

Parents who apply competent leadership skills can do it in many different ways. There are some common elements, however. These include providing a family environment that stimulates, motivates, guides, and challenges children to develop themselves. *Focus on the Children* defines sound leadership as making adjustments based on four adaptation principles: maturity, preparation, goodness of fit, and balance.

In the foregoing sections, you read some suggested ways to organize work, rules, and relationships during the "Family Consolidation" period. Let us consider some additional ways competent parents apply these principles to promote their children's development and growth.

Organize a Teaching Program

The thought of teaching children frightens some of us. Usually, this is because the word "teaching" calls up the image of standing before people and telling them what to do or how to do it. We get this idea from our experience in school. In families, however, (as in most other places) this is the least effective method of teaching.

Instead of thinking about teaching in this light, suppose we include going places to learn about what we see there, talking while we are working together, playing games, and doing other fun activities. Let us also include using teaching moments connected to some emotional need, misbehavior, or crisis.

Ronald Haroldson, a shop teacher at the local high school, built one home each year. As his children grew, all of them worked with him, and in the process, learned how to construct their own homes.

Sue and Larry Thornton spent one night a week with their children teaching positive social skills. They read stories, played games, performed skits, and did pantomimes. As their children grew, they involved them in the teaching and the older children learned while teaching their younger siblings.

Children do not always know what to do or how to act appropriately in every situation, but their ability to observe and imitate is truly remarkable. They are quite intelligent when it comes to understanding how to survive and succeed. Even with this extraordinary ability, their development is more positive if we organize a teaching program and introduce success ideas to them.

Think about a school teacher who teaches her own children to read and write, or the naturalist who involves his children in caring for the environment. Some families bring people into their homes such as artists, musicians, and teachers of foreign languages. Families can discuss world events, local political issues, and matters of moral and social concern. Further, we can teach by telling stories and personal experiences. We can help children learn social skills like giving compliments to others, being kind, and sharing.

Organizing a teaching program during the "Family Consolidation" period will help solidify your family, demonstrate the importance of learning, strengthen the relationship with your children, and promote their development. The happiest and most memorable experiences children recall are those times when they were sharing something with a parent and learned a life lesson from it.

Of all the reasons to teach there is one greater than any other. There are times in every parent and child's life together where we know we should make it very clear that some event or act should or should not take place. The happiness and success of our children are at stake. It might be whom they choose for a friend. It might be whom they choose for a mate. It might be going some place where there is a great risk to them.

Our children trust us when we have spent time teaching them. When we ask them, even without logic or evidence to support our view, they are more likely to follow us believing that we are acting in their best interest. Parents who do not teach are less likely to be trusted and believed.

Correct Misbehavior Positively

Because children make mistakes and misbehave, we develop discipline techniques that may include spanking, scolding, restricting a privilege (i.e., grounding), isolating (e.g., "Go to your room!"), or imposing some extra work or assignment. These are the most common methods of correcting misbehavior because they work at least some of the time. Further, they give us the benefit of immediate response. We feel as if we are doing the right thing to prevent further misbehavior. However, all these techniques share one limiting characteristic: All focus on what the child did wrong and teach no positive alternative.

There are two reasons why most children between the ages of five and eleven misbehave. First, they misbehave because they do not understand something they should and need to know. Second, they have knowledge but willfully choose to disregard it for some other emotional reason. In this case, they are making a bad choice or a choice to do something wrong or do something at the wrong time.

During a scolding you might remember having previously given instructions and say, "Why did you do that? You know better!" If children really knew better, they would probably do what is expected and desired of them. Telling is not the same thing as teaching. If they did know better, they still did not know that a certain act was important enough to draw your attention and frustration. Therefore, they know what to do but do not have knowledge about its importance.

Instead of using the most common discipline methods (as outlined on the last page) try using a more positive learning approach. Use punishment as a teaching process. Simply have them practice doing "correctly" what they failed to do when they made a mistake or misbehaved. For example, suppose two children get into an argument while playing a game and hit each other. This means they do not know how to talk things over, regulate their emotions, and cooperate.

The consequence you can impose is to require them to play another game "happily" all the way through, practice talking and listening to each other, and doing something that will promote cooperation. They will have learned to do what they did not do when they misbehaved.

Correcting misbehavior positively means that instead of focusing all your time on what was wrong or incorrect, you are shifting the focus to what your children need to learn. Further, instead of making your children feel stupid, guilty, or ashamed, you are constructively helping them learn to be better and more successful. This is a more effective use of time and it leads to more growth and learning.

Be Situation Specific

When children are five or six years old, they are in a position to learn some of the more important lessons in life. In our effort to manage our children we often overlook something very significant. We are trying to help our children be "good kids," or develop some lasting personality trait, such as honesty. We forget that these are adult ideas and only become part of children's lives after many years of repetitive experience. In contrast, young children think about specific situations and how to adapt and succeed in each one.

Two children may be playing together at home quite happily, but start to argue after getting in the car for a ride. This may seem confusing until we recognize that being in the car presents a very different situation from playing in the living room.

We can probably think of many other specific situations in which children participate. A few examples include eating in a restaurant, playing a team game, going to church, talking to a new friend, mealtime at home, going on a trip or vacation, shopping in a grocery store, or riding in a plane. If you want your children to be confident and successful, instead of giving general instructions to "be good," you will teach them what to do in each specific situation. The more specific we are, the more easily they learn.

This might be done in a conversation, but usually it will require some practice or rehearsal to help children understand what they are to do correctly.

A mother put three children in the car to run some errands. Two of them began to fight as she drove out the driveway. She immediately pulled back into the garage and took the children back into the living room. She made them practice "car riding" while explaining who would sit in which seat and the best way for them to act. Then she took them back to the car and tried it again. This time they knew what do and she praised them for succeeding in this situation.

The more children know about situations, the more likely they will adapt themselves correctly or remove themselves from situations that may be harmful to them. In addition to giving "general" instructions, it is fairly easy to apply instructions to the very situation in which children are about to participate. Playing school, having tea parties, and adopting other adult roles in pretend games are examples of their efforts to learn how to act in specific situations.

They will need to know the correct words and the correct way to name them. They will need to know about and rehearse appropriate emotional behavior (e.g. reverence at church, good manners at a restaurant) for each situation. They will benefit from knowing who else will participate and how to relate to each person. Being situation specific is an effective way to help children learn.

Selectively Approve and Disapprove

Parents have many ways to approve and disapprove of children. For example, when children act as we desire, we could praise them, display affection for them, tell others about their accomplishments, provide recognition in the forms of rewards or prizes, and give many different types of attention.

When children do not act as we desire we can also use several disapproval alternatives. We might explain what they need to do to improve, criticize them, scold them, yell

angrily, ignore them, require some penalty, restrict a privilege, isolate them, spank them, or any other punishment
we have practiced.

All methods of approval and disapproval have great
power to influence children. It is so powerful that what our
children think we believe about them, good or bad, will be
directly tied to our methods of disapproval and approval.
Further, approval and disapproval exert real influence on
what they eventually come to believe about themselves.

When we too frequently disapprove, we risk telling
children we think they are wholly inadequate, unable to
successfully achieve or perform. Rather than assume that
consistent approval is the antidote to this difficulty, we
should recognize that too much approval also has its problems. It can be just as controlling and can accelerate children's
dependence on us. Plus, if used too extensively, parental
approval can help children develop unrealistic notions
about what they can and should do.

The best thing to do is to apply disapproval and
approval selectively. This means that we use both, but that
we use each (and the methods of each) for specific purposes and in specific situations. To illustrate, parental styles
of disapproving and approving are described in the box
on page 204. Examine them and match them with the
"Consequences" listed below the box. Answers are provided on page 205.

While you are thinking about approval and disapproval, please remember these final points. Expressing

1. You display much more disapproval than approval.
   Consequence for children: _____

2. You often show anger when children misbehave. A loud, angry voice accompanied by angry gestures and movements may indicate the intensity of your feelings about something.
   Consequence for children: _____

3. You withdraw love and affection. This means you avoid talking, touching, or problem solving when children do something you do not like.
   Consequence for children: _____

4. You explain and talk with children before imposing any approval or disapproval and discuss what they need to do to improve.
   Consequence for children: _____

5. You frequently communicate your love for them and make a point of doing so even when children misbehave or make a mistake.
   Consequence for children: _____

6. You display only approval.
   Consequence for children: _____

Consequences:

a. Children learn that mistakes are an acceptable part of life and that they need not fear trying something new. They are more likely to avoid making the same mistake again. They believe in their own abilities and have more confidence in you.

b. Children will learn their relationship with you is enduring and is not threatened by their errors. This fosters healthy self-esteem and self-confidence but also increases the possibility that children will try to please you and will accept what you want for them.

c. Children develop an unrealistic sense of how to live in the world. They may develop a sense of superiority over others and believe they do not have to work or comply in order to be successful.

d. If children comply, they do so because they fear you. The older they get, the more likely they are to oppose your authority.

e. Children show a lot of frustration and anxiety. Some may argue, some may act helpless, and some may become aggressive, controlling, and critical of other children.

f. Children display intense anxiety about any kind of judgment from other people. Some will respond by hiding their emotions. Some will show indifference to anything important to them.

Correct Answers: 1. (d) 2. (e) 3. (f) 4. (a) 5. (b) 6. (c)

approval or disapproval implies that you are making judgments (which is our right and obligation as parents). Your children will link your judgment to your love, and will measure your love for them by it. As a result, many children become adults believing they are only loved when they have others' approval.

We can send a clear message of love for them even when we disapprove of their behavior. Taking the time to discuss and motivate improved behavior is a sign of love. Finally, if we approve or disapprove too frequently we will give no space for freedom. Children may sense excessive control and may distance themselves. It is better to use approval and disapproval selectively while more consistently displaying affection, warmth, caring, and acceptance. This implies acceptance even while judgments are being made.

Teach Children about Themselves and Their Relationships

Growing up offers a mixture of many experiences, including making mistakes, at least occasionally breaking rules, and having periodic conflict with other people. It also usually includes doing some things well, complying with rules, and succeeding with people. Children participate in a variety of social situations. These call on them to understand themselves and others, understand rule conditions, and do what is appropriate for that situation. In other words, children have many things to know and think about. Suppose we reserve approval only if they follow rules. Or, we pay most attention to how much work they do or do not do. Where we place great value, our children will tend to place value as well.

Furthermore, it is probably easy for us to think of people who commit most of their energies to their work as a supreme value. We might know of someone who gives their greatest focus to positive or negative application of rules, laws, policies, or procedures. There are, of course, good and bad things associated with each. In a discussion about their relative merits, it is easy to miss the important idea that these represent choices people make based on what they have learned early in life.

A dysfunctional family is a family in which the work and rules are considered more valuable than the development of children and relationships. In American society we see the terrible consequences that result when parents neglect to teach their children about themselves and their relationships with others. These consequences are well known by the names of gang membership, chemical abuse, sexual exploitation, violent crimes, dishonesty, and varieties of social aggression.

All are the results of inadequate emphasis on the development and healthy growth of children and the failure to

ure to foster their ability to participate in high-quality relationships with other people. When they fail in these efforts,
they try to meet their emotional and social needs in aber-
rant forms. It is not difficult to keep your focus on children and their abilities to participate in relationships with
others. You need only include it in a timely manner in your
conversations and other involvement with them. Read the
examples below which illustrate what you might do.

What do you do? If your response is similar to Option
1 or 2, you are leaving the "relationship" out of the dis-

Example 1:

Your eleven-year-old daughter avoids her work, delaying it to the last
moment, and sometimes does not do it at all.

Option 1: "You will be grounded for three days."

Option 2: "You haven't done your chores, so I am going to give you more
to do."

Option 3: "When you don't do your part everyone else has to do more."

---

cussion. If you usually take Option 3, then you have a
balance which includes a relationship emphasis. Read
the next example on page 208 to see how you might handle another difficult situation.

There are four things to be discussed when you focus
on your children's success, mistakes, or misbehavior:
(1) the deeds themselves, (2) any rules that may apply, (3)
the consequences for the child, and (4) the results for their
relationship with any other people involved (including us
as parents). When you address all four levels, you will

Example 2:

A ten-year-old boy is caught telling a lie.

Parental Response:

- "I want to talk with you about what happened. Please tell me what you did." (Paying attention to the task).
- "What have we decided about being honest?" (Paying attention to the rule condition).
- "What happens to you when you are not honest?" (Paying attention to the child).
- "Dishonesty creates mistrust between us. Do you want me to mistrust you?" (Paying attention to the relationship).

---

give your children a balanced, healthy, view of life. They will learn to perform, obey when appropriate, and be successful with other people. You will have balanced your family environment effectively so that it fits your children, prepares them for future development, and matches their level of maturity.

Summary and Transition

At the end of the family-consolidation period neither we nor our children will be perfect. But, we are not finished yet. There is room for improvement, but there is also room for self-congratulation. We did some things well. We will do them even better in the future. There is also the opportunity to communicate unfailing love for our children whether or not they follow all the rules perfectly or do all their work exactly.

Close and loving family ties do not depend on whether children or parents are perfect. They depend on our willingness to spend worthwhile time with each other, to communicate often, and to make our time together more rewarding than frustrating. They also depend on our using the considerable feelings we have in our families to form shared memories.

If we have done these things in our children's early years, to provide a solid foundation for them, we can look forward to the next stage of family life with interest and hope. The teenage years are some of the most enjoyable for parents and children. If we are confident about parenthood, we can find the rewards we expect and the next few years will hold the possibility of good things. It is sometimes useful, therefore, to remind ourselves of what is good about our children and to recall constructive things we have done.   ✸

Summary of Developmental Tasks
(Children 6-11)

Physical Development

1. Fascination with specific physical skills such as whistling, spitting, skating, bicycling, facial contortions, sound effects, writing on arms and hands, and making false tattoos
2. Increasing gender interest around the age of five or six—this "false courtship" gradually diminishes as children lose interest in favor of same gender friends
3. Growing awareness of gender, refined concepts of male and female, increased interest in knowing about sex and reproduction
4. Growth surges usually preceded by weight gain that naturally becomes integrated with new body size

Mental Development

1. Identifying and becoming aware of specific thought processes, such as strategies for remembering, solving problems, and creating new ideas
2. Increasing vocabulary; learning how to use new words and sentences and apply them correctly
3. Discovering they are naturally interested in and better at learning some things than others—they will be learning about physical movement, people and relationships, math, music, language, and arranging objects (art)
4. Organizing their thought processes to become effective thinkers in order to take more information into account while they are solving problems

Social Development

1. Communicating with and adjusting to authority figures
2. Talking and listening as part of communication
3. Appreciating the give-and-take of friendships
4. Understanding what other people think and feel; perceiving others accurately
5. Learning how to act appropriately in many social situations
6. Practicing fairness, loyalty, and cooperation

Emotional Development

1. Understanding a broad range of positive and negative emotions
2. Regulating and controlling anger, frustration, and aggression
3. Talking about their own emotions
4. Seeing and understanding the emotions of others
5. Adapting their emotional responses to fit many situations

Moral Development

1. Understanding what helps and harms themselves and other people
2. Looking for and understanding their own intentions or motives, and those of other people
3. Developing a sense of personal responsibility for their own actions

4. Learning caring, acceptance, and empathy for other people

5. Applying rules and performing tasks that will help people, and modifying harmful rules or tasks

6. Participating in communication with people who can teach them moral concepts

7. Understanding that good or bad consequences, for themselves and others, inevitably follow their actions

8. Describing their own thoughts, feelings, and actions accurately in situations in which they participate

Summary of Adapting Your Family Environment

(Children 6-11)
Adapting Tasks and Activities

Family Chores

1. Make the chores specific
2. Link the completion of chores to a time (before 5:00)
3. Set an achievable standard of performance
4. Use encouragement rather than nagging
5. Put low-probability chores (such as vacuuming) ahead of high-probability behavior (such as watching TV)
6. Show appreciation and recognition by praising children when the chores get done—after a child completes the tasks regularly, expand your attention by suggesting that doing chores responsibly means a child is organized, dependable, and efficient (this helps children develop an "identity" or "self-concept" as a positive worker)

Physical Activity

1. Parent and children participate in the same activities
2. Parents give attention to children's participation and help children develop physical skills
3. Positive participation is regarded as more important than outcomes (winning or losing) of any event

4. Parents discuss with children how they are participating and use activities to teach important lessons

5. Children participate in a variety of activities, but not more than one or two at a time

6. Performance and participation should seldom be accompanied by parental criticism or pressure

7. Learning to be active will be accomplished because children find it satisfying and fulfilling—not because of rewards or incentives

Achievement Motivation

1. Discuss with children the positive possibilities achievement will have for them

2. Ask children to predict how long it will take to perform a task and what the outcome will be

3. Start them working and then return to follow up—express abundant praise for achievement (criticism may motivate temporarily, but it creates fear of failure rather than incentive to achieve)

Creating and Adapting Family Relationships

1. Develop a conversation relationship

    a. Ask open-ended questions that invite children to talk about their activities, feelings, and any other personal impressions—express genuine interest and ask follow-up questions that show your depth of concern

b. Listen attentively without being critical or defensive

2. Recognize emotions

a. Notice what your children feel

b. Help them describe their feelings

c. Ask children to pay attention to the feelings of others

d. Disclose your feelings about yourself and situations (especially those that are positive)

e. Help children learn an emotional word vocabulary for many positive and negative emotions

3. Teach relationship concepts

a. Discuss the concepts

b. Demonstrate them

c. Ask for compliance

d. Reward compliance

e. Rehearse when children fail to comply

4. Gradually change formal rules

a. Become more flexible as children mature; move to more informal rules

b. Exchange formal rules for individual disclosure and compliance with what children say they will do

Applying Leadership Skills

Competent leadership is necessary to make your family successful. It will help you consolidate your family and help make all family members take pride in being a member of your family. Read the following leadership skills and select one or more that you would like to apply more effectively. Describe what you would like to do.

1. **Organize a teaching program.** This may include one night a week where family members meet together. It might consist of one-on-one teaching activities. What will you do?

2. **Correct misbehavior positively.** The word discipline usually means using some form of scolding, spanking, isolating, or removing a privilege. These might be useful at times, but they are not more effective than correcting misbehavior by requiring children to practice or rehearse correctly what they did not do in the first place. What will you do?

3. Be situation specific. Helping children learn how to act in specific situations is better than giving them general commands like "be good." You can explain, demonstrate, or rehearse so children know exactly what to do in any situation. What will you do?

4. Selectively approve and disapprove. Your approval and disapproval exert a significant influence. Both approval and disapproval are highly evaluative, however, and need to be balanced with acceptance and understanding. What will you do to selectively use approval or disapproval?

5. Teach children about themselves and about their relationships with other people. You can help them be successful if you will help them focus on how other people will be affected by what they do. What will you do?

Chapter Seven

FAMILY FLEXIBILITY

Recognizing the physical changes that come with puberty, members of primitive societies participate in ceremonies marking the end of childhood and the beginning of mature adulthood. These "rites of passage" help children understand they are entering into a new period of life with new expectations and responsibilities. The ceremonies, which may include fasting, bathing, and other rituals and celebrations, help individuals see the characteristics of children and how they differ from those of adults. Usually, children also learn the characteristics of successful adults and are encouraged to proceed toward those. After the ceremonies, children are recognized by others as full-fledged members of society and are accorded the rights and privileges given to adults.

These ceremonies provide a fairly clear path showing children their developmental destination. The children receive recognition for what they have accomplished as well as a new and important status. Children are valued because of their new development and are informed about how to make important contributions. The path from childhood to adulthood is made clear.

In more advanced societies like ours, children typically reach and go through puberty very differently. Where we could do much more to help our children along the way, we actually do very little. This is because we do not have a clear picture of what takes place, and what we, as parents, might do to contribute.

For example, little social recognition is given to the series of physical changes that turn a sexually immature individual into one who is reproductively mature. We could give correct knowledge, as well as much more support and encouragement when children are not quite children and not quite adults. Even in this day of increased openness about such matters, most children report they do not learn about sex and reproduction from their parents.

For many of our children this stage in life is reached with apprehension and unhappiness. Girls who mature early are usually ridiculed by friends and ignored by adults. Boys who mature later than most of their peers are so ignored they often give in to attention-getting behavior. Collectively, we fail to attach enough importance to these issues to give children sufficient guidance. One could easily see why, in the absence of clear-cut directions to adulthood, many youth flounder, make unnecessary mistakes, and find adolescence a difficult time. This is largely the reason why many parents believe that adolescence is a time when young people will have stormy, unstable experiences. Incidentally, many studies report that age fourteen, instead of being the happiest time, is generally considered the period during which youth are more discouraged about themselves than any other time in childhood.

Most youth go through puberty and adolescence gradually and the negative possibilities their fears suggest are not realized. Adolescence can be a time of great opportunity if parents are appropriately involved and the parent-child relationship is positive.

Factors like the right kind of involvement and a positive relationship are important during "Family Flexibility.". This stage begins when the oldest child reaches puberty and continues for the next six or so years. It is called the period of flexibility for several reasons. For one thing, if you have more than one child, when the oldest enters adolescence you will have children of the greatest age variation. Each of these children are in their own period of development and working to achieve the developmental tasks of their age. This requires increased parental flexibility simply to accommodate each child.

"Family Flexibility" is required for some additional reasons. For example, older children typically have greater mobility than do younger children and they spend more time away from home than in previous years. Families need to adjust to their comings and goings. Because of school and other social opportunities, older children are faced with greater numbers of situations requiring personal decisions. These decisions almost always affect the rest of the family because teenagers are not old enough to make decisions for which they can assume full responsibility. As a result, their decisions might need our involvement and actually increase the need for parental support. Adolescent children also need and will request more family resources such as money and transportation. And because social groups are one means of helping our children achieve independence, they are members of a larger network of friends, teachers, and employers. They are, therefore, more likely to learn from and be influenced by people outside the family. As a group, teenagers bring more influence into the family from external sources.

Increased elasticity or flexibility is also necessary to accommodate children and to help them retain the sense of family unity we have previously worked to create. Although we are prepared to help children continue developing themselves, outside forces may make increased flexibility difficult to achieve. Ironically, children's developmental tasks have added significance because there is less of childhood left in which to experiment. A bad experience early on allows more time for adjustment and recovery. Life is often less forgiving for those mistakes made in adolescence.

Knowing this can intensify our feelings as we watch our children progress toward their adult destinies. We may take pride in new changes and growth. At the same time we are more aware of potential pitfalls. Further, their new maturity makes them less innocent and less willing to naively accept what we say or want. Ordinarily, such increased awareness enables them to better recognize and understand us, which permits them to be more appreciative. If, however, our parental approach is inconsistent or illogical, teenage children are more likely to point that out (and sometimes in a less than subtle and gracious manner).

Furthermore, adolescents are more likely to express their opinions openly, and some of these opinions may be different from ours. We may have once been able to make statements and have them received and respected with little discussion or few questions. Our ideas about the world are now met with our children's views about the same things. For some of us it is a difficult adjustment to allow for additional perspectives and to accept children's rights to their own ideas.

With apprehensions increased and our authority sometimes challenged, we may respond by becoming more rigid rather than more flexible. This is the greatest decision during this period of family life. Should we maintain support for our children by increasingly regulating them, or should we gradually adapt the family environment so it is more flexible?

It is, of course, sometimes appropriate to impose firm guidelines and to regulate children, but doing so merely for the purpose of maintaining parental authority is rigid and limiting. Only in a very few situations will this promote healthy development. In contrast, it usually will prevent us from creating the amount of flexibility needed to adjust to the new tasks facing children and the rest of our family. A family becomes more complex as the number of members (and their ages and maturity) increases. The elevated complexity of family life usually requires increased flexibility.

The decision we make about rigidity or flexibility is influenced by another factor. Feelings shared between us and our children are intense, and by now we have firm, established perceptions of each other. These established ideas or opinions may lock everyone into emotional positions and create defensive impulses. This often evidences the anxiety we and our children feel when we enter this period of time.

If it results in a defensive struggle, and if it endures, it can cause attention to be removed from the real purpose of this stage of life. The purpose is still to focus on the children and their development. If we retain this focus, we can make this period of time enjoyable, like the others that preceded it. The period of "Family Flexibility" has major sources of fulfillment for both us and our children.

Children's Developmental Tasks

In American society, age eighteen has legal and social implications. Many laws indicate this is the dividing line between childhood and adulthood. Eighteen is the age when most individuals leave the structure and safety of "required" school programs and face personal life decisions including career, living conditions, and marriage. When children approach age eighteen, they judge themselves and are judged by others in terms of what they have previously done. This age signals a time to measure and be measured. It represents a milestone of significant achievement or failed attempts.

This is because the preceding six years are filled with many opportunities and challenges. Many separate paths of development are linked during this period. To illustrate, consider how physical, social, emotional, and moral development come together. The biological ability to procreate, as part of physical development, usually is combined with positive social relationships (dating and courting), emotional behavior (love and liking), and moral concepts (right and wrong). New mental abilities are combined with forms of achievement and social (career) opportunities. It is an understatement to say this is an interesting time.

Like all the other periods of life, at age eighteen, children have developmental goals to achieve. They are laid out in front of them like new clothes waiting to be worn. The clothes look good, but no one knows for certain whether they will fit just right.

Physical Development

The path of physical growth follows an irregular pace during childhood. This is also the case during ages twelve through eighteen. At some time during this period, a fairly rapid surge of growth will be preceded and followed by a slowing of growth. The range of possible changes is quite remarkable. Some general statements could be made for all of us, but mostly children develop on an individual schedule triggered by the "biological clock" in their brains. Once begun, however, many changes take place.

These changes include secondary (observable) sexual characteristics, increases in weight and height, firming of male and female contours, fat and muscle distribution, changes in complexion, and in some cases changes in hair color and form (e.g., from straight to curly). Children can begin the period of "Family Flexibility" looking one way, and, in some respects, end up looking quite altered.

As physical development happens with all its obvious signs, adolescents increase many of their less obvious physical abilities. Changes include increased strength, agility, and small and large motor coordination. This can be seen in such activity areas as work, sports, and dance. Important physical developmental tasks are summarized in the following list:

1. Achieving Puberty/Reproductive Maturity

Females start maturing nine months to a year before males. Each gender follows a fairly consistent sequence of physical changes until children are reproductively mature.

2. Regulating Increased Sexual Motivation

Puberty increases sexual motivation, which is usually displayed by increased awareness of how one looks to other people, need of acceptance by others, interest in heterosexual attention, and improved social skills. Mature individuals regulate their sexual impulses and the display of sexual behavior to the conditions of love, commitment, and responsibility present in their relationships.

3. Adjusting to Physical Abilities/Limitations

Physical changes during adolescence pose a "reality test" for individuals, creating a situation in which children become more realistic about their physical abilities or lack of them.

4. Desiring Adult Acceptance

Gains in physical stature increase motivation to be accepted and treated like adults.

5. Solidifying a Gender Identity

During this period, individuals acquire information about themselves, which is used to form a concept of "adequate" or "inadequate" masculinity or femininity.

6. Achieving in Focused Physical Tasks

Adolescents seek to achieve in tasks that require physical effort and abilities. These range from exercise and body building to organized programs of sports, dance, and work. This achievement plays a major role in determining their overall success.

Mental Development

The human brain continues to grow and mature through adolescence. It becomes more complex and adds new neural connections. This growth brings new mental abilities that will be demonstrated in many settings. Children will display them in their families, at school, in choosing activities in which they wish to participate, in demonstrating career choices, in clarifying religious and other social values, and in forming an individual style of thinking. It is one of the most interesting periods of child development.

When we understand what is taking place, it is exciting to watch this period and fulfilling to contribute to it. The following list includes some goals for this period.

1. Displaying a Unique Style of Thinking

During adolescence, children progress toward a unique style of thinking that they demonstrate in their likes and dislikes. They also show it in the way they think about other people and conditions in the world.

2. Formalized Reasoning

Children demonstrate an ability to organize "thinking sequences" to solve problems, to create new ideas, and to make decisions. For example, they will typically see solving a problem as a sequence of (1) identifying the problem, (2) thinking of alternatives, (3) testing the options to find the best one, and (4) reaching a conclusion. Forming these types of sequences makes the children's thinking more efficient.

3. Developing the Mind

During adolescence, young people can use their minds to understand things their senses cannot see, touch, taste, smell, or hear. Further, the ability to understand ideas goes beyond the basics of logical thought and reasoning. Abstract ideas like love, ethics, integrity, empathy, political philosophy, enjoyment, and religious faith are among life's most important.

4. Making Judgments

The ability to make finer and better judgments accompanies other mental abilities. With improved mental abilities, children make both positive and negative judgments about themselves, other people, and conditions they find in the world. In a mature form, this ability is displayed in better discrimination between truth and untruth, good and bad, trust and mistrust, and so forth. Children are better able to realize subtleties. In an immature form, this ability will be displayed in critical self-judgments, prejudice toward others, excessive cynicism, and harsh sarcasm.

Emotional Development

The task of regulating and adapting emotions to appropriately fit many situations continues in this period of development. A teenage girl is more comfortable meeting new friends, people in authority, and responding to the emotions invited by dating a handsome boy. She, and her male counterparts, are better at adapting and controlling themselves. Where there may have been unrestrained jealousy, anger, or anxiety, children now show progress regulating the display of both negative and positive emotions.

From the beginning to the end of this developmental period, most children continue to improve these adapting abilities. Children who do not improve are considered delinquent in their development and demonstrate this by trying to satisfy their less mature desires in the absence of emotional control. This is but one of several challenges to development during this period. As we read the following descriptions to learn about specific developmental tasks, notice the real potential for both success and failure.

1. Increased Emotional Independence

During adolescence, children seek to move from a more dependent position to one of greater independence. They can acquire increased self-reliance, confidence, and security by learning how to regulate and create emotions themselves rather than depending on others to do so.

2. Matching Emotions to Gender Requirements

Every society has expectations for developing individuals. In our society, the emotional requirements differ for men and women in some respects. Males, for example, have the developmental task of regulating and constructively channeling their aggression and the anger that usually accompanies it. Females have the developmental task of regulating and constructively channeling their competitiveness and the anxiety that usually accompanies it.

3. Emotional Readiness for Commitment

Making promises and keeping them is a significant emotional skill. It takes a true awareness of feelings at the time the promise is made and it requires the ability to regulate emotions when the time comes to honor the promise. Individuals must know several emotions, have awareness of the intensity of their feelings, and focus them on some things while ignoring other distractions. These emotional abilities are involved in major commitments such as schooling and work, career selection, courtship and marriage, financial decisions, religious faith, and value orientation.

4. Balancing Momentary Desire and Achievement

During adolescence, children are faced with new achievement opportunities and challenges. They also retain the emotional desires of earlier childhood. Achievements (such as high grades, music competence, debate, and sports) require more focused attention than a momentary impulse. To achieve, children need the ability to focus, and focusing depends on the ability to regulate and control desire. On the other hand, children's quality of life is enhanced if they recognize the importance of satisfying some of these desires. Mature people are able to strike a balance between these two opposing forces.

5. Achieving Acceptance and Autonomy and Resolving Adolescent Peer Pressure

A sense of belonging, security, and affection can be obtained through receiving the acceptance of others. For adolescents, these positive emotional needs can become negative if they are not balanced by a strong sense of autonomy. Autonomy is acceptance of responsibility for oneself, and the ability to make emotional decisions by oneself.

6. Enjoyment

One component to a happy and successful life is the ability to have fun and to find enjoyment. During adolescence, this developmental task is important because it is more than simply finding sensory satisfaction. It is identifying those situations and experiences that are truly fun without harming property, self, or others. It involves laughing at oneself, finding humor in people and situations, and knowing how to turn negative events into something positive.

7. Forming Positive Attitudes

Hope, faith, and a belief in oneself are ingredients of a successful life. Adolescents who develop these positive attitudes have achieved a developmental milestone. Such hopeful attitudes help children survive life's adversity, overcome failures, and persist when stopping seems welcome. Most adolescents pass through a period of self-criticism and have feelings of inadequacy, discouragement, and despair. These negative conditions set the stage for learning the benefits of a more positive approach to life.

Social Development

Adolescence is a critical time for social development. Social experiences during these times may have lifelong implications because the ability for intimacy and friendship expands considerably, increasing the possibilities for fulfillment or unhappiness. Children's developmental tasks include friendship skills, more effective communication, better application of social skills in new situations, participating in heterosexual friendships, and complex social reasoning. These tasks are achieved when children learn and apply specific social abilities. Helping them achieve improved social skills can create a foundation for future success.

1. Communicating to Understand

If people would like to be understood, they must first understand. Adolescents need to communicate information about themselves without defensiveness (withholding information or blaming other people) and they need to acquire other positive talking and listening skills. Social skills hinge on the development of positive conversation and communication skills.

2. Improving Acquaintance Skills

Added maturity means greater exposure to other people. This developmental task during adolescence involves learning how to meet new people, being comfortable in making their acquaintance, and forming a variety of social contacts.

3. Improved "Person Perception" and Tolerance

Successful "person perception" is the ability to be aware of and to communicate about oneself, another person, and the nature of any relationship between self and others. It is also the ability to understand that any person is influenced by several things and that it is usually best to reserve judgment about someone until more information is learned.

4. More Accurate Social Reasoning

Social relationships are fairly complex. One developmental task for adolescents is to reason about social situations by taking more, rather than less, into account. For example, it is considered more mature to link sex to love and commitment than to think about sex as something separate and isolated. Mature social reasoning also means that children understand about themselves and the larger social world. They can reason about society and government, social issues of the day, money and the economy.

If adolescents are successful, their understanding will permit them to see the world as an interesting place in which they have the power to achieve goals and master challenges. If unsuccessful, adolescents will view the world as a frightening and forbidding place where they may be controlled or intimidated.

5. Increased Social Confidence

Developing social confidence is a major task during adolescence. It comes from the willingness to take reasonable social risks to communicate, to be in front of people, to offer opinions, and to be skillful in conversations. Further, social confidence emerges when adolescents receive approval from others instead of criticism or mistreatment.

6. Readiness for the Experience of Intimacy

During adolescence children discover the experience of emotional intimacy. This happens first with same-sex friends, and later in dating. Feelings are personal and very intense. This is shown by long and deep conversations, strong liking, and genuine caring for another person. Mature individuals participate in intimate relationships and also retain a sense of autonomy. Immature individuals feel controlled by intimacy or feel they must control others. In these cases their performance (school work) declines and they may violate rules to participate in intimate (sometimes sexual) experiences.

Moral Development

At a very early age, children understand that some things are more harmful for people than are others. For example, four year olds are similar to nineteen year olds in their judgments that hitting someone is worse than doing something embarrassing like wearing pajamas to school.

Most children learn about rules before they are five years old and know that obeying or disobeying rules results in consequences. In the next few years this concept is followed by applying rules to relationships with others in order to establish and maintain a social morality of fairness, justice, and/or equality.

We can conclude that this early understanding of rules and their consequences for people and relationships merges with additional emotional and social skills. For instance, we learn how our actions may affect others by the way we ourselves are affected in similar situations.

We use our own emotions to understand the emotions of someone else. We understand what hurts us, and we better know what will hurt others. Likewise, we improve our ability to act consistently with what we believe or value.

We learn new things all our lives, but there is more integration of moral concepts in adolescence than in any earlier time. During this period, children confront new situations in which moral or immoral behavior can result. Further, they do so whether they understand they are responsible for themselves or not. Sometimes they seek only for increased freedom in their decision making.

During the time of adolescence, children lay a moral foundation for much of their remaining lives. It is true that moral mistakes can be corrected, but those made during adolescence last longer and are tougher to correct. In the context of caring about our children's growth, it is fairly easy to understand why adolescence is a fertile time for promoting moral development. Adolescence is an extremely important period for us to focus on our children. We can notice, for example, how their developmental tasks orient them toward a personal concept of morality in which each person is responsible for what might help or harm himself and other people.

The objectives of moral development include a strong sense of personal integrity which includes a sense of responsibility for our own actions. Another objective is the ability to appraise situations and understand when we or someone else might be harmed by what happens. We need several optional ways to help rather than hurt ourselves or others. These general moral objectives are easier to achieve if children accomplish several specific goals.

1. Identifying When Their Actions Help or Harm Someone

People may be moral simply because they are obeying a rule or doing what they have been taught by a trusted person. Most of the time, however, morality is based on knowing what helps or harms people. This is the basis of a mature concept of morality. Adolescent children refine their understanding of themselves and others enough to appreciate what may harm or help.

2. Improved Appraisal of Social Situations

Morality is more than a rule about behavior. Morality or immorality takes place in situations in which people are at risk. These are called moral circumstances. Morally mature people appraise situations by recognizing whether they or someone else is in duress or can be harmed by what happens. This is followed by recognizing responsibility and thinking about optional courses of action. To decide what to do, they identify rules that may or may not apply, other people, and their relationships with them. By thinking about situations in this way it is possible to identify what might help or harm themselves and others.

3. Developing a Standard of Personal Integrity

Successful human beings have a strong sense of personal integrity. This begins with emotional control (required to successfully adapt from one situation to another). It includes the willingness to accurately describe their own thoughts, feelings, and actions as part of any situation. Then, as adolescents, they learn to act to avoid harming other people. They learn how to retain their own sense of integrity even when receiving peer pressure. This often requires teenagers to choose between what they value and what is popular. Those who conserve their integrity become exemplars of morality.

4. Understanding Connections to Other People

Morality is about people and their relationships. During adolescence, children develop an increased understanding of the many ways they are connected to other people and they improve their abilities to act caringly. Recognizing these connections helps them avoid the isolation that characterizes the lives of many who engage in immoral or hurtful behavior.

Adapting Your Family Environment

I have proposed that we begin families with the idea that growth and development move from a simple form to something more complex. The wise course of action is to not wait until change and adaptation are forced on us, but to get ready for it by preparing ourselves and our children. The "Family Flexibility" stage is a time when increased adaptability is required. Children of different ages who have their own style of participation in the family are doing an increased variety of things. One or both parents are faced with personal life decisions, and these matters are coincident with and contribute to all the variation provided by the children.

Some of us are frightened of change. There are some changes that are risky and difficult. But, as older, experienced parents know, change is necessary to promote life. We would, however, like changes to be controlled, moving in a direction suitable to us, and beneficial to our children.

> **Change is necessary to promote life.**

We should not be confused or mistaken about the concept of flexibility. While flexibility means to increase the variety of possible ways to work with and respond to children, it does not mean that parents cannot or should not be firm and sometimes inflexible. Being flexible means that we hunt for alternative ways to help our children and increase our capacity for the many things required of us. It does not mean that we can or should remove ourselves and make indifference a part of flexibility. Flexibility may mean a new or different way of responding to a child's behavior from one situation to the next, but it is because the child's situation warrants it, not because we are inconsistent or uncaring. Flexibility suggests that we find new ways to make family membership possible, while at the same time allowing for children's individual opportunities. It does not suggest that either one or the other is ignored.

It is during this family stage that we can recognize the true importance of the four adaptation principles. Combined with children's achievement of their developmental tasks, they provide a standard to measure how well we are doing. We can adapt to children's level of maturity. We can discover new and better ways to make a good fit between what we do and the things that make each child unique. We can create a different and more appropriate balance between rules, tasks, and family relationships. Further, there is significant added importance to continuing to find ways to improve our abilities to teach and prepare children for their future tasks.

During the beginning stages of our family, it is crucial to learn how to promote the growth and development of our children in each of the five areas described herein. During the period of "Family Consolidation." I proposed that we continue by first learning about children and then using the elements of the family environment to help them learn and adjust. Children's developmental tasks were described, followed by examples of how to use work, rules, and relationships to contribute to them.

In this stage, we are integrating our knowledge about children and the conditions in the family environment with the four adaptation principles. "Family Flexibility" is an appropriate name, because to be successful we must increase our knowledge and be better at organizing and adapting our family to promote the welfare and well-being of our children.

Moving toward More Mature Family Relationships

Good family relationships are usually viewed as close, useful, and enjoyable. At their best, they are the resource for love, tenderness, commitment, and all other positive exchanges between people. Good or bad, the influence of family relationships is lasting. Among other things, they are the means for teaching many of life's lessons, a method of influence, and the first line source of support. They can be rich in personal fulfillment, because through them we find meaning and discover many of life's best kept secrets. Through healthy relationships we understand the deepest feelings, we experience the most profound moments in life, and we find our greatest satisfaction.

When our relationships are not successful, we still learn of their significance. In these cases, however, we learn because the sorrow is great, the emotional pain is extreme, and the anger is intense. All the negative conditions will continue (just as the positive ones do) unless we are willing to commit considerable energy to improving them. While working to do so we discover that relationships are amazingly stable. If we have started early and maintained good relationships, they tend to continue through adolescence. If relationships have not been of high quality, they will change from bad to good only by tremendous effort to rehabilitate them.

Parents in this situation recognize with newfound clarity that it would have been easier and better to have worked to make and keep relationships positive in the first place. It is especially important when our children are adolescents that we do well at creating and maintaining high-quality relationships. So, it is worth whatever it takes to make them more mature and satisfying. Our children need strong, positive relationships, and so do we.

During the period of "Family Flexibility", it is usually a good idea to make it clear that good relationships are important to us. If you need a reason to add emphasis, tell your children that they are going to participate in situations that you want and need to share with them. Good relationships will help us feel comfortable and give them the support they want.

What we do or do not do with our side of the relationship will not be lost on the children because they have matured enough to better understand what relationships should and ought to be. They will still imitate what we do and use it as one source of information about the way they should act. Although they are still in the formative years, the natural course of development allows them to think more discriminatingly about how they act toward us as measured by how we treat them.

Suppose, for example, that one of your children breaks a rule or makes a mistake and that your response is intense, critical anger. Rather than focus on their own actions to assume responsibility for what they have done and try to improve or change, most children would be wounded by your anger because it is a violation of the relationship. If you repeat your response, your children will become suspicious of you, less willing to accept what you value and more likely to repeat the behavior you criticized as a means of showing their resentment. The social demands they face in their lives make the relationship with you paramount. Their increased sensitivity to relationships raises, rather than reduces, the importance of the family.

Many women have told of having loving, affectionate experiences with their fathers in their pre-puberty years. When the girls matured, many of these fathers withdrew their displays of affection because their daughters were no longer "daddy's little girl." Adolescence, however, is usually a time when a girl worries most about herself and could benefit from a father's attention and warmth. Instead, these girls were abandoned.

The quality of your family relationships during adolescence is the principal reason why children comply or fail to comply with your rules, do or fail to do their tasks, and accept or reject your leadership. You cannot ignore the importance of a good family relationship if you expect to contribute effectively to your children's lives.

Adapting relationships during the "Family Flexibility" stage calls for relationship skills including positive attention, high-quantity communication, companionship time, displays of respect, approval, and regard. For adolescents, however, there are some additional things you can do. Adapting to their level of maturity, for example, may mean that you increase their participation in making decisions that affect them so they can assume greater responsibility. This enables them to feel more freedom, but also allows you to teach them about responsibility to others, to them-selves, and to those who depend on them.

You can further promote their sense of responsibility in one additional way. Coupled with inviting them to participate in decision making, urge them to openly and frequently discuss their thoughts and feelings about their relationship with you. "How do you think we are doing?" you might ask. "From your point of view, what do you think our relationship is like?" Help them examine the relationship from the point of view of their responsibility to it, just like you have a responsibility to them. "What do I need to do to have a good relationship with you?" "What do you think you need to do to improve our relationship?"

"Would you rather have a good relationship with me, or a lot of rules?"

Because successful participation in relationships is important, you may wish to use one additional motivational method. Offer to exchange some of your rules in favor of a "good relationship." You might, for example, ask, "Would you rather have a good relationship with me or a lot of rules?" Children usually choose a good relationship, but without knowing the elements of a high-quality relationship or how to successfully participate in one. Their desire to reduce the rules, however, will stimulate further interest. This will enable you to teach them about trust, which is created when people say what they will do and then do what they say. You can help adolescents learn the importance of clear and frequent communication because such communication contributes to trust, helps solve problems, and strengthens emotional ties. You can introduce affection, warmth, respect, and consideration as means of being aware of the other person.

Think about this for a moment. If you make establishing a good relationship your primary focus, you can take a positive approach to your children's development. The approach is active, and it makes a great deal of sense to children because they are in the period of time when their relationships with others have accelerated in importance. They will benefit by transferring what they learn with you to their relationships with friends. This means that you are promoting their social and emotional development as outlined earlier. Further, we will see that such emphasis on the relationship part of the family environment is a principal method of encouraging high-quality moral development.

What might happen if you choose to emphasize something other than trust, communication, or affection? Suppose, for example, that you place greater emphasis on work or rules. Children are smart enough to know how to please you, and even if not fully aware of doing so, they will try to learn and to do what you emphasize. They may, for example, become good at working. However important work habits and a strong rule orientation are to a successful life, they are not the same thing as relationships or social skills. The evidence supporting this conclusion is found in the most common situations where children fail to perform adequately or simply disobey. When you have neglected to emphasize the value of your relationships with your children, these common conditions easily progress to "power struggles" in which there are no winners.

Emphasizing the importance of your relationships will mean that you must spend the time to be aware of, informed about, and attentive to your children. You can be available for conversations and ask your children to come and talk with you. You can also be ready to show abundant amounts of warmth, respect, and affection. This will help you create the right emphasis and set the context for other important interactions.

Use Your Relationship To Teach about Sex, Chastity, and Social Relationships

Your children are on the threshold of adult life. They deserve some of the innocence we reserve for children and the opportunity to "play" before they assume all the burdens of adulthood. Most children are offered ample opportunity for this experience. Others, because of trauma or choice, have their innocence removed from them and learn too early that much of life is not play or fun.

For all children, however, the beginnings of adult-hood ought to contain preparations for what is to come. Such preparation can happen gradually and still be sufficient to enable children to move on with minimum struggle or error. That is the hope of most parents who, instead of worrying that children will grow up and leave, as earlier generations of parents did, now worry that children may not mature and may not become independent. There is much we can do to help them if we adopt a teaching and preparing attitude.

During adolescence your children undergo puberty. This biological process produces physical changes, as earlier indicated, and it does much more. It increases the attention children give to bodily changes, appearance, and social acceptance. It stimulates interest in sex and attraction. Because these natural motivations are fairly intense, children are ready to learn if parents will take advantage of the opportunity to teach and prepare.

You can promote the quality of your relationships through the sensitive attention you give to the physical changes that are emerging. For example, you can appreciate and give added support when you see increased self-consciousness (which is usually displayed by self-criti-cism, attention-getting behaviors, withdrawal and avoid-ance, or defensiveness).

Your recognition of their experience is a powerful indication to your children that you understand and care. Your conversations, encouragement, and understanding make them more receptive to what you wish to teach.

Further, relationships have two sides. Though it is not true in every case, children typically respond with behavior similar to what parents offer. Thus, we must offer the treatment we would like from them.

Not all children will be open to talking about themselves and participating in intimate communication. You can improve this possibility by complimenting them on how they look, asking questions, showing interest in their social experiences, and sharing some of your own experiences (although you need to be careful that you do not always switch the focus from them and put it on yourself). You can, for example, tell about yourself to explain the physical changes they are experiencing. You can help them understand that sometimes they will worry about their adequacy, their appearance, and whether they will be liked by others. You can help children understand that all the changes they are going through have a goal. Once this is achieved, they will like and delight in themselves. Let them know that your support and encouragement will always be available to them.

By creating a relationship of trust, communication, and affection you also create a context to help your children develop reproductive maturity and understand the close ties between sex, love, maturity, and commitment. In addition, you can present the idea that chastity requires the integration of love, maturity and commitment. In this context, chastity is more easily taught as a symbol of love, because to achieve it, people regulate themselves to avoid harming themselves or another person. The following are suggested ways to accomplish teaching about chastity.

    a. Ask your children to share with you their attitudes about sex and chastity.

    b. Ask them to appraise situations where it may be easy or difficult to regulate their sexual desires.

    c. Provide some "resistance training" or methods of asserting their desire to avoid inappropriate sexual behavior.

    d. Invite frequent conversations with your children about the link between sex, emotions, intimacy, and commitment.

    e. Help children understand the connection between self-control and their religious faith. A belief in God gives reason to be chaste. Sexual self-regulation helps create confidence in themselves and a sense of control over their lives. These values are usually found in ethical and religious principles. Religious belief stabilizes behavior when children establish a loving (not fearful or guilty) tie between their faith and the management of sexual behavior.

In addition to puberty and sex, there are other significant things you need to teach about and prepare your children for. Adult life usually involves the process of making decisions, organizing time, and planning. Some of your children will allow you to sit with them and show them what to do and then will practice doing it. Other children resist and wish to learn by themselves. And others are so caught up in following the attractive stimulations of the day that they go through their entire adolescence without cultivating these abilities.

Your family relationships are the basis of what your children know about emotions and how they make them a part of their lives. If you talk about "feelings," your children will be more aware of their own emotions and those of others, and will be more adaptable. If you tell about yourself, including what you think and feel, they will learn to do this and will be able to demonstrate positive intimacies in their friendships. If you are able to display a desire to understand, they will know acceptance and increased confidence. If there is affection and encouragement, children will feel more confidence. Interestingly, but less well known, these expressions of confidence and openness are the very conditions that promote gender adequacy in both males and females.

To further illustrate how family relationships lead to positive social and emotional development, consider the need for children to develop successful social reasoning. Such reasoning necessarily involves understanding people's motives and intentions and appraising situations for what might help or harm someone. Children also need to know how to cooperate to accomplish joint tasks and how their behavior affects others.

All of these abilities can be learned inside your family. They are learned during wide-ranging family conversations about people and world situations. They are taught during attempts to resolve conflict between children if you insist they talk through feelings until they understand one another. They are taught by their learning to pay attention to someone other than themselves and by examining the effects someone else has on them.

Finally, positive family relationships stimulate mental development. Communication and positive emotional exchanges add stimulation and encourage exploration into new mental domains. When you and your children introduce ideas into the family dialogue you are reinforcing the idea that learning is important and enriches everyone's life.

Balance Emotional Support and Rule Conditions

Adolescent children make their way into society and, while doing so, expose to other people what we have done as parents. If our children represent the best values, we can bask a little and feel some comfort and relief.

When children are not successful, many parents feel like their children are negative reflections of their parenting. To feel more secure, these apprehensive mothers and fathers often try to resolve this situation by increasing their children's compliance to existing family rules.

To some extent, enforcing rules may remind children that you are attentive and involved with what they do. Sometimes, in the process of increasing your attention to children's performance and compliance to rules you gradually remove or diminish expressions of emotional support. You might reduce the amount of praise, touch, affection, encouragement, warmth, concern for their feelings, and shared humor. You might be so interested in "telling" your children what to do that you forget to ask what they are feeling, or you do not listen when they speak. If your children are experiencing social pressure, distress, or feelings of inadequacy, this withdrawal of support is a significant parental blunder.

Yet, we want our children to have a realistic view of life and to face up to their responsibilities. Some of this requires that we confront them, tell them where improvements need to be made, and correct unwise choices. There are no magic fairies who come and make things easy. There are few, if any, shortcuts to a successful life. There are, however, rewards for hard work, integrity, and social competence.

The solution to this seemingly unresolvable paradox is to balance emotional support with giving the facts about life's lessons. You can identify what you would like to do to express your concern, support, affection, and approval. Then commit yourself to communicate these regularly. You may even have to create opportunities like "going for a ride" or "getting something to eat." Constant support for children helps them find the resources to face their challenges. If and when they do make mistakes, your emotional support will enable them to communicate the mistake and recover from it faster than if they feel distant from you. Emotional support includes:

a. Displaying touch, warmth, and affection frequently
b. Expressing sincere praise and approval

c. Asking for companionship time

d. Asking about personal matters in a nonjudgmental way and respecting your child's privacy

e. Clearly expressing what you would like your child to do in a direct and encouraging way and focusing more on what could and should happen than on mistakes or past behavior

f. Sharing methods for success

Fit Rule Conditions to Each Child

The older your children are, the more they wish to be thought of as separate individuals who are unique, at least in some respects. Most parents recognize the need to adjust their rules and how these rules are enforced based on their children's level of maturity. Unless you consider conditions outside your home worrisome to your children, or believe your children to be unreliable, you are likely to relax some of your rules for older children. This symbolizes increased trust and recognizes their increased maturity.

Whenever you exercise your authority, you are also communicate something about your child's freedom, responsibility, autonomy and dependence. Adolescent children generally want their parents to remove the rules and relax their authority so they can have more freedom. There are two important freedoms in life. One is the freedom *from* external pressure or authority. Many children seek for this by demanding that parents "back off" or "relax." Often, parents concern themselves with how much freedom to allow and how much authority to retain.

The answer to this question is found in the second type of freedom—the freedom to perform, make choices, achieve, and act to promote one's own welfare. This freedom is different from the first because it is related to internalized values, awareness of responsibility for choices, autonomy, and independence. It develops gradually, based on a child's own experience, mingled with much contact and communication with parents.

Many parents are unaware there are two types of freedom, and in trying to adapt rules they confuse the two. Some remove their attention and attempt to completely turn over most, if not all, rule and authority to their children. Done in the name of "giving space," this approach often borders on neglect and leaves children without the important support and preparation they need during this crucial period of life.

Other parents, who believe the first approach to be too permissive or indulgent, retain authority and use it intrusively, compelling too much compliance. These parents prevent the formation of freedom to act and to create internalized values in their children because they feel reaffirmed and temporarily secure by their children's submissive responses. The whole thing has gone haywire if children are either rebellious or submissive. In either case, success for children is then measured, not by their initiative, self-control, or character, but by their compliance.

There is a third, and better, alternative—to use a measured, gradual process over a long period of time. This process includes the following steps:

a. **Discuss Rule Conversations:** Talk with children about how rules should be created and enforced. This permits children to become aware of rule conditions. Awareness increases a child's sense of responsibility for rules.

b. **Be Selective in Retaining Authority:** Retain authority where you think it important, but select some (at least one) situations in which you are willing to entertain your children's opinions and accept and rely on their decisions. Correspondingly, children need to be given responsibilities and asked to fulfill them effectively. Notice their efforts and communicate praise regularly.

c. **Make Joint Decisions:** During communication with children, it is important to listen attentively, and then to clarify and summarize what the children say they want. Your child also needs to listen to and understand what you want, so that you both comprehend each other's viewpoint.

Sometimes, the decision will be what the child wants. Sometimes it will be what the parent wants, but most decisions should be mutually satisfying. No decision should be reached until this form of communication has taken place. Encourage this type of communication and show appreciation for the children's participation.

d. Designate the Decision Maker, Communicate the Decision, Carry It Out: The last step is to designate the child as the decision maker for a gradually increasing number of decisions. Depending on your situation, these decisions may include curfews, social plans, completion of homework assignments, choice of friends, or performance of chores. In any case, parents and children must communicate openly and understand the agreement completely.

You can suggest options so that their decision is amended somewhat to be more satisfying to you. Then, it is important that you communicate your expectations that the children will carry out the decision just as you all have discussed it. If they do not, it is important to communicate to learn why not, and to reaffirm the need to for the decision to be carried out.

However, there will always be the need for decisions that only parents can make. One of these is deciding how to adjust the rule conditions for each individual child. Because children develop at somewhat individual rates, flat age rules are insufficient help in making the decision (e.g., at age sixteen every child can drive). Sometimes it is hard to determine how responsible or irresponsible a child will be. In such cases, we discover the answers by trial and error. Always focus on the development of your children.

Your decisions should be based on trying to help your children learn, develop, and achieve. Fewer errors occur when you do this than when you base decisions on observations alone. Further, if mistakes are made they are usually less damaging because your decisions have a useful and coherent purpose, rather than a personal-emotional bias.

Fit Children to Their Work & Prepare Them To Be Effective

Habits and attitudes adolescent children develop about work are usually carried with them into adulthood. This is because adolescence is a trial period. What teenagers learn and believe about themselves becomes integrated into their self-concepts ("hard worker," "lazy," "smart").

Further, children's work habits and attitudes become linked to their development. Effective work, for example, also requires social skills such as communication. It requires emotional abilities like autonomy and self-regulation, physical skills, and the use of energy. It is linked to moral concepts of responsibility, dependability, and honesty.

You have probably given each of your children some tasks to perform in the family. By now you have employed methods of teaching children how to work and how to supervise what they have done. You know that each has his or her own style of doing work.

One child will be thorough while another is sloppy. One will be organized while another is undirected. One will pay attention to detail while another does not. Some will have achievement goals and work toward them, and others will seem impulsive and distracted. All children, how-

ever, have the same developmental objective: To participate in worthwhile efforts and to achieve.

Physical activities such as individual and team sports
offer children an opportunity to work with others and to
achieve. Parents who join with children in these activities
help them set the foundation for an active, healthy life.

Most parents want their children to work, and to work
effectively. It is hoped that these work habits will be applied
toward school achievement, family chores, part-time work,
or work related to a career. Yet, in the age when fewer
children work alongside their parents, it seems more parents
have difficulty getting their children to work and helping
them develop work-related values that will permit them
to succeed.

In addition, as recently as one generation ago, children needed to work in or out of the home because it was
economically useful for them to do so. That is true also for
some of today's adolescents, but many others are not expected to add to the family income. In other words, young people find less reason to work.

Increased numbers of these individuals enter adult
life without a desire to work, and without valuing the ability to work. Consider the following suggestions as ways
of helping your children learn to be positive workers:

Assign, Organize, Do, and Complete: Make sure that
children have important work and a specific time to do it.
Give them recognition for organizing the work, doing it
well, and completing the job. A.O.D.C.—assign, organize,
do, and complete.

Set an Example and Point to Other Good Examples: Adolescents benefit from seeing positive examples of work and its effects. Some good work examples could include shared work between you and your children.

Commit To Supervise: Your supervision indicates what you think is important. Assigning something and failing to supervise it will typically produce unsatisfactory results. Schedule an assignment (just as you would schedule an evening out) and use your supervision to teach good work habits and values. Discuss how the children organize their work, what they think about it, and make positive comments, if possible. Talk about the importance of work, liberally sprinkling your conversation with "truisms," such as the following:

Examples:
- "It is better to keep up than catch up."
- "If you are really trying, then you are succeeding."
- "The people who are really successful will do one thing more before they quit."
- "You get credit only for what you finish—not what you start."

Prime with Incentives and Move toward a Personal Standard of Work: Everybody works for incentives, even if the incentive is to finish something that needs to be done. Giving children an incentive (money) is all right if elsewhere they contribute to the family work without payment. Some children may need to have other activities restricted until they complete their work. While children are working, help them apply the following slogan to themselves: "A good worker organizes, does it well, and completes what is started." Give your children encouragement by telling them in a positive manner what you have observed.

Face Resistance with Calm Persistence: Do not nag, argue, and repeatedly demand. Just assign the task and tell the children how to perform it. The more you talk with children about their work the longer they will take to do it. Ask that it be done; ask if it has been completed. If the task is not finished, ask, "What does it mean that you are not able to do your chores?" and "What are you going to do to finish?"

To early teens:
"Why do you expect things from us if you cannot do your work?"
To late teens:
"What kind of person do you expect to be?"

Incorporate Many Types of Development into Work: The more types of development you can incorporate into work, the more likely children are to do it. Work will more likely be done when it includes mental, emotional, social, and physical activities.

Adolescents, for example, are especially intrigued by the mental aspects of work because they are developing new abilities and want to apply them. If mental stimulation is not available in the work itself, many young people will resort to other types of stimulation such as listening to music while studying or thinking about some problem while working.

Many types of development during adolescence are linked to children's ability to work, and work effectively. Most of the time, work gives children a sense of purpose and accomplishment. After childhood is over, much of our mental, emotional, and moral lives are tied to the work we engage in. Thus, as our children enter adolescence, we can make work an important part of our family environment and promote our children's happy growth toward increased maturity.

Applying Parental Leadership

During childhood there is a premium on the present moment, and with it, the spontaneous innocence made possible by secure and capable care of loving parents. Teenagers (who are ending their childhood) are exposed to both the good and the bad of the world. Their orientation moves away from the past and present as they think about what lies ahead. The growth of their bodies and the expansion of their minds, combined with their enlarged social experiences, convince adolescents that childhood is ending. Although there is much to look forward to, the future is not certain.

This uncertainty of the future creates a need for true leadership, for someone who is a few yards ahead on the pathway of life and who influences those who follow with a vision and a hope of future possibilities. A vision, however, is just the beginning. Parental leadership includes preparing children so they can meet and master the uncertainty they will surely face.

All children deserve to enter their future optimistically—with enthusiasm—and with the hope that they can "climb any hill" and survive any problem. When children do not have this optimism, they are more likely to fear the future. Any parent who has seen a child suddenly begin to evade moving toward the future trembles at the realization. Nowadays, too many of our children are finding the future too complex and difficult. Increasing numbers of adolescents try to solve their fears and despair in death.

Your parental leadership, if you apply it well, is the solution. Your very life is evidence that the future is survivable. The emphasis you place on preparing for life in your teaching further confirms that if you can do it, so can they. That happy thought is expressed by the man who taught his children that he would be a successful father only if they found some way to surpass him.

Lead into the Future

We remember the past, live in the present, and imagine the future. If you stop to think about it, you can appreciate how important time is to adolescent children. Happiness and success are between the present and the future. If you wish your children to experience these feelings, you must anchor their thoughts to this time (present and future) so they will live in it.

Suppose one of your children has experienced a major disappointment. After you have listened carefully, understood, and shown empathy, what do you do? Almost instinctively, most parents will try to take their children's feelings out of the present and direct their thoughts to the future. Examine the following statements that reflect this idea:

- "Things will get better"
- "You have a lot to look forward to"
- "Just imagine what you can do"
- "You have special abilities and you need to get ready"

Comforting and encouraging children includes providing hope about a better future. By describing future possibilities you are helping them anchor their thoughts between the present and future, the place where happiness can be found. But, it can be found only if the child is willing to prepare for it.

Suppose you have watched a child try to do something and then give up. What will motivate that child to try again? Persistence is based on hope that what one does now (in the present) will produce something worthwhile (in the future). You might say, "Keep trying—you will need this skill where you are going."

Many parents use this approach to help children understand at least one reason why they need to practice a musical instrument, learn to work, do well in school, or be honest. These ideas are embodied in the statement, "Keep going—you need to prepare now for what is to come." If children ask why you want them to participate in family activities, you can apply the same principle. "If we want to always be a close family, we need to be together now and get to know each other."

Leading into the future represents the true purpose of parental leadership. In fact, we are part of our children's past, present, and future. Because we love them and want them to be successful, we must tell them about their future. Then, we need to monitor them when they are both on and off the path and exult with them when they make progress or reach their sought-after milestones.

Consider the specific things tied to the concept of preparing for the future. Some examples include saving money, doing well in school, developing good work habits, making and keeping friends, developing a strong sense of integrity, and improving talents. In fact, nearly everything adolescents do can belong in the present moment and at the same time be linked to the future.

Take Advantage of Achievement Opportunities

Children strengthen or validate themselves through healthy relationships with others, through their achievements, and through compliance to positive rule conditions. There is abundant evidence showing these three conditions as the basis for self-esteem and self-confidence. When children feel opportunities for validation do not exist, or when they believe they have failed at them, they are more likely to have large—even impairing— doubts about themselves. During adolescence, when they are especially vulnerable and impressionable, there is great wisdom in using your parental leadership to take advantage of achievement opportunities.

Achievement opportunities can include many things. Some parents, for instance, ensure their children have positive skills in at least one area such as music, sports, academics, or student government. A talent is a medium of social exchange and a "ticket" that permits participation with other similarly interested people.

Another way of taking advantage of achievement opportunities is to consider the milestone achievements that normally take place during the seven teenage years. Some of these achievements are school awards, making a sports team or music group, getting a part-time job, completing requirements for scouting awards, getting a driver's license, and having a first date. These achievements and others like them provide opportunities for us to encourage participation, provide support, and enthusiastically give recognition.

In an effort to motivate, however, some parents withhold one desired goal unless a son or daughter achieves another. This form of leverage reduces the value of any achievement. Consider a common example in which parents may want a son to complete his Eagle Scout requirements, but he is not motivated to complete them. They know he is highly motivated to get his driver's license, so they use it as a form of leverage, saying, "You will not be able to get your license or drive until you have your Eagle Scout Award."

Another common situation includes school achievement and driving. In some states, for example, insurance rates are lower for students with grades at or above a "B" average. Consequently, some parents will attempt to motivate their children to study and do homework by announcing that they will have to pay for the increased insurance costs if their grades are below a "B" average.

On the surface, using a highly-valued goal to motivate the accomplishment of one that is less valued may seem a useful approach. However, although all the achievements (i.e., scholastic achievement, scout awards, and driving) are important, these situations are not the same. For one thing, the relationship between grades and insurance rates is imposed by the insurance company. Eagle Scout Awards are desirable, but only two percent of Scouts ever achieve them, which means that many successful people do not. A son, therefore, does not "have" to get one. (It is not a social requirement in the way that good grades are required for low insurance costs.)

Second, there are several reasons why children resist achievement. Simply using one important and valued achievement as the leverage to produce the other often places a child in a hypocritical situation. Is the achievement for the parents or for the child? This robs the child of the sense of freedom and accomplishment one ordinarily expects from achievement. The good that could have resulted has been diminished.

Third, children may not always be in agreement with their parents. While this is not uncommon, it could be a sign of deeper problems. Parents who use leverage to motivate children in this situation will build resentment. Often the child shows the resentment by leaving the arena (i.e., getting out of the situation) or by failing to achieve either of the alternatives in question.

In contrast to the leverage approach is the idea that every achievement is important. That is, achieving in school is important, getting an Eagle Scout Award is worthwhile, and getting a driver's license is significant. They are all sufficiently valuable and should not be tied to another (except in cases in which conditions are imposed by someone other than the parents—grades and insurance costs, for example). Keeping achievements separate from one another means that it is best to build a motivational program rather than holding one option hostage to the achievement of another.

Use your parental leadership to start the achievement process. First, you can expose your children to positive examples of achievement. You can be an example if you are willing to tell about the steps you have taken to choose a goal and achieve it. Second, children also like to hear about the real emotions that are part of achievement— apprehension about not succeeding, but elation and feelings of worth after succeeding. Third, participate with your children as they select areas to pursue. Fourth, talk about your children's goals and help them create a vision of future possibilities. Fifth, share some of the work and use abundant encouragement. Always share in family members' achievements and enthusiasm as well as their discouragement. In short, be involved in their achievements. Being involved is more important than most people think. Not being involved in your child's achievements hurts more than we imagine.

Describe the Situation

By the time children are teenagers many parents have formed habits of commanding, regulating, and correcting them. Such statements usually emerge because parents learn they are the simplest and most effective way to get what is wanted. These verbal habits are sometimes difficult to change even when failure to adapt may create serious leadership problems.

Young children are more inclined to depend on people with authority because their youth and vulnerabilities require direction as well as support. As they mature, however, their world widens and they are likely to reduce their dependence on a person (parent) and rely more on understanding social situations to determine how they should act. Often they will indicate this ability by responding with irritation to something you tell them: "I know, I know!" or "Whatever!" This happens mostly because as they grow they have increased experience where parents are not present. Children sharpen their understanding of social situations because they have to adapt and make judgments about themselves and other people based on their interpretations of each circumstance. Their understanding of situations becomes more important, while their dependence on authority figures moderately diminishes.

Use your leadership to take advantage of this positive condition. When you ask your children to do something, you will probably get more compliance if you take the time to explain the situation as you see it, rather than simply giving them a command of some kind. Contrast the following statements.

First, a frustrated parent might raise her voice and say, "Get your band instruments out of the living room!" Or, in the same situation, the parent could say, "Let me tell you about the situation. I come home tired and look forward to relaxing. Sometimes I invite people to visit. Also, neighbors drop in to talk from time to time and I would like the living room to be clean. Those instruments make the room look cluttered and I would like you to take care of them. Besides, if you leave the instruments out they are more likely to be broken."

Examine the preceding paragraph. Notice that it took more lines to describe the situation than it did just to tell someone what to do. Even though there are times when telling and correcting are quite appropriate, our goal is something different. We want our children to be obedient without excessively controlling them. Therefore, discuss the situation with them as you view it, invite them to tell their point of view, and then indicate what you want them to do. Except for cases in which children are angry and rebellious, they will more often do as you ask without your having to argue with them.

Find the Two "Want To's"

Conflicts over limited resources and between two interests are a regular part of any relationship. One person's desire will often contradict that of the other person's simply because people are different from one another. Rather than fear this conflict and attempt to suppress it, one should develop a leadership plan which accommodates conflict and attempts to solve it.

Puberty, mental development, and increased social mobility all contribute to something parents can use to successfully reduce the amount of conflict they have with their children. During adolescence, most individuals develop increased awareness of themselves in at least two areas. First, adolescents begin to understand their personal hopes and dreams. Second, they understand the extent of their obligation to others. The self-consciousness of the teenage years appears to bring them into more familiar terms with what they want, feel, and desire.

At first glance, many parents will see this as selfishness coupled with arrogance and indifference toward others. It often appears to be this way and it sometimes is. However, if channeled correctly, this development can be used to reduce conflict.

The climate for conflict exists when there is real or perceived disagreement, disobedience, rudeness, or unwillingness to communicate. When any of these are extreme, it is often difficult to restore a conflict-free relationship. However, to prevent conflict in the first place, the best way is to separate what should or ought to happen from what you and your teenager want for yourselves. What you want might be the same as what your teenager wants, but often it is different. Children frequently perceive parents as imposing "shoulds" and "ought to's" and believe that parents care little for what they want. In this case, children are also likely to ignore what their parents want. The definition of a good solution is one in which both parent and teenager get some of what they want while addressing what the situation suggests should take place. When you can identify and talk about what each person wants and what each person thinks should happen, you will discover that solutions are more easily reached. Besides, voice tones are softer and people are more willing to listen when the conversation is about "want to's" rather than "shoulds" and ought to's."

Mel and his son Todd were arguing about Todd's late hours and his failure to do his chores. Mel was angrily asking, "Why do you stay out so late?" Todd's reply was a sullen, "I don't know." When tempers accelerated, Todd told his dad that he "never understood," and that his rules were "stupid." Ordinarily such statements were inflammatory and Mel's anger increased. Rather than blowing up, Mel asked in exasperation, "What do you want?" Todd sat without speaking, sullen and angry. Taking advantage of the sudden lessening of tension, Mel more sincerely asked again, "Really, Todd, I would like to know what you want." When he finally spoke, Todd said he didn't know. Then he said he couldn't tell his dad because he knew he wouldn't care. After being reassured, Todd finally told his father, "I want a guitar and I want to take lessons." Mel was stunned. "I never knew that," he replied in a muted voice.

Todd didn't ask what his father wanted, but Mel eventually told him that he wanted to know that Todd still cared about the family and respected him. It took them awhile, but they were able to figure out some way to get more of what each wanted. With your teenage children, practice having them explain what they want in certain situations. Without being demanding, communicate the same information about yourself. These statements might be similar to, "I want us to get along," or "I want you to come in on time because I worry," or "I want to spend a thousand fun times together."

In any negotiation between two conflicting parties, the most important information is to learn what people want (not what they say they want, or what they pretend they want, but what they really, sincerely want). This information is not easy to get, so you must practice asking this question frequently: "Tell me what you really want. I would like to know." Children's willingness to search for what they want is an indication of how close or far apart you are. If children understand what they want and can talk about it, there is at least the beginnings of an agreement. If they do not know what they want, or cannot say it, you will need to help them by asking questions until they can form a clear idea for themselves.

Helping your children match what they want with what you want is the highest order of skilled parental leadership. Pursuing this objective suggests you are willing to be cooperative without always giving in. It means you want to consider your children's point of view. The best part about it is the amount of angry conflict you can avoid in your family. You and your children will be honestly considering each other in terms of what you both "want."

By now you might be thinking about whether people can go through life avoiding what they should do. Of course not, but when authority is being applied by a parent, it is easier to gain compliance to what should or ought to happen if children know that their personal desires are being considered at least some of the time. Real commitment to a course of action happens when a person wants to do what he or she ought to do.

Leadership and Laughter

Laughter bonds family members together, lightens our burdens, smooths out rough spots, and takes the sting out of disappointments. Being able to laugh at yourself is a sign of real maturity. Laughter is a form of affection. It smooths difficult times and it helps us enjoy life more. We do not do enough of it.

It is hard to get a sense of humor if you have not been busy developing one, and it is hard to use one if you think life is grim and stressful. Telling funny stories and jokes, and playful, good-natured kidding seem to be a part of nearly all successful families. If you cannot or do not laugh much in your family, you are missing something terrifically important to your teenage kids. Even though your family may have a lot of stresses, it will greatly benefit from the temporary respite laughter gives. If nothing else, try reading and telling funny stories. Laugh at strange situations and invite family members to tell "good" jokes at mealtimes. Injecting humor and fun into a family makes family life more pleasant. Besides, it is an important part of leadership because it improves morale, productivity, and unity.

It is a true compliment when a parent tells children they are fun to be around. It is the same when a child wants to be around parents because they are fun. Humans like to be around and learn from those people whom they find rewarding. Laughter and humor make companionship rewarding.

Exercise leadership by eliminating distractions one night a week for "family home evening." Begin conversations that include funny stories, pantomimes, jokes, riddles, and fun personal experiences. Teach or make up a limerick. These family times do a great deal to contribute to positive family experiences.

Summary and Transition

There is obviously much more to the period of "Family Flexibility" than described here. However, I have included the most important things. "Family Flexibility" includes understanding children's developmental tasks and organizing your family to promote successful achievement. This will put you in a positive parenting position and will help you think of alternatives you would not think of if you were simply worrying about how to control your children or get them grown and out of the home as fast as possible.

Further, you deserve to enjoy this period of time. Remember, it is easier to take the time to learn how to do something right than to solve problems after they have been created. You might be enticed by friendships, career, or activities outside the home. But, your children still need your association. There are few tangible rewards for parents who invest in the development of their children because it is done privately and no one pays for it. However, if parents are not committed we all pay, literally and figuratively. Committed parents say the intangible rewards of love, peace, happiness, and fun are worth it.   ❀

Summary of Developmental Tasks
(Children 12-18)

Physical Development

1. **Puberty and Reproductive Maturity.** Females start about nine months to a year before males. Each gender follows a fairly consistent sequence of physical changes until puberty is concluded.

2. **Regulating Increased Sexual Motivation.** Puberty increases sexual motivation. This is usually shown by increased awareness of how one looks to other people, the need for acceptance by others, interest in heterosexual attention, and improved social skills. Mature individuals regulate their sexual impulses and gauge the display of sexual behavior to the conditions of love, commitment, and responsibility.

3. **Adjusting to Physical Abilities and Limitations.** Physical changes during adolescence pose a "reality test" for individuals, creating a situation where children become more realistic about their physical abilities or lack of them.

4. **Desire for Adult Acceptance.** Increases in physical stature increase motivation to be accepted and treated like adults.

5. **Establishment of a Gender Identity.** During this period of time, individuals acquire information about themselves

that is used to form a concept of "adequate" or "inadequate" masculinity or femininity.

6. **Achievement in Focused Physical Tasks.** Children seek to achieve in tasks that require physical effort and abilities. These range from exercise and body building to organized programs of sports, dance, and work. This achievement plays a major role in determining the overall success of their development during the adolescent years.

Mental Development

1. **A Unique Style of Thinking.** During adolescence children progress toward a unique style of thinking that they demonstrate in their "likes" and "dislikes." They also show it in the way they think about other people and conditions in the world.

2. **Formalized Reasoning.** Children demonstrate an ability to organize "thinking sequences" to solve problems, to create new ideas, and to make decisions. For example, they will typically see a problem as a sequence of (a) identifying the problem, (b) thinking of alternatives, (c) testing the options to find the best one, and (d) reaching a conclusion. Forming these types of sequences reduces their impulsiveness and makes thinking more efficient.

3. Developing the Mind. During adolescence, children can use their minds to understand things they cannot see, touch, taste, smell, or hear. Abstract ideas are among life's most important. They include forming a deeper understanding of things like love, ethics, integrity, empathy, political philosophy, and religious faith.

4. Making Judgments. The ability to make finer and better judgements accompanies other mental abilities. With improved mental abilities, children make both positive and negative judgements about themselves, other people, and conditions they find in the world. This is shown as better discrimination of truth and untruth, good and bad, humor, trust versus mistrust, and seeing subtleties as well as the obvious. In an immature form, this ability will be shown in critical self-judgements, prejudice toward others, excessive cynicism, and sarcasm.

Social Development

1. Communicating to Understand. If people want to be understood, they must first understand. Adolescents need to learn to communicate without defensiveness, and they need other positive talking and listening skills. Social skills hinge on the development of positive conversation and communication skills.

2. Acquaintance Skills. Added maturity means greater exposure to other people. The task for adolescents is to learn how to meet new people, be comfortable in making their acquaintance, and form a variety of social contacts.

3. Mature Person Perception and Tolerance. Successful person perception is the ability to be aware of and communicate about oneself, other people, and the nature of relationships. It is also the ability to understand that any person is influenced by several things at any given time, and it is usually best to reserve judgment about someone until other things are learned.

4. Successful Social Reasoning. The task for adolescents is to reason about social situations by taking more, rather than less, into account.

5. Social Confidence. Developing social confidence is a major task during adolescence. It comes from the willingness to take social risks to communicate, speak in front of people, and offer opinions. Social confidence emerges when children receive approval from others instead of criticism or mistreatment.

6. The Experience of Intimacy. During adolescence, children discover the experience of emotional intimacy. This happens with same sex friends, and later in dating. This is shown by long, "deep" conversations, affection, and genuine caring. Mature individuals participate in intimate relationships and retain a sense of autonomy.

Emotional Development

1. **Emotional Independence.** Adolescents acquire increased self-reliance, confidence, and security by learning how to regulate and create emotions themselves, rather than depending on others to do so.

2. **Gender Requirements.** In our society, emotional requirements differ for men and women in some respects. Males have the developmental task of regulating their aggression and anger. Females have the task of regulating their competitiveness and anxiety.

3. **Readiness for Commitment.** Making promises and keeping them are significant emotional skills. It takes a true awareness of feelings at the time the promise is made and it requires the ability to regulate emotions when the time comes to honor the promise. These abilities are involved in major commitments, such as schooling, work, career selection, courtship and marriage, financial decisions, and religious faith.

4. Balancing Momentary Desire and Achievement. During adolescence, children are faced with new achievement opportunities and challenges. They also retain the emotional desires of earlier childhood. Achievements (such as high grades, musical competence, debate, and sports) require focused attention. To achieve, children need the ability to regulate and control distracting desires. Mature people are able to strike a balance between these two opposing forces.

5. Achieving Acceptance and Autonomy. Positive emotional needs can become negative if they are not balanced by a strong sense of autonomy. Autonomy is acceptance of responsibility for self, and the ability to make emotional decisions by oneself.

6. Fun and Enjoyment. Children learn to identify experiences that are truly fun without harming themselves, property, or others. They learn to laugh at themselves, find humor in people and situations, and how to turn negative events into something positive.

7. Forming Positive Attitudes. Hopefulness, faith, and belief in oneself are essential characteristics for a successful life. Adolescents who develop these positive attitudes have achieved a developmental milestone.

Moral Development

1. **Identifying When Actions May Help or Harm.** Morality is based on knowing what helps or harms people. Adolescent children refine their understanding of themselves and others.

2. **Appraising Social Situations.** Morality is more than a rule about some behavior. Morality or immorality take place in situations where people are at risk. These are called moral circumstances. Morally mature people appraise situations by thinking about the options, the rules involved, the people involved, and their relationships with each other.

3. **Develop a Standard of Personal Integrity.** Successful people have a strong sense of personal integrity. This begins with the willingness to describe their own thoughts, feelings, and actions in any situation. Teenagers are often required to choose between what they value and what is popular. Conserving integrity becomes a very personal thing.

4. **Understanding How They Are Connected to Other People.** During adolescence, children develop increased understanding of the many ways they are connected to other people. They improve their ability to act caringly toward others.

Adolescent Case Studies

Case 1: The Girlfriend

Your son is spending excessive amounts of time at his girl-friend's home. He is sixteen and somewhat immature. You are worried because when they are together, they seem to hang on and cling to each other too much. In fact, one evening you saw them kissing while they were in the TV room. You have a pretty good relationship with him, but now you need to do something more. What will you do?

Case 2: The Work Ethic

Your fourteen-year-old daughter is doing well in school, has some very good and close friends, and has ample par-ticipation in social-religious activities. One day, you received a phone call from the science teacher who informed you your daughter was failing the course. She said it was because your daughter had not turned in any homework since the beginning of the term. While thinking about what to do, you notice that she is also resistant to doing any work around the house, and does so only if you get upset. What are you going to do?

Case 3: The Self-Esteem

Your thirteen-year-old son lags behind other boys who are going through puberty. Although his voice has changed, he is still quite short. He also has a bad case of acne. He reads a lot and avoids spending time with kids at school or at church. He mumbles when he talks, seems to be shy, and when he does talk about himself, he says critical things. Occasionally, he has even talked about hoping he would die. He gets through these discouraging times, however, and seems to enjoy being with the family, at least some of the time. What will you do to help him?

Love and Emotional Support

Children need love and emotional support. They need these even when they are resistant, angry, and non-compliant. The purpose of this assignment is to rehearse and improve your ability to express love and emotional support. Read the following lists and then select some expressions to work harder on in the future.

Expressing Love

Praise

Affection

Listening

Shared laughter and fun

Giving

Showing empathy

Companionship time

Saying loving words

Expressing Emotional Support

Contribute to a child's goals or desire

Make statements of positive belief in a child

Show concern

Show hopefulness in a child's future

Chapter Eight

FAMILY LAUNCHING

F amilies form a life cycle designed to have no beginning or end. Over time there is change (through the
emergence of new characteristics, the addition of new people, and the passing away of old), but the essential family
usually continues. This is often not easy to see while we
are in it, but someone surveying several generations of the
same family could note similar occupations, shared religious faith, similar mental abilities or deficiencies, and
other attributes in common. These, along with certain emotional characteristics, appear to be passed on from one
generation to another inside our families.

Like it or not, we pass both the good and the bad on
to subsequent generations. By recognizing this, each generation could be the one that stops what might be less
desirable and starts something better. It is a liberating and
satisfying thought that we can discard at least some of what
makes us unhappy and create something better. This is
possible during a window of time that, if taken advantage
of, can produce positive results. One of these windows
opens when a child readies himself or herself to leave
hearth and home. Like the other stages, "Family Launching"
adds its important contributions to the ongoing path families

travel. It is called "Family Launching" because individual family members participate in the process of separation.

"Family Launching" starts when a child leaves to establish a separate life. This phase continues until all the children leave home and family members adjust to living apart from one another. It continues while the parents reorganize their lives without the significant effort of child rearing. It is a time of transitions where children go and return, go and return. Each cycle teaches both children and parents something more about living separately. "Family Launching" includes the addition of new people, the deaths of others, and the establishment of new families. All these transitions take getting used to, but also can be used to create new and better possibilities.

"Family Launching" is not the end of the original family. It is a new family form with its own relationships, tasks, and rule conditions. Of the four family stages, it is the longest, and, like the others, it is filled with challenges and opportunities as well as enjoyment and satisfaction.

During this period, for example, we and our children confront anew the requirements to live successfully in our world. Sending family members out into the world gives a burst of added significance to social values, friendships, cultural traditions, and customs. As we do for ourselves, we want our children to succeed in their communities, their churches, and the larger society. We have been working to promote competence in many forms and now we have a chance to see what we and our children have accomplished. The launching stage confronts us with the realization that our children will demonstrate what they have learned about long-standing family beliefs and other family practices. In addition, they will represent our definition of competence because they, as part of separating from us, will learn about and adjust to new conditions and people.

This is only one reason why separating from each other is a time of strong emotions. There are several others. For example, when children marry, the addition of new spouses is accompanied by many feelings. We learn to understand the sadness of departure and the excitement and anticipation of the future. There will be new worries and new loneliness, just as there will be new satisfaction and fulfillment.

With all these feelings involved, "Family Launching" is a mixed experience for parents and children. For many reasons we want our children to go, but they are such a part of our lives that a little of us goes with each one. For the children, home is familiar, and they feel secure and safe. Yet, even though they are on life's threshold and uncertain about themselves, most understand that leaving is natural and they anticipate what is to come. These two powerful opposing forces create tension, producing a mild crisis that only decision-making can solve.

Despite the tension for both parents and children, most of us prepare for this time. Children want to test themselves in the adult world. They have learned the lessons of childhood and desire to experiment in an environment that is not controlled by anyone else. Ironically, for reasons of security, most children leaving home seek a very similar situation to the one they left. Just like birds leaving their nest, however, the world they find away from home is foreign to them.

The desire to test themselves in the world is a main motivation for children. The desire is both personal and social. It is personal because every person must be willing to try out things by himself (even if accompanied by friends or roommates). It is social in the sense that every group of people carry notions about the age when important life events are supposed to take place. This age consensus may apply to the time when we think people should finish their education, get married, move away, and find work. Sometimes these ideas are influenced by socioeconomic factors.

In North America, people with a high school degree or less agree that the most common time for women to marry is between the ages of eighteen and twenty-two. College-educated people expect women to marry between the ages of twenty-four and thirty. The agreed-upon ages for males are somewhat older but also illustrate these societal expectations.

Young adults are aware of age expectations and recognize that progress is necessary to avoid being wholly out of step and suffering social embarrassment. They see friends and acquaintances move forward and feel impelled to do something themselves. It is not comfortable to be living at home at age twenty-nine, and have a friend ask what you are doing and where you are living. This motivates young adults to search for ways to leave home and often puts them in a decision-making crisis, a notable hall-mark of this period.

The options available to young adults are not simple and most decisions are not easy. These options include choosing a place to live and people to live with, educational choices, and career selection. Young adults are confronted with mate selection, moral choices, decisions about religious values, and political persuasion. All these invite decisions that have significant consequences because they lead to heavy time and resource commitments. Mostly, however, they loom large because they require decisions that typically cannot be made by anyone else. The young adults who make the decision will live and experience the consequences.

A few shrink from the stress of deciding and attempt to extend childhood—the time when more decisions can be made by others. Some children are simply shy or insecure about moving away. Others engage in a more serious form of avoidance. This usually includes delinquent or antisocial behavior, or learned helplessness where a child cannot or will not perform. These children present special challenges to parents. They use various tactics to delay their departures or try to prevent leaving altogether.

Some children face another type of challenge. Their parents are so distressed about the prospect of their departure, they attempt openly or subtly to restrain them. In some situations this serves the desires of both parents and children, and the children remain at home. Many letters from mothers to college freshmen contain suggestions, or cues, for children to come back home.

Abundant scientific literature informs us, however, that these conditions, while meeting some security needs, are almost always difficult and can even be tragic for the young adult. Development is slowed and a full expression of potential is impossible. To promote development, parents need to support and encourage children to leave home. The world may look like a frightening place and children may worry, but if they don't leave, a new fear may develop. Where parents may have dreaded the day children would grow up and leave them, they may eventually dread their growing up and staying forever. Many parents also find their children returning home, sometimes with their own children. Large numbers of parents are now parenting their grandchildren.

Leaving home is easier when children have been prepared along the way. Such preparation is usually accomplished by a process of structuring children's expectations so they learn to desire something they expect will happen.

The Thompsons helped their children prepare to leave by talking about this "time," when they would go to school, find an apartment, and seek work. They also helped them explore some possibilities by getting to know others who have made a successful transition, or by visiting the place where they will live, study, or work. Then, when it was about time for their children to go, they gave encouragement. Their preparation helped all six of their children leave successfully and live successful lives.

Children's Developmental Tasks

When are children independent? Suppose you asked young adults living away from home to identify the point at which they were independent of their parents. They would probably identify one or more of eight conditions which measure independence. These conditions are: (1) personal control (they make the majority of their own decisions), (2) financial independence (they earn and pay for their own living), (3) a separate residence, (4) longer amounts of time between physical contact, (5) a network of friends and acquaintances who have replaced the family as the center of life, (6) broken ties (choosing to be with other people during some traditional family times such as holidays), (7) emotional separation (feeling like they do not belong or like a visitor at home), and (8) significant personal achievement (graduating from college, getting married, or getting a good job or promotion).

Suppose we consider the foregoing as some of the conditions children need for independence and development. We can understand how to help by reviewing these eight conditions and identifying the specific developmental tasks of this period. Consider the following:

Physical Development

Three physical tasks are important when someone is in the process of leaving home and family to become independent. The first task is to develop and maintain good health by forming healthy eating and sleeping habits and a program of exercise. In addition to completing natural growth in height and weight distribution, the second task is to be physically attractive. This may include body shaping, grooming, or other methods to enhance appearance. The third is to develop sexual and reproductive capability.

Good health is a prerequisite for productivity, successful social participation, and overall well-being. These objectives motivate individuals to examine their eating and sleeping habits, along with exercise programs, to ensure their health will permit them to do what they want. Good health is also beneficial in helping them cope with the tension of trying to achieve. Like always, if one has good health, it is possible to have most of what else is important.

Attractiveness is so much a part of our current American scene that we sometimes fail to fully appreciate how much we devote to it. If we measured it in terms of dollars and cents we would find that a majority of money is spent on clothes, makeup, and other items designed to make us attractive. Meeting one another in heterosexual rituals creates a powerful motivation.

Attraction hopefully leads to deeper relationships. Casual dating turns into courtship, which is the "thinking and considering" part of mate selection. Attracting potential partners to this

> **Attraction hopefully leads to deeper relationships.**

process is probably the single major focus of the young adult period. Making oneself attractive brings continued focus on physical appearance, including weight, shape, and complexion. Achieving a positive appearance is a significant developmental milestone.

Attraction, of course, has powerful sexual overtones. Unless we are thinking of "interpersonal attraction," the reason for one to be concerned about his or her appearance is to increase sexual attention from others. This does not mean just "bedroom" attraction. It includes all forms of emotional and psychological attraction between males and females. They are driven, of course, by the motive to mate and reproduce.

From a physical perspective, sexual behavior is an activity that requires some physical skill and ability. It involves another person and takes place within other social and emotional circumstances. One can have sex, of course, without these other components. However, sexual and reproductive competence includes more than sexual union. It includes a committed, legal, loving relationship in which one purpose is to procreate. Reproductive competence, therefore, is a set of physical abilities combined with self-control sufficient to manage impulses. It is a sense of responsibility to physically care for one's sexual partner and any children that may result. Because this usually requires a long-term commitment, these physical abilities must be of sufficient quality to endure.

Social Development

There is often considerable experimentation when an individual begins a life separate from his or her parents. Young adults experiment with lifestyle possibilities that are manifest in the type of car they own, the amount of education they desire, and the clothes they buy and wear.

They test religious, political, and social beliefs and experiment with ways to express their beliefs publicly. They participate in the financial community by acquiring and spending money. They form networks of friends and acquaintances, enter long-term, committed relationships, and experiment with new social roles like spouse, parent, in-law, and supervisor. These permit them to establish the following things: (1) a life style that suits them, (2) a set of social beliefs and values, (3) financial competence, and (4) social stability. These are the tasks of social development for which we can help them prepare, and at which they must succeed if they are to achieve independence.

Launching a life independent from parents includes finding a style of living in which satisfaction and fulfillment are achieved. Lifestyles are representations of the amount of money we wish to acquire, the types of careers we wish to have, and organizations we seek to join. During a five- to ten-year period, young adults will learn from social contacts and establish for themselves a style of living, which, once created, tends to be fairly consistent for the rest of their lives.

The financial and physical aspects of their lifestyles often are representations of their social beliefs and values. For example, someone willing to marry with less money is clearly suggesting that material goods are less important than love.

The social beliefs and values of young adults will, however, go beyond their attitudes about material versus other more emotional relational values. A full participant in society expresses beliefs and values in such areas as religion and politics. Religious faith is manifested by the type of religious participation chosen. Political philosophy is indicated by the way one feels about and acts toward government and social issues.

Young adults experiment to find ways to participate that accurately represent their personal beliefs and values. They adjust what they believe over time until beliefs become more formal and definite, and are matched by actions. At the point of getting them clear for themselves, many young adults desire to communicate their beliefs and try to persuade others to accept them. They accept teaching or training roles that allow this to happen.

In America, virtually all social participation and life style decisions involve money. Money is not required for everything, but money affects our thinking about what we do. The force of the role the market economy plays in our lives is truly substantial. There are few decisions that young adults make where they do not think about financial implications.

Also, social participation includes acquiring and spending money. In the few years after leaving home, young adults try to become competent at working, spending, saving, borrowing, and investing. All these tasks are part of achieving financial competence. Many parents fail to teach children about money and how to use it (instead of being used by it). Instead, increasing numbers of young adults learn about credit card debt, impulse buying, and failure to save. They often put themselves in financial jeopardy because they do not use the same financial wisdom and prudence they observed in their parents.

While they are creating lifestyles and formalizing their social beliefs and values, most young adults establish networks of friends and acquaintances. This is often motivated by the desire to increase one's stability and security. If they should marry, this usually adds even more stability and allows them to progress toward assuming more responsible social roles.

They might assume the roles of spouse, in-law, and parent. If well-prepared, they will learn how important these roles are, and how to succeed at them. If unprepared socially, financially, or emotionally, their first attempts at being responsible may fail. Many in this situation will have begun these roles too early and their inadequacy will result in increased burdens of failed marriages, children they must care for, and substantial debt. All these exist at the same time these individuals are starting over and trying to get themselves better prepared for a stable life. It is easier and happier for us as parents to be diligent in our efforts to prepare our children.

Emotional Development

Leaving home to create an independent life is possible if there is sufficient emotional maturity. Emotional development is a gradual process and is never complete. Consider the example of caring for others and how it continues and changes over time. As adolescents, we may find out a little about caring for ourselves and some about caring for others. As young adults, we learn whom we care to be with. Then, in adulthood, we learn what and whom to take care of. The ability to care for someone else is a major developmental task for young adults.

Another emotional skill young adults must develop is the ability to establish intimacy. This is necessary to successfully participate in marriage and parent-child relationships. This skill involves the management of anxiety and fear. If these are not managed successfully, young adults will not enter into relationships requiring intimacy. They may, for example, date seriously and even profess their love—but when commitment is required they will find some reason to withdraw.

Love, warmth, affection, tenderness, and gentleness take center stage because effectively displaying them is necessary for success in intimate relationships. Then, to maintain these relationships, young adults must develop methods of displaying other positive emotions, such as optimism and patience, while regulating negative emotions such as discouragement, frustration, and anger.

In addition to learning about emotions and how to express them clearly and frequently, young adults are faced with the tasks of regulating and managing their emotional behavior. As part of self-management, adolescents typically develop increased self-awareness, as well as the ability to reveal themselves to others. This is amplified during the time they are young adults. Increased self-awareness allows a person to understand his or her emotions and what creates them. Being able to think about ourselves leads to increased self-control and permits us to assume responsibility for what we feel. This emotional step is highly important. It helps us avoid depending on others, blaming them for our bad feelings, and manipulating them to create good feelings in ourselves. It is more "mature" to avoid blaming others, eliminate excuses, and solve problems by assuming our share of responsibility. In addition, more mature individuals talk about and skillfully incorporate rewarding feelings within marriage and family relationships. That is, they know how to generate love, fun, happiness, and warmth. Being able to do this effectively is highly valued, and throughout adult life this skill takes on increasing significance.

In addition, emotions have to be regulated in order to maintain commitments to others. Focusing interest, affection, and love on one person is necessary to stay married, and can only be done if young adults have learned self-management skills. Otherwise, they will respond to others with promiscuous feelings, creating potentially harmful possibilities.

A common social myth suggests that being emotional is a form of childishness, whereas adulthood is characterized by the ability to be logical and unemotional. Managing and expressing emotions is an important part of every stage of human life. For young adults, understanding and communicating emotions may be even more important than in childhood. This is because this time requires a combination of personal decisions that involve emotions and the establishment of relationships.

Consider the importance of knowing and expressing emotions related to a major emotional task required of all young adults. They are faced with the task of learning to care about how they act, what they do, and who they are with, in addition to learning care for others. Caretaking has many forms which combine several emotions. These include sacrifice, warmly giving to others, sensitivity to one's own and others' feelings, and the ability to talk about emotional issues. During this period, a young adult will be faced with the challenge of managing all these emotions in relationships with a spouse, children, in-laws, parents, siblings, and good friends. If we want to truly understand young adults, we will need to watch their efforts to demonstrate emotional skills, testing and trying their abilities until effective caring is learned.

Caring is a great form of love and commitment. In the early stages of marriage, love is a combination of intense attraction and sexual desire. It becomes also a willingness to sacrifice, to provide long-term caretaking if necessary, and to regulate oneself so as not to harm the other. Parental love has all of the above components, except sexual desire. Developing the ability to love deeply by truly caring for self and others is a major part of a successful adult life.

Ironically, the motive and need to learn more about caring for others is pitted against a powerful opposing force. This is emotional fear, as demonstrated by pessimism. Leaving home means going into a wider, uncertain, and potentially dangerous world. Making financial and emotional commitments invites a sense of responsibility. It is developmentally more mature to face these commitments with reasonable optimism and to forge ahead than it is to let fear and anxiety rule life. Young adults, however, must learn a method of developing reasonable optimism and managing their fears.

This is usually accomplished by focusing on their ability to create positive emotions. If they are busy learning to create love, warmth, and happiness they are less likely to experience fear. Besides, these positive emotions help us feel complete. When young adults have a proactive method of creating situations that allow for positive emotions, the result is a stable self-concept and a sense of personal identity that reduces the influence of others. It helps us organize our own lives based on what we value. This is the true solution to fear.

Mental Development

The human brain matures gradually until the late teens or early twenties. Connections between brain cells become more efficient, varied and elaborate. This growth improves our ability to handle complex thought and helps us organize increased quantities of information. In this process we develop formalized methods of thinking we call logic, creativity, and memory. Even during adolescence, when physical growth begins to slow, the brain continues its development until it is able to learn most efficiently. If young adults choose, they can add to this development by perpetuating mental stimulation and learning.

Young adults learn about their interests, abilities, and talents by observing themselves. They participate in many different types of learning environments. They also understand when it is easier and more exciting to learn. In the early years of the launching period, many apply their mental abilities to endeavors they think will reward them with success. Such individuals are less likely to trust their own knowledge about themselves. They often do not pay attention to what is most interesting and stimulating to them. This is why many choose careers that will give them financial rewards, for example, but that are not inherently interesting to them. As they progress in their lives and their work, they discover the unhappiness that results when people fail to be true to themselves. If they discover this, they move toward these interesting contexts and focus their attention on achieving in these areas. We can conclude from this that it is easier and more effective if we help our young-adult children trust what they know about themselves.

This includes whether they believe themselves to be smart or less smart. Unhappily, this question arises from the limited way the education world views intelligence. Instead of thinking about smart versus "not smart," as we are led to do, it is much wiser to understand the type of intelligence each person possesses and focus on that.

The reason for this is that young adults are in the process of narrowing their options. The decision to pursue an education after high school, for example, is usually based on what one believes his or her mental abilities to be. It is the same with career and mate selection. The recognition and development of mental abilities becomes a more focused effort. This means that young adults continue to learn but usually apply their knowledge in focused areas. Application of mental abilities in this way increases their creativity and inventiveness toward some specific end. In the ensuing twenty or so years, more than one-half of all adults will make their greatest creative contributions in their chosen fields of business, literature, natural science, the arts, or the social sciences.

The energy associated with these focused contributions is truly remarkable and is one of the most noteworthy characteristics of the launching stage of life. Harnessing this energy to make creative contributions is a major part of full participation in society. Young adults may require encouragement to help them make their greatest contribution, but when their mental abilities (such as interests and talents) are linked to a stimulating environment they become self-motivated and self-invested.

All this is happening while a less obvious mental ability is appearing. It is the ability to form an integrated view of life. Increased independence permits young adults to makes assessments of themselves and their lives. It permits them to make mental connections between ideas, between themselves and others, and between the many other aspects of their lives. This helps them develop an integrated view of life in which everything has a place. Relationships with others gradually assume greater importance and become linked to religious beliefs. Single or isolated perspectives (about the importance of work, for example) are mingled with other values. For most, this added integration helps them view life as good, helping them increase their appreciation for good people and good relationships.

All this occurs because mental development continues. It is alive and growing through this period, much like any earlier period of life. We can take advantage of it by asking questions and learning from our young-adult children.

Moral Development

The more highly developed and mature we are, the more we understand and appreciate the importance of morality. Newfound independence lets young adults see firsthand how people, including themselves, can be helped or harmed by what they do. One of their developmental tasks is to refine this knowledge until they clearly appreciate any situation in terms of what might help or harm the people in it.

They are faced with added responsibility for moral decisions and the recognition of potential consequences. In part, this is because they face many more complex situations and are more likely to be alone with their own thoughts and feelings. The more they mature and develop themselves as part of these experiences, the more they can refine their sense of personal responsibility. In moral circumstances, mature people see what might happen to themselves and others and are not passive in the face of threat or potential harm. Young adults will have opportunities to learn this and often learn because they make mistakes.

There are many moral dilemmas, and anyone may make moral or immoral judgements, but when someone is developing a sense of personal morality, the overriding objective is to act with integrity. This becomes the focal point of moral development for young adults.

> **When someone is developing a sense of personal morality, the overriding objective is to act with integrity.**

Personal responsibility also means that the motives for one's actions change. During adolescence, for example, individuals might act morally to seek the approval of other people, or because they are afraid of the guilt they will feel if they do not comply with a rule. These reasons are adequate if they result in moral behavior.

Increased moral maturity, however, means that people are motivated to act consistently with what they value, especially if these actions help rather than harm someone. Satisfaction comes when one acts morally, regardless of whether others approve. In the best sense, morally mature individuals have a highly individualized integrity which perpetuates their sense of freedom and autonomy.

This is not the same thing as self-centeredness, which occurs when a person seeks to promote his or her welfare at the expense of someone else. Integrity is a personal commitment to the idea that one's actions are connected to other people. Therefore, what one person does or does not do can have dramatic effect on someone else.

Morally-mature people balance their own welfare with that of others and are capable of making sacrifices for them, but can also regulate themselves in the face of extreme, improper influence. Such maturity is evidenced both when an individual freely gives time, money, and effort toward helping other people and when pressure to participate in some harmful activity is successfully resisted.

The young adult years are a fertile time for our children to learn that a life lived without integrity is a life of less worth. Integrity needs to become a significant part of everyone's self-concept and should be used as the basis for making judgements about what one will or will not do. That is, we should ask the question, "Will this action cost or retain integrity?" This measure of one's self produces strength of character and promotes stability and lasting relationships. Under these conditions, the greatest love can be given and received. Under these conditions, the greatest security can be found and experienced.

Part of this responsibility to others is demonstrated by the willingness of mature people to teach other, less experienced, individuals about moral concepts. They may teach it in school, church, or through civic involvement. They may teach it to their children. Teaching includes providing examples, having conversations, giving advice, storytelling, and using formal lessons. Such willingness to teach means that individuals have accepted morality themselves and believe it to be a vital part of a mature and successful life.

As part of this period of time, many young adults begin a gradual process of refining their sense of responsibility in moral situations. In the press of life, there are many circumstances in which individual responsibility is expected and hopefully present, but where excuses can be used without producing dramatic consequences. Some of these responsibilities include dependability at work, promises in relationships, and proper conduct in private.

These situations are often "winked at" by us because they do not appear to have major effects on anyone. However, they often do, and we do not realize it. In this case, experience is the teacher and young people learn that assuming responsibility for themselves does in fact help themselves and others. Being punctual, for example, will help themselves at work and in relationships with others.

To respond to those many situations in which moral questions arise, young adults gradually refine their concept of personal integrity so they will know in advance what they might do if faced with a moral dilemma. Such refinement creates a foundation that can be relied on when difficult situations occur, rather than merely reacting impulsively to what others do or do not do. They have the opportunity to refine their thoughts and make it clear to themselves what they will or will not do.

In summary, moral development while our children are young adults is further refined and made more personal. Moral concepts, such as integrity, are used more often in interpreting themselves and other people. For successful young adults, integrity becomes an identifying characteristic they use to think about themselves, weighing most decisions by whether it will preserve or detract from their integrity.

Adapting Your Family Environment

The foregoing are developmental tasks for all who strive to acquire the positive qualities of mature people. They are descriptions of challenges young adults face and represent things they can learn to become competent. As parents, we hope our children will have this desire. Even though they are launching their own lives, most of us still want to contribute to their growth. Our methods will be somewhat different than in earlier family stages but, if effective, they can still be useful and are still important.

As our children leave us, they demonstrate both the force of what they brought with them into life and what they have learned from us. Their genetic characteristics have acted on them to create highly unique people. We can also notice they are mixtures of strengths, which we admire, and undeveloped possibilities that we try to accept. We imagine who they are going to be with. We hope they will make good choices, and that they will provide positive experiences for these other people.

Whether on happy or unhappy terms, the separation between parent and child is significant. For one thing, we discover that parenting does not end (as we rather hoped it would several years ago when we grew tired of it). The form changes, but the relationship does not. Further, when a family member leaves, it pushes us to make adjustments that are new to us. One child's departure changes the dynamics of the family, both extending its scope and reducing the number of people to which we pay close attention. When the next child departs, we extend our family even farther. We must develop new forms of communication and make adjustments to relationships. The original family environment we created exists as an anchor for our memories and a platform we use to adjust to new things. It is important to our children, and necessary for us, that we retain what is good and adapt to what is new.

Mature Relationships with "Good Fit"

Necessity forces us to adapt our relationships during the time children are leaving us and after they have established themselves. We have less time with each other (sometimes distance intervenes) and their desires need to be focused on their own lives. Parents and children still need contact, communication, the opportunity to share love, and the enjoyment of all the new happenings. In the most successful circumstances there is little conflict and much laughter and enjoyment.

Success can be realized if a few adaptations are made that "fit" our children. More specifically, we need to increase encouragement and decrease advice giving. To make this change, begin by examining your communication style. You might, for instance, communicate more frequently with children who are away for the first time and send more encouraging and advice-giving messages than you will later. If you communicate too frequently, however, you will send the message that you worry, that they cannot be trusted, and so forth. As time and distance continue to intervene, however, you can further adjust your communication, filling it with many tidbits of information, some encouragement, and even less advice.

While living away from home, Todd Anderson (not his real name) was thinking of proposing to a young lady. He called his dad, whom he had always respected, to ask him for advice. "What should I do?" the son asked. Because he knew the young lady in question, the father could have told his son "Marry her" or "Don't marry her." Correctly recognizing his son's maturity and the nature of the decision, the father answered by encouraging rather than by giving advice. He said, "I have confidence in whatever you decide." The decision was rightfully the son's, and by resisting the temptation to give advice, the father showed he recognized his boundary and signaled his son's responsibility.

There are many other adjustments we need to make in relationships with our children. Adjusting relationships is easier if accompanied by conversations about the nature of the new circumstances. Unfortunately, many parents and children do not talk openly about adaptations that need to be made and hope that better conditions will evolve over time. This increases the risk for difficulty.

In contrast, it is useful to discuss and reach agreement about: (1) your expectations that children are free to say yes or no in response to your requests (e.g., coming over for dinner), (2) the types of contact you would like with them and vice versa, (3) the forms of communication that you think are appropriate (such as letters and phone calls) and how frequently they are used, (4) how to treat grandchildren when they come, and (5) how to solve communication problems.

Having these conversations will set the stage for a good adjustment, making the relationship conditions fit the desires of both parents and children. In addition, these "adjustment" conversations set the stage for any other change if it becomes necessary. The inability to talk in this manner is often the beginning of conflict. If conflict develops, failing to communicate will prevent solutions from being found.

One young couple failed to have enough communication with the man's parents about adjusting their relationship. After their wedding, they moved a moderate distance from his parents and began to set up their own home. His parents started to visit twice a month, usually for an entire weekend. When the parents came they insisted on cleaning the apartment and even washing the car. The young married couple protested, but the parents did it anyway. The couple decided to give the parents an "appreciation gift," but were surprised when they received an even more expensive gift in the mail the following week.

Once this had happened, the "kids" felt controlled, but believed they could not communicate without offending his parents. The parents seemed like they wanted to visit regularly and help with the work when they came. This problem was only solved when a counselor suggested that, during the next parental visit, the couple sleep in, lie around, and go play golf while the parents worked. They followed this suggestion. At the end of this visit, the parents informed the couple that they thought it unwise to continue visiting as often as they did because the "kids" were not facing their responsibilities like they should. The young married couple was appropriately contrite, but pleased with the decision.

Making Loving Each Other the Most Important Part of Your Relationship

Whether good or bad, old communication habits can last a long time. When children return for visits, for example, they soon begin to participate in their respective roles as daughter and son and communicate as they used to do. If communication is healthy and positive, parents and children will return to that. If not, there is some possibility that old, negative patterns of communication will return and make a short visit less than pleasant.

Knowing time is limited, avoid this distress by developing methods of communicating love before the children arrive, the moment they arrive, and during the periods while they are staying with you. Obvious gestures of love soothe unhappy memories and act to prevent the recurrence of old miseries. Sometimes, when parents cannot do this, children must.

One man was in his forties before his father and mother visited during a Christmas holiday. His early life had been marred by intense family conflict and abusive parental behavior. As a result, his parents had never visited him in his home. He was, of course, afraid his parent's visit would be unpleasant. He wrote to them the week before they came and communicated his appreciation for them and for their coming. When they arrived he welcomed them warmly and gave each a present of a new bathrobe. One evening during their stay he showed them some pictures that represented happy memories of his childhood. He could only think of four. He purchased small tokens to represent each experience and these were given to his parents by their granddaughters, while he explained the significance of all four. His mother and father wept, clinging to their small gifts. After they left, his father called him and told him it was the best Christmas he had ever had and thanked him again. They have continued telephoning each other, which has made both the parents and the son happier.

This is an unusual example, but it illustrates why communicating love is more important during family visits than anything else. The visits usually are of short duration. They are about reviving emotional connections and family ties. They give our children a chance to steady themselves by retouching their origins. The brief return, if positive and loving, can provide a rejuvenation, supplying new energy to go out again and face opportunities and challenges.

Reframe Old Bad Experiences

Leaving home permits children to turn back and look more objectively at their experience. If and when they have their own children, they repeat our experience of parenthood and have greater insight into what we as parents went through. When this happens, children are typically more understanding toward us and also have increased desire to talk about their experience. Some of these experiences will be about our mistakes and their unhappiness. Some will be about real or imagined mistreatment during their childhood. Such memories might be authentic, but most children are simply interested in understanding their early years better because they are, as adults, trying to deepen their understanding of themselves. Therefore, their conversations will move to memories and to questions concerning why parents did what they did.

Unless you are truly unusual, you will have had failures as a parent, but you will have done the best you could under the existing conditions. This is what your children desire to know. Listen intently to their questions and be prepared to tell and retell stories that explain why you did what you did. If you keep calm, allow them to question and talk openly, the gratification of these moments will reframe any bad memories into positive perspectives. Happy memories will be reframed into a deeper regard and respect.

The added perspective of a few years helps our children better understand why certain events happened. It also takes some of the bitter sting out of the way they remembered their unhappy childhood experiences.

Balance Relationships, Tasks, and Rules

Soon after children leave home, many parents experience a reduced amount of day-to-day responsibility and assume their parenting duties are diminishing. Actually, this is more illusionary than real. As I have already suggested, parenting continues even though its form changes. To illustrate, consider the following questions: Should children help with the family chores when they visit, or are they guests? To what extent, if any, can parents rightfully expect adult children to comply with family rules, and punish them if they do not? How much financial help should parents provide for their children? How much baby-sitting should parents do? If children have financial or emotional reverses, should parents allow them to return home to live? For how long and under what circumstances?

> **Parenting continues even though its form changes.**

There are few general answers to these questions because each family and situation are unique. There is, however, a way of finding answers. Remind yourself that you are most concerned about the true development of your children. This may require some things from you. If, for instance, children are not complying with the values and rule conditions you taught them, then judging whether to do or say anything depends on the quality of your relationship. You are never obligated to be silent, especially if your children are doing destructive things. The effect of what you say and do, however, will be determined if things are balanced and your relationship with them is positive.

How much you do for children can be determined by the consequences for them and for their development. Too much help from you without any real effort on their part can weaken even adult children. Your effort and involvement may make you feel exploited and frustrated, affecting your feelings toward your children. However, giving some help may be necessary. The amount can be determined by whether children are willing to do their share.

High-Quality Parental Leadership

When children leave home, parents have little authority over them (as far as regulating rules, work, or conduct). Yet you are the originators, protectors, and preservers of your family. If you wish, you can exert leadership to maintain the strength of your family unit. This can be done by communicating the importance of unity and mutual care. You can continue to share information about the members of your family so that all keep informed about one another. You can organize reunions to foster renewal of emotional ties that create a sense of belonging. You can teach a concept of the family as a lasting organization where individuals can find security and love. Through your example and teaching you can demonstrate positive emotional virtues so your children continue to benefit from your kindness, patience, and love. In addition, you bring enjoyment to the lives of those you love. Shared happiness and adventure are bonding experiences, which remind us that the family has an incredible capacity to support, nurture, and fulfill.

> The family has an incredible capacity to support, nurture, and fulfill.

Good parental leadership is always worthwhile. Young adults need the wisdom experience gives and they need encouragement from significant people. They also benefit from a trusted person who occasionally warns and make firms suggestions about what might be wrong or too risky. When it is possible for parents and children to have these conditions, and have little conflict, children still get guidance along with the freedom to choose.

Leadership is supplied by our example. They see how we are facing our challenges, making decisions, and represent what we have taught them. If we stay steady on course we provide a powerful motive for them to follow. If we do not, they are not as obligated. Parents who divorce later in life learn that divorce hurts children of any age. Parents who violate the lessons they taught their children may think their children will not notice or should be able to manage without a positive example, but learn instead that the parent-child relationship always influences the children.

Good parental leadership is provided through the reinforcement we give to the progress our children make. We have watched them and seen them grow and have taken pride in what they have done. Now, it is important for us to continue to reinforce them, as they are living lives they have chosen for themselves.

After a visit to a married son and his wife, Reldon and Nicole Greene wrote letters to their son and daughter-in-law, telling the positive things they had observed in them. Their son was working in a local steel mill while taking a computer class at night at a nearby junior college. His wife was going to school full-time hoping to become a nurse. The Greenes wrote about their son's willingness to work hard, to care for his wife, and his continued involvement with a group of Boy Scouts.

The pride these parents communicated provided an implicit suggestion that the good things should continue. High-quality parental leadership includes teaching. This usually does not mean giving lectures and persuading, but it does mean parents have an opportunity to bring some new things to their children and promote learning.

Ronald Shumway, a successful investor, meets one Saturday morning a month with his young adult children to discuss money management and investment strategies. Maralyn Henderson invites her daughters and daughters-in-law to attend seminars of mutual interest. Afterwards, they have dinner together. They do this once or twice each year. She also shares cooking tips, home management ideas, and child care suggestions. Most of the time these come up as part of routine discussions during visits, but she still sees the ideas appear in their lives.

As time passes, you will have enlarged your perspective of yourself as a parent. You will recognize your shortcomings and your strengths. That is why it is important now to focus on the children's development. The rewards of parenting appear when you are able to make a useful contribution. Your children will benefit, of course, and there is much to be said for living out the rest of your life with more happy than sad memories. ❀

Summary of Developmental Tasks

(Young Adults)

Physical Development

1. Health: Good health is a prerequisite to achievement, productivity, successful social participation, and well-being. This motivates individuals to examine eating and sleeping habits, along with exercise programs, to ensure their health will permit them to do what they want.

2. Attractiveness: Casual dating turns into courtship. Attracting potential partners is a major focus of this period's early stages. Making oneself attractive brings continued focus on physical appearance. Achieving a positive self-image is a significant developmental milestone.

3. Sexual and Reproductive Competence: From a physical perspective, sexual behavior is an activity that requires physical ability. Competence, however, includes more than the sexual union. It includes a committed, legal, loving relationship where one purpose is to procreate.

Mental Development

1. Adapting Interests and Abilities to Career Selection: Young adults search for those life situations that match their interests and abilities.

2. Focused Energy and Thought: A good match between mental abilities and interest unleashes mental energy. A mature person organizes life and carefully works toward valued objectives.

3. Generate and Create: After leaving home, the next two decades and beyond will be filled with generative tasks. Work, marriage, and raising children are some major examples.

4. An Integrated View of Life: Increased independence permits young adults to develop an integrated view of life where everything has a place.

Social Development

1. Lifestyle: Independence from parents includes choosing a lifestyle. The task is to experiment until a satisfactory lifestyle is acquired.

2. Social Beliefs and Values: Young adults experiment to find types of social participation that accurately represent their personal beliefs and values. Many begin to communicate about their beliefs and to persuade others to accept them.

3. Financial Competence: Young adults attempt to become competent in the areas of work, spending, saving, borrowing, investing, and so on. All these tasks are part of achieving financial competence.

4. Social Stability: Establishing networks of friends and acquaintances increases one's stability and provides security.

Emotional Development

1. Caretaking: Young adults have the task of learning to care about how they act, what they do, who they are with, and how to treat others.

2. Love and Commitment: In marriage, love is a combination of intense emotion, sexual desire, a willingness to sacrifice, and the ability to regulate oneself so as not to harm the other. Parental love includes all the above but sexual desire. Developing the ability to love deeply is a major task of adult life.

3. Self-Awareness, Communication Skills, and Responsibility: This task can be described as the ability to understand the causes of emotions, to discriminate between different emotions, and to clearly communicate emotions.

4. Reasonable Optimism and the Management of Fear: Leaving home means going into a wider, uncertain, and potentially dangerous world. It is developmentally more mature to face challenges with reasonable optimism than to let fear and anxiety rule one's life.

5. Identity and Self-Management: Positive emotions help us feel whole and complete. Such integration results in a stable self-concept.

Moral Development

1. Refining Moral Responsibility: Young adults begin a gradual process of refining their sense of responsibility in moral situations.

2. Refining a Personal Standard of Integrity: What is right or wrong has been linked to what helps or harms people. By responding to situations where moral questions arise, young adults gradually refine their concept of personal integrity so they will know how to react when faced with moral dilemmas.

3. Teaching Moral Concepts: Moral maturity includes the recognition that moral concepts are necessary to a successful life. When one is aware of the importance of moral concepts, one has a desire to teach them to others.

Chapter Nine

YOUR IN-LAWS

LOVING THE PEOPLE YOUR CHILDREN LOVE

G roucho Marx, a famous comedian of the past, once heard a report that he had died. He wrote to the source of this message telling them that the stories about his death were greatly exaggerated. The stories about mean and bad mothers-in-law or fathers-in-law are greatly exaggerated, too. Relations between in-laws are usually quite positive. The incidence of problems in these relationships is no more frequent than in any other family relationships. Our in-laws are also a source of great reward and happiness (if we can learn how to take advantage of the opportunities presented when our children marry). This means to actively bring them into our family, make them welcome, and organize ourselves to promote their growth along with what we do with and for our children.

We have committed ourselves to promote the well-being of our children. When they marry, one form of helping them is to love the people they love. This makes them feel successful, reduces stress and tension, and indirectly helps them stay on positive paths of development where they choose good things for themselves. As it turns out, this is one of the most, not least, important things we can do.

Like the quality and size of our family, parenting does not end—it just changes shape and form. When our children marry, new members of our families offer new possibilities. They are the ones our children have chosen to love, and by this choice have indicated they are going to be influenced by these people. If we wish to continue to promote the development and growth of our own sons and daughters, we will love the people our children love.

Sometimes this is not easy. By the time our children marry we have invested mountains of emotional concern, worry, and effort. We have protected them. We have hoped, cheered, and cried for them. It is fair to expect that some of us think no others will be good enough for the children for whom we have worked so hard. On the other hand, it is also reasonable to assume that some of us will be grateful for those willing to marry our children after we have tried and not completely succeeded with them. It is also possible that the people our children find attractive are less so to us, making it a challenge to form close attachments with them. Sometimes, the in-laws do not like us, making it difficult for us to care for them. In this case, some of us have mountains to climb.

In contrast to these problems, those of us who easily love our in-laws are fortunate. Our lives are enriched by the contribution they bring to our family. When we are able to create these happy circumstances, it is then that we find the true importance such effort has to our children. They are gladdened by the realization that we accept, care for, and include their spouses. Thus, to continue promoting the growth of our children, we are again required to expand our abilities, taking into our lives those they bring us to love. Whether done with ease or effort, our labors in the enterprise will challenge and improve us.

Our Children's Developmental Tasks

When our children marry, they are confronted with one of life's best (and most challenging) times. Every couple learns that marriage, as a union of legal and public commitment, is quite different than dating or courtship. There is, for example, a great deal of evidence suggesting that the course of most marriages is largely set within the first three or four years. Whenever two people expect to live together a long time, whatever is good or bad (as the case may be) tends to be learned and repeated thereafter. This is because what one person does is reacted to by the other. After one or two trials, these interpersonal exchanges become fixed between any two people and usually are repeated. Older couples could testify that forms of communication or certain arguments are the same even after ten or fifteen years of marriage.

The early stages of marriage are usually periods of adjustment. Marriage brings with it certain requirements that give rise to the need for each person to adjust to the other. These might include: (1) adjusting to how fast or slow each person works, (2) a personal style of organization, (3) their sexual relationship, (4) attention to and time with each other, (5) learning successful methods of solving problems, (6) the amount and kind of communication preferred by each,

(7) displays of commitment to each other and to the relationship, (8) social and religious values, (9) financial and other career goals, (10) balancing work and career goals with relationship quality, and (11) building relationships with in-laws.

With all these requirements in mind, we can identify some of the major developmental tasks for our children during this period of time. We can also note that they involve physical, emotional, social, mental, and moral behavior. When our children marry is one time we can see how well they have developed themselves and how well we have helped them. Making a marriage successful usually requires effective and successful skills that we hope our children have learned. If they (and we) have been reasonably successful, they can approach the following developmental tasks with confidence.

Communicating Positive Feelings

Marriages are made more successful if the two partners are skillful at displaying several forms of positive emotions. This simply means that many forms of kindness, love, optimism, cheerfulness, tenderness, passion, and warmth make a marriage relationship happier and more enjoyable. The number of emotional rewards compared to the amount of frustration, fear, and anger determines whether the marriage lasts and succeeds. When individuals start marriages with the ability to communicate many positive emotions, they create solid foundations. Once these skills and habits are learned, they tend to be repeated.

Other emotional skills are also useful in making marriages happy. They include the self-disclosure of feelings so that both can understand the other, correctly interpreting the other person's emotional behavior, and regulating emotional behavior so that the other person is not hurt. Some believe that the ultimate display of love is to have sufficient emotional control to ensure that the other person is not harmed.

Bridging and Balancing Family Ties

High-quality social skills are required to form new ties with in-laws, balanced with an increased separation from one's own family. One must learn to communicate with new people, decide what to call them (e.g. "Dad," and "Mom" vs. Ralph and Shirley), participate in their family activities, and respect family traditions and rules. At the same time, each person is involved in balancing attention to the needs of their partner (and their own desires) with the desire to be with their own parents and siblings. How young married people bridge and balance does much to determine the success of their marriages. These matters involve intense feelings, accelerating the need to communicate well, being sensitive to others, and appraising situations accurately.

Organizing and Using Problem-Solving Skills

Sometimes we think mental abilities apply only to school or work. In marriage, however, mental skills show up clearly in a couple's ability to organize themselves to achieve desired goals and to creatively solve problems. Successful organization includes communicating about and agreeing on goals or desired achievements, scheduling time efficiently, making and keeping promises, and working to accomplish required tasks. The most effective way to solve marital problems is to recognize a problem exists, avoid blaming, accept a share in the responsibility, identify and talk about one issue at a time, identify new and creative solutions, support and empathize with each other, and try out the new solutions. We can see this inevitably involves a positive set of mental skills.

Making Personal and Relationship Adjustments

Morality is any intention or act to help someone, and likewise, immorality is any intention or act to harm someone. Marriages offer numerous opportunities to hurt one another. Marriage partners may lie, say hurtful things, ignore and reject, be more interested in control than intimacy, and fail to care for and help one another if things are not equal or fair. These things happen when one or both individuals lack a sense of integrity or self-control.

Marriage also offers opportunities to demonstrate high-level moral behavior. Marriage partners can agree to tell each other the truth, to avoid saying mean and spiteful things, to pay attention to each other in tender and loving ways, and learn to sacrifice and care for each other when it is needed, rather than measuring everything by equality.

These are moral skills. When new marriage partners know these skills, they can talk and make adjustments without harming each other. When they do not know them, they express their irritation, frustration, and anger. In their minds, they justify doing this because they believe the other person is responsible for their unhappiness, and the other person has done hurtful things. Under these conditions, adjustments are more difficult to make, plus both people are more likely to hurt each other. Many problems may be solved by talking and communicating clearly. Most marital adjustments, however, involve making a change of behavior. Changing oneself is often a difficult task. Except in cases where one or both people are abusive, change is made more difficult if one is pressured, coerced, ridiculed, or blamed.

If couples have a marriage climate of helping each other, these changes can be talked about and made in the context of helpfulness and consideration. When people have hurt each other in the process of trying to make adjustments, change is less likely because each feels a lack of caring from the other. The fear felt by a person who does not trust the other makes it extremely difficult for any change of behavior to take place.

Morally mature individuals are more likely to accept their rightful share of responsibility for any unhappiness. They can understand their partner's emotional position with compassion

> **Both must change in order for one to do so.**

and empathy. They may even see how their own behavior is linked to what the other person does. Therefore, both must change in order for one to do so. There is little derision and gratitude is expressed for each other's efforts.

Effective Parental Leadership

In early periods of the family cycle, parental leadership was aimed at organizing a family environment made up of rules, tasks, and relationships. We needed to supply the type of leadership required to help our children with specific developmental tasks. When we have married children, the need for our leadership is just as great. Our leadership needs to be focused on the developmental tasks of our married children.

If we are effective, we can help them start their marriages with the skills to be successful. Further, we can form relationships with our in-laws that will bring happiness and satisfaction to our children. We only need to remember that we will always have influence with our children. It is up to us to apply it responsibly, in ways that will help them be successful.

The forms of parental leadership described in the following paragraphs are designed to promote achievement of children's developmental tasks. They are based on research by behavioral scientists who have sought information regarding how parents can continue to help their adult children without assuming too much responsibility for them.

In the Beginning, Maximize the Moment

I learned a very real and important life lesson from a friend. Sadly, he and his wife discovered their daughter was afflicted with an advanced case of leukemia. Their physician said nothing could be done to save her and advised them to simply go on with their regular routine. Taking him at his word, they continued to work and to live as they usually did. In a few months, this daughter died. Both had an extremely difficult time adjusting to her death. His wife was greatly depressed and only the happy adoption of another daughter helped her recover.

Years later, a man came to my friend for advice because his seven-year-old son had the same illness. My friend had learned something. He told this gentleman about his experience and said, "If I could do it over again I would have quit my job and spent time with my daughter. We would have done all the things we could as a family. We would have taken short trips, gone on picnics and done everything she liked. We would have done this to make certain we honored our daughter's life."

Some life events are not routine, and they deserve more than simple recognition or passing notice. Because they are unusual, it is important to make changes in order to maximize the moment. We validate these times as something remarkable when we shift from our normal course and do something to heighten the memory. To succeed at this, we only need to appreciate that we can go through these experiences worried about details, pressured about success, and wishing they were over. Or, we can think of ways to celebrate the significance, find the symbols, and give honor.

Dating, courtship, engagement, marriage, and childbirth are some of these moments. All are pivotal events. They stick out as mile markers to other experiences, and we use them to remind us of time on life's calendar. Thinking

about them enables us to latch onto things less easily remembered. This is because they fulfill dreams long-dreamed,
symbolize some of the best in us, and predict what is to
come. These times are also significant for us because we
have a built-in mechanism that responds joyfully when
we see our children repeat what we experienced.

There is another reason, however, why these times are
important. When our children date, court, become engaged,
and marry they are having their own personal experience,
but they are also introducing someone to our family. Also,
the emotionality of these events makes those experiencing
them more vulnerable to what others may do. Prospective
in-laws, for example, may be exceptionally worried about
whether we will like them, and will be looking for signs that
we do. They may act immaturely, showing their anxiety in
displays of frustration. After all, they have never had us for
in-laws before and are trying to find the best way to belong.

Yet, we must measure the feelings of our own children and match our response to them, otherwise we risk over-
stepping the boundaries and being perceived as interfering.
It calls for a little sensitivity and willingness to appreciate
what the situation brings for all of us.

Increased emotionality creates some risk for unfavorable
things, but it also gives us one way to maximize the moment.
The social event of an engagement, for example, is more
than an exciting moment. It is a symbol of what love is. If
we cannot appreciate this, then engagement is only the
announcement of marriage.

If we can recognize the symbol, however, we can use the engagement announcement and the engagement period to set the stage for future and continued harmony with our in-laws. We can, for example, use this period to find special and unique ways to communicate affection and regard for new family members.

One father wrote a note to a prospective son-in-law after they both participated in a family activity. The father told of some positive things he noticed about the young man. He also described his daughter's happiness and indicated that he believed her to be a young woman of good judgment. The prospective son-in-law therefore, must be a high-quality person, otherwise she would not have agreed to marry him. He closed his letter by indicating that he looked forward to being together with him again.

Two sets of parents met with their children the night before their wedding day. Both parents told their love stories to their children. In his conversation, the father of the young woman turned and talked to her. He said, "Your mother and I have loved you all your life and we always will. As your father, I now give you permission to love another family and be loved by them." The women wept and the men were pleased but a little uncomfortable. Neither family has any in-law problems.

Another family "maximized the moment" with their son. He and his new fiancée had announced their engagement. In a conversation with his parents, he asked them what they would advise doing during the four months of the engagement. The parents suggested that he find every way he could to communicate his love for this girl and to do it often. They told him, "You only do this one time in your life. Let's make this the most fun and loving time possible." The son took his parent's advice and wrote notes, poems, gave gifts, and spent caring time. He learned to be more explicit about his feelings and told his fiancée he loved her frequently. At a family meeting, his mother stood and asked everyone to be quiet. She looked down at the prospective daughter in-law and told her that she loved her and was grateful for the wonderful influence she was having on her son. In this one statement the mother welcomed the new daughter, validated her son's choice of a wife, and make it clear that love awaited them both. Neither family has any in-law problems.

The Foundation of Praise and Freedom

In-law relationships would be much happier if, for the first year of our children's marriage, we decided to display only warmth, praise, and love for new in-laws. Our children's marriages would have a better chance if we committed to only tell our children about the good things we see them doing. They would also be much happier if we accepted their right to great freedom so they could choose exactly as they wish without worrying about us. Both of these conditions apply to the early years of marriage and deserve our parental leadership to ensure they exist in abundance. This means that we can make both of these conditions explicit by telling our children of the good things we notice. We can reinforce the idea they should not feel undue pressure to comply with our invitations and requests, but to feel free to do as they wish knowing that is acceptable to us. We can say, "We love having you here, but we want you to feel free to come when you want and leave when you think you need to." The more freedom we communicate, the greater their security. The greater their security, the more likely they will be responsible for themselves. The more responsible they are, the more likely their chances of making their marriages succeed, and fostering their happy and successful marriages is the best way we can promote the ongoing development of our children.

> **Fostering their happy and successful marriages is the best way we can promote the ongoing development of our children.**

Assuming and creating the positive is better than trying to solve problems when we have failed to be proactive. It is surprising, however, that so many of us fail to appreciate this rather simple idea. In any relationship, the eventual outcome is determined by the quality of the feelings people experience in the beginning.

Suppose a new in-law visits and talks with the new family ten times during the first year and ten times he or she has positive feelings. These positive feelings build a foundation for more good things and also set the stage for handling any difficult problems should they arise.

In contrast, suppose that we fail to pay attention to the need for positive feelings. We go through the wedding and our children return from their honeymoon. Life settles into its routine. We all know that it is easy to take offense. Our child might tell us too much about his or her marriage adjustments and be a little critical about the new spouse, hoping to get some support. When they visit, they may spend less time with us than with the other family. As a newly married couple they might say or do something impolite or critical. They also might mismanage money, fail to be responsible in some area, and make choices other than we would make. Now, what do we do?

All these occurrences are likely because of the nature of a new marriage. If they happen when we have not laid a solid foundation of praise, warmth, and freedom, any constructive criticism on our part toward the new couple may be interpreted as intrusive instead of caring.

This sets the stage for the exchange of negative emotions and difficult communication. If and when this happens, problems await us, rather than peace.

The Power of Hope and Emotional Support

There may be good reasons why we need to provide financial support for our married children. They may be in school or they may have legitimately incurred some unusual expense. Even if we have good reasons, however, maintaining this type of support for married children will delay their assumption of responsibility for themselves. Further, we need to remind ourselves that children who excessively depend on their parents are usually angry and resentful toward those they depend on. Many parents get into the cycle of giving resources, only to discover they are not only not appreciated for it, but resented and sometimes exploited.

If we have to give what they do not earn through their own efforts, then at the time the decision is made to give it, the decision can be accompanied by a time limit. In cases where children could—but choose not to—assume responsibility, we can use a form of tough love, and say no.

The power of responsibility for oneself comes from the time-honored notion that we must work, earn, and do all that is necessary to care for ourselves. In addition, responsibility comes from being around supportive people. Miguel de Cervantes, the Spanish philosopher and novelist, is reported to have written that it is easy to be self-reliant when we are around caring people.

In lieu of money and other gifts that have strings attached, suppose we accelerate our encouragement and emotional support. Most people, at the beginning of something new and unfamiliar, benefit from expressions of encouragement and support from others. When children seem unhappy with their marriages for example, they may want to tell us some part of it. If we ask too many questions and give too much advice we will assume a responsibility role that we do not want. After listening and understanding what has been said, it is generally better to move the conversation toward expressions of encouragement and support. "You can work this out," we might say. Or, to a child who is a nervous expectant parent, we might say, "You will be wonderful." We might send a note, give flowers, or have lunch and talk. We might be capable of helping them see positive possibilities for themselves. Our motivations to provide support and contribute to their hope and confidence should come from the realization that they will become more responsible for themselves.

One young married woman discussed her disappointment in her parents. She was their youngest child and the last to marry in her family. The day after her wedding ceremony, her parents left on an extended trip to Europe. Returning from her honeymoon, she wanted someone to talk with and she wanted it to be her mother and dad. They did not arrive for another three weeks. When they returned she was angry at them for leaving for such a long time and communicated her frustration to them. Instead of getting involved in the rightness or wrongness of her logic, her mother said, "Honey, your dad and I have all the confidence in the world in you. We knew you would handle everything just fine. Tell me how things are going." The daughter proceeded to talk about the honeymoon and what she and her husband had been doing since. Her mother pointed out several positive things as examples of her daughter's competence.

Most of us miss our children, worry about how they are doing when absent from us, and understand the challenges they face. We do not help them when we let our anxieties get the best of us. Nor do we help by habitually solving their problems and taking away their challenges.

A single mother of five children had reared them mostly by herself. When they began to marry she suffered the loneliness of the separation and with difficulty watched them assume responsibility for themselves. It was difficult because she no longer felt as important or necessary. At first she worried that they were not spending as much time with her as they did the "other family." Then, she worried about whether her daughters-in-law *liked her. On one or two occasions she regretfully assumed too much responsibility by telling her married children what they needed to do in their marriages and in relation to her. She was surprised and hurt when they withdrew further from her. Gradually she learned about and used a different strategy. She started holding family gatherings at holidays and other important times. She tried to make each of these positive for her children and took pains to communicate how well she thought they were doing.*

At first there was no change in them, but she felt better. Her feelings improved when she was able to reduce her need for control and feelings of responsibility. She was even able to over-look those times when a child or an in-law forgot something they promised to do for one of these family activities. She learned that if she said something about it, the statement would place her in the responsible position. In addition, it would reduce the pleasantness of the evening. As she improved her ability to express confidence and support, her children began to spend a little more time with her and their sense of responsibility improved. There were fewer times when she needed to remind them of something, and when she did they accepted responsibility for it.

Promote Continuous Learning

There are several ways to promote children's mental growth. One of the best for adult children is to continue the idea of learning. It is not necessary for learning to be the same as "school learning." Talking about books we have read, places we have gone, or current events will contribute. One man who had suffered financial reverses in his life held a monthly meeting for his adult children and hired an investment counselor to come and speak to them. Then, he proposed they invest a modest amount of money and meet each month to talk and discuss ways of managing it.

Learning is a worthwhile activity if the knowledge is good and useful. It also is a good reason to talk and spend time together. When we take our children and in-laws to educational places (such as museums, concert halls, or theatres) so they can learn, we are promoting their mental development in a way that does not intrude on their lives.

Remember the Fun

When asked what he wanted to be remembered for, one father replied that he most wanted to be remembered for the fun he contributed to his children's lives. Like anything, fun can get out of balance, but as he watched his children leave his home and start their own, he said, "I am most thankful for those times when we were having fun together." We sometimes forget that fun is a tradition.

One set of parents who did not forget the importance of fun took their children, in-laws, and grandchildren to a family-oriented resort every other year. The week they spent in the Utah mountains together allowed them to renew their traditions of fun. One tradition was playing a card game called "Make a Million" (similar to the more familiar "Rook" game). The father and grandfather played this game with his siblings while growing up. His father was a prisoner of war during World War II. The family could not afford much and television was not available.

So, they played this game. Over the years, the father taught it to his children and to their spouses when they married. Finally, the cards wore out.

He called Parker Brothers, the original makers of the game, and obtained permission to reproduce the cards. He went to a printer and made 1,000 new copies and gave several to each of his married children. When they arrived at the Utah resort, the children took to their own activities, but the adults found time to play this game. It was a lot of fun as they paired up and played against each other. Little competitions were secondary as memories were retold. This fun time together helped them reunite themselves and made another memory. The father said, "It might be true that the family which prays together stays together, but I think it is also true that the family which plays together stays together."

A Good Relationship with Your In-Laws Benefits Your Children

It is well-known that how we are treated influences the way we treat others. In the case of our in-laws this is especially true. If, for example, we treat our in-laws with integrity and with a willingness to be of help to them, our children are more likely to be treated the same way.

There are numerous stories of parents who learned to love their daughters- or sons-in-law. Later, when their children made serious mistakes (such as having affairs), the in-laws were loyal and caring when just the opposite could be justified. When asked why, one of the most common reasons given was love for their parents-in-law.

This unusual example illustrates many other possibilities. Kindness inspires kindness and giving motivates giv-

> **Kindness inspires kindness and giving motivates giving.**

ing. Taking the time to put these types of moral attributes into our relationships with our in-laws can have both immediate and lasting results. We are on the pathway of life, fifty yards or so ahead of our children.

By our examples we show them what lies ahead. When we treat these new "children" in a fair, just, and caring fashion we say to them, "Come and follow me." Their attempts to follow our examples will often be manifest toward our own children. So, our children will benefit from our examples in two ways.

We pass legacies of behavior through our children to our grandchildren. The most common things parents pass on are their successes or failures with moral behavior. We may pass on meanness or kindness, but we will pass on a legacy. It is obviously better for our children and grandchildren if we pass on the positive things we want them to know. ❀

Chapter Ten

GRANDPARENTING

Grandparenting is more than "putting up with" your grandchildren, indulging them, or playing with them. High-quality grandparenting includes companionship, personal attention, expressions of warmth, and a passing of wisdom. It is the magical experience of love between one old enough to understand its importance and one young enough to learn. It is not the same as the love between parent and child. It is more accepting and less judgmental. It is based on the grandparent's desire to take a permanent place in the grandchild's bank of loving memories. In return, the grandchildren learn about their parents, and learn some of the best lessons of life. Being cared for by an older person is an important part of a child's development. Children who have this high-quality experience are more likely to achieve, to be emotionally stable, and to accept their parent's values. Grandparents have much to contribute.

We have a ready-made condition for whatever we do. One wry comedian pointed out that grandparents and grandchildren get along so well with each other because they have a common enemy. Whether this is exactly true is less important than the idea that grandparents and grandchildren find each other attractive if given the chance. Grandparents have many motives to know and be with their grandchildren. We are fascinated with human growth and enjoy watching the steps they take. We feel rewarded when we see them demonstrate the same important life lessons we have tried to teach our children. Grandchildren, while less aware of what they want, find comfort, stimulation, and security in their grandparents.

A majority of Americans become grandparents when they get to middle age. When this happy day arrives, we find that the idea of grandparenting is much different than the aged person, rocking quietly in a rocking chair and spinning yarns and stories. Currently, more of us are active and involved with our children and grandchildren. For one thing, there are more dual-earning families and many of us are the primary care takers for our grandchildren. Secondly, there is a strong social tendency for families to move closer together and maintain or re-establish close extended family ties.

You can decide to play an active role in the lives of your grandchildren or simply wait to see what unfolds. The principles of good family leadership suggest, however, that you formulate your plan, communicate it to your children for their approval, and carry it out in a way that is comfortable and pleasing to you and to them. Exercising this kind of leadership allows you to retain a sense of control over your time and ensures that your efforts will have positive results. If you take the initiative, you can work toward positive events rather than having to solve some of those delicate situations where children expect more than you want to give. Positive and proactive grandparenting, like positive parenting, is usually more successful.

The times in which we live do not afford everyone the same opportunities. The tradition of grandparents, two parents, and grandchildren is less common in current American society. Some of us have children who, because of divorce, are not able to be active parents to our grandchildren. If our child is the custodial parent, then our grandchildren are being reared by one parent. Our grandchildren may have come into our families when their mothers (our daughters) were not married. In these cases, we might need to be both parents and grandparents. Some of us have to be parents to our grandchildren because our children cannot or will not be proper parents.

Much of what we are able to do depends on our situation. Yet, there are many things we, as grandparents, can do to support our children (which is the first requirement of our leadership). These actions will continue to give us the opportunity to promote their growth and well-being.

Shirley Saunders and her husband had reared four children, two boys and two girls. The children were all teenagers or older and she looked forward to the time when she and her husband, Harvey, would have more time to be alone together. Harvey was a construction supervisor and his work often required that he live away from home for a few days at a time. When he was home his ability to contribute was limited because he was a heavy drinker. On several weekend nights, Shirley had gone to the local bar and brought him home because he was not able to drive himself.

Shirley decided to surprise Harvey one day by visiting him in the town where he lived while he was working. What she found there surprised her. He was living with another woman.

Their divorce was accompanied by the usual hurt, distress, and anger. The four children were caught and affected by this unhappy situation. In the next few weeks, one daughter became pregnant and married a boy who had a serious drug-abuse problem. This daughter was the most fun, happy, and loving child in Shirley's family. They were especially close. In the next three years this daughter had a second child, even though the marriage was not solid or happy.

Then, misfortune struck again. While driving, the daughter slid off an ice-covered road and was killed. Shirley was faced with the choice of rearing these two grandsons by herself, or attempting to force the father to do so. She chose to raise them herself. Over the next several years she worked, she mothered, and she hunted for ways to help these boys. She did it because she loved the boys, but this was not the entire reason. Shirley said once, "This is what I think my daughter would want me to do. I am trying to rear her children the way she would want."

This true story demonstrates the commitment some grandparents have to their family. It also demonstrates the need and significance attached to grandparenting. Even if we are not in circumstances as extreme as Shirley's, what we do or do not do can have great influence. To be more effective, we can understand our children's developmental tasks and help with them.

Our Children's Developmental Tasks

Yogi Berra, the well-known Yankees catcher, has a seemingly unintentional quick wit. Once, after telling a story, he explained it by adding, "It was déjà vu all over again." His possibly unintentional joke also describes what it is like to be a grandparent. Our children better understand what we went through and did for them. As we watch them, we get a chance to remember what it was like to have and rear children. The range of possibilities includes empathy for the effort and sacrifice required, gratification when they repeat something we did well, elation and satisfaction at their successes, support when they are discouraged, and justification if they have difficult children (like they were to us). Like it or not, one measure of our parenting will be demonstrated when our children become parents. Hopefully, they will have learned all the good things we did and will add upon that to make themselves better than we were.

> One measure of our parenting will be demonstrated when our children become parents.

Grandparenting is still a time for us to carry out the two original commitments we made to our children. When we conceive and give birth to them we commit to rear them as well as we know how. When it comes to the task of teaching and raising children, we commit to promote their development and growth. This is central to everything we do. That is why one of the most important things we do is to learn about them and use this knowledge while trying to help them grow.

In the following descriptions of their developmental tasks, notice how the five forms of development merge into adult roles. Our children are now parents. What our children do as parents will require social, emotional, mental, physical, and moral skills. This means that over the years, our efforts to promote their development in these five areas come together on the stage when they perform as parents with their children. They have the primary responsibility, of course, but if we choose to be involved in a positive way, we can help them, help our grandchildren, and create happiness and fulfillment for ourselves.

Nurturing

Nurturing is the name given to what one person does to sustain and promote the life and well-being of another. Hardly anyone is fully prepared to do it when his or her first child is born. We must learn how to do it as we go along. Our children have the task of learning to be good at nurturing their children. It may be emotional nurturing in the form of physical affection, stimulation, and love. It may be nurturing by giving attention and predictable care. Nurturing is also sacrifice and inconvenience. In the early stages of parenthood, our children will be invited to learn nurturing as part of what they will do with their children.

Focusing on the Children

Having had us pay attention to them and learn about them, when our children become parents it is their turn to learn about and focus on their children. One of the most important developmental tasks for parents is to learn about their children. They then use this information in organizing a family environment that promotes the children's growth. To be successful at this, our children need to focus on their children to understand development and how to stimulate it.

Applying Proactive Family Leadership

New parents can react to what their children do, or they can assume a proactive position. They can take an active and positive approach to parenting, or get caught in the trap of struggling with the added burdens they feel. They can organize and lead, or they can feel the resentment and frustration that results from feeling controlled by children who require sacrifice and effort. If they wish to promote the welfare of their children and have successful families, they will assume leadership by identifying the type of family they hope to create, organizing themselves to achieve it, and committing time and energy to ensure their ideas are applied.

Proactive leadership can take many forms, including organizing an active teaching program, giving children positive experiences, setting an example of desired behavior, and supplying other growth and learning opportunities. When parents apply their own style of leadership to their family, there is less conflict and more unity. This means they have thought through and clarified what is important to them, rather than simply using someone else's ideas.

Making the Family Fun and Happy

Parents of any age can subscribe to the idea that families could and should have fun, happiness, and joy, as well as serious life experiences. However, many parents do not take time to do what children find enjoyable. When our children become parents, they will take the sense of fun and enjoyment they learned from us, plus whatever they choose to offer themselves. They will not have applied these skills in a family before, and doing so will be new to them. They will need to seek out what gives them enjoyment with their children. They may get so busy, however, they forget to have fun.

Our Grandparent Leadership

Most recognize that leadership with grandchildren is much more indirect and less involved than when we have the full responsibilities of parents. We can do many indirect things, however, that help our children in their tasks of parenting and help our grandchildren in their efforts to grow and learn. By acting to help our children develop themselves as parents, we can continue to honor our commitment to promote their growth.

Research has suggested that grandparents perform four central roles. The first is simply being present, or "being there," for their grandchildren. The second is to be a protector or a support during crisis. A third role is as arbitrators who negotiate or try to achieve reconciliation when problems arise. Lastly, grandparents maintain the family biography through record keeping and oral traditions. These important roles may be part of everyone's grandparenting opportunities. They are not, however, descriptions of leadership designed to promote growth in our children. Since that is our commitment, let us examine how we can do that.

Organize an Extended Family Environment

When we spend time visiting with our children and grandchildren, we may think we are just visiting with each other or maintaining some tradition. We are doing much more than that. When more than one immediate family gets together, cousins meet, in-laws visit, and time is spent in an organized way; a new family environment is created. We may get together monthly, once every other month, or as infrequently as once a year. Yet, this new organization offers several possibilities.

We can organize these events and teach important things through the activities we create. For example, if we have fun we will communicate that to our grandchildren. If we also have discussions about family traditions and learn about family history (genealogy) our grandchildren will learn that. If we spend time talking with each other, our children will hear these discussions and seek to participate in them. Whatever we do, if we do it together, we will teach that family ties and relationships are worth creating and retaining.

We only need to generate the ideas, get others to help, and carry out the experience. This is indirect leadership. It is a form of family leadership that can be proactive but not controlling, and it effectively helps our grandchildren. It also gives our children time to renew themselves and learn more from us and from each other. Family gatherings help our children succeed at their developmental tasks.

The Andersons held an annual family reunion. Their four married children alternated responsibility for it with the grandparents. That way, the duties would fall on each family once every five years. The reunions were three days long and involved a variety of activities. They agreed to make "learning," "fun," and "service," their guidelines. Each time they came together they organized an activity where family members shared what they had learned the previous year. They did many fun things, and they organized service activities in which everyone could participate. One time it was cleaning a widow's yard. Another time they conducted a car wash and donated the proceeds to the local shelter for homeless people.

Through these events, the grandparents provided a family environment where their grandchildren could meet and know each other. As they grew older, the grandchildren helped organize activities and were praised for their individual achievements. They learned about helping others and had a chance to compare rules in their families with their cousins' rules. Finding some similarities, individual grandchildren soon saw themselves in a unified family organization. Grandma and Grandpa Anderson, in their early seventies, were still providing a healthy family environment.

Communicating

Living in the information age as we do, it is somewhat surprising that anyone would forget the importance of communicating. It is not only the information in any message that might be important. Rather, it is the fact that relationships are maintained by communication. When we communicate with our children and with our grandchildren we are sending at least two messages. What we say or write is one message. How we feel toward one another, as evidenced by the effort to communicate, is the other. Grandparents who make efforts to communicate obviously care, while grandparents who do not communicate might not.

Communicating with grandchildren on birthdays, holidays, and other special family occasions is just part of the task. Calling just to talk and writing at other times are also important. Think of the symbolism. A positive message from a grandparent to a grandchild is a message from the future, telling what can be expected. This message tells grandchildren that the future holds interesting and safe possibilities they can look forward to. After having communicated many such messages to our grandchildren, they become messengers we send into a time we will never see.

Communication becomes the tie that binds, the meaning we give to events in the world, and a source of satisfaction. It is the method we use to keep track of our grandchildren's development and the means by which we can promote it. This is especially true when grandparents know enough about their grandchildren to communicate excitement about their achievements and successes.

One grandfather of yesteryear usually carried some gum or mints with him. It was available for any grandchild's sadness. It was available for a small moment of fun or enjoyment. The children thought the candy was the important thing, but as they lingered on in his lap and learned to talk with him, they discovered the gum was caring and the mints were kindness.

A college student left school just before an important test. She went to her professor to ask permission to take the test late. She explained her grandfather had passed away and she was flying several hundred miles to be at his funeral. "You must have been close," the professor suggested. "For most of my life, my grandfather used to call me just to see how I was doing," the student replied. "He called just last month to find out how I was doing here at school." She began to weep. "I will really miss him," she said.

There is great power in communication if it is timely and if it is arranged so that a grandchild knows care is given and genuine interest is being shown. It is the medium by which we deliver ourselves to them.

Reinforce the Positive

During a father-and-son fishing trip, the son began to tell of a problem he was having at home. He described one of his children as "undisciplined," and "unmanageable." His father (his child's grandfather) listened. After awhile, his father said, "You know, you were a lot like that. I have come to understand it is the way very intelligent boys sometimes adjust to their situation. He is very intense and he may cause some difficulty, but he will grow out of that and one day this intensity will be ambition." The son grew *quiet and finally replied, "I had never thought of that. I guess it [the emotional behavior] has a positive side."*

This is the part of parenting that never ends. It is always the older generation that has the responsibility of sending messages of hope and positive possibilities. As grandparents, we can play a vital role for both our children and our grandchildren.

Someone once said the most important characteristics of a good leader is that he or she leads. This means that a good leader needs to identify and suggest the direction where developing people might go, and encourage them to select a successful path. While we do not have the same obligation to our children as we used to have, there is never a time when our moral or spiritual leadership will go unnoticed. We are still demonstrating parental leadership by the way we live in our middle and older years. We are setting an example when we enter retirement, when we age, and even when we die. Equally important is the leadership we supply through our wisdom, our suggestions, and occasional attempts to display our opinions more strongly. Parents have the primary responsibility to do this for their children at every age, and when we have grandchildren our obligation for this type of leadership expands rather than diminishes.

We can, for example, tell our children and grandchildren about life lessons we have learned that bring success. Rather than preaching, we can link lessons to teaching moments and tell them in the form of a story. This is a better form of teaching.

We can notice important moments and give recognition to those who have achieved. Many grandparents attend school honor assemblies to be present when their grandchildren receive awards. Many parents still give gifts of time and material goods to their adult children.

There is an underlying purpose for reinforcing the positive. We need to practice and keep ourselves proficient, because one day grandchildren will ask questions about their parents or about themselves. These questions come in the form of speculation, apprehension, or disbelief. We only have this moment, and if we miss it, we may not be able to recover it.

When grandchildren doubt their parents or doubt themselves, we have the power to refocus their thoughts if we are committed to reinforce the positive. As respected and wise people, we listen until the person speaking has had a chance to vent the frustration. Then, after showing we have understood, we can suggest that we disagree with a bad idea, provide an alternative perspective, and suggest there is reason to have hope.

It is no small thing when a grandparent reinforces or agrees with the frustration of a grandchild toward his or her parents if the parents are trying to do well. Likewise, there are negative consequences when grandchildren speak to us as trusted people, say self-recriminating things, and discover we do not disagree. It is much better if we learn to disagree with the negative and communicate the positive. We have the power to shape some parts of reality for

Communicate the positive.

our children and grandchildren. For the purposes of growth and development, it is better if we use our influence to encourage positive and happy views of themselves and of each other.

Be Loving Biographers

Historians teach about past events and the importance of paying attention to them. For families, knowing about the past offers many potential benefits for the present and for the future. We live in a time where many people are exploring the past to understand the difficulties of today. Knowing what has happened in the past might help us solve problems in the present and future. However, we too often fail to see connections between choices we made and what happened to us, attributing the responsibility to others, and to the mistakes of the past.

Life is not better when we attribute responsibility to someone else. It is obviously the case that what others do to us as children affects us as adults. Negative things affect us severely. We tend to continue to anchor ourselves to the past by repeating unhappiness and ineffectiveness. The more we do that, the more likely it is that bad experiences will continue to exert their distracting influence, preventing us from finding love and happiness in the present and future.

This provides a valuable lesson. We learn through the analysis of mistreatment, trauma, sadness, and other forms of misery, that any person's history shapes and influences life in the present. If a negative and unhappy history can do this, so can a history filled with realism about the aches and pains of living, plus the memories of joy and love. Many children have been motivated by an expectation they derived from their forbearers. One familiar example includes teaching children certain values by telling them of ancestors who demonstrated them. Another is to provide motivation to excel because others did, or because they did not have the opportunity. Still another example includes specific family characteristics that grandchildren learn and try to apply.

The role of family biographer is not insignificant. Every person who has grandchildren can play a major role in defining the history their children and grandchildren come to believe. We have lived it and we are carrying a momentous message with us. We only need to find the best and most appropriate way of using it.

The memories and ideas in our respective family histories meet receptive minds. And, if it is necessary to set our grandchildren free from the misery of the past, we can do so by explaining accurately, adding understanding, and helping them to assume control over their own lives. Many of us do not have to worry about bad memories. For one thing, our memories are failing a bit and it is good if we forget some things. If we have a chance to tell our experiences, it is possible to also provide useful lessons about the greater and grander things life offers.

Let us consider several ways we might do this. We recognize it will happen in the normal course of family communication. Family history is what we talk about when we are together. In addition, many people write personal histories of their ancestors, detailing their experiences and what might be learned from them. We might write our own history to make it available to our children and grandchildren. We could visit a former residence that triggers memories and stories about the people and the times in which they lived. We could make certain that memories of people and times long gone are brought to light by setting up certain traditions. One family chooses one ancestor and sets a place for him or her at the table for each holiday dinner. This person is talked about, and in the minds of the grandchildren, reinvited back into the family and made a part of their history.

Is it better to live knowing nothing about the people who preceded us? Or, is it preferable to live knowing the good things about those people? The answer depends on the uses we give to the history. When it comes to helping us and our children learn very specific traits, like kindness, or habits like hard work, it is much better for them, and for all of us, to know about the struggles and successes of our ancestors. Again, knowing specific things about specific people adds leverage to the lessons we try to teach. If ancestors show a long record of public service, charity, honor, and sacrifice, knowing about them and what they did strengthens attempts by parents to teach these same values. At first glance, this might seem more true for younger children. But this idea applies even to teenagers who, as researchers suggest, are more likely to accept parental instruction if grandparents support it with family history.

If our desires for our grandchildren can be supported by actual events, then, we are the most effective by transmitting a family history told in the language of love. This comes by understanding those who preceded us, giving each story a realism that is tempered by compassion and forgiveness. If there are few positive events in our past, we can emphasize those. If there are more, we can tell about the people who made happiness possible. This means that we learn to elaborate the good, the loving, and the joyful, and tell of the positive consequences. We will let our grandchildren know about the people who loved us, and it will strengthen our efforts to love them. We can identify the useful lessons to be learned in all people's lives and give our grandchildren a perspective that helps them.

It Takes a Family "Village"

A wise African is reported to have said that it takes a whole village to raise a child. This statement was an explanation for the question of why all the members of a village appeared to cooperate in rearing children. One family helped another, and many village ceremonies were devoted to child rearing.

In Native American tribal histories, there are traditions that apply this same idea. One is about the time when puberty signals the onset of adulthood. All the members of the tribe participate in bathing to symbolize new life, feasts to celebrate, and educational rituals. One of the ceremonies is about the role men and women have in sustaining the lives of their children. Then, as a final gesture, the entire village honors the new adult.

Reflect on this a moment to imagine the possible thoughts of the young person. All the important people in his or her life are communicating their affection and the importance they attach to him or her. The whole village is giving time, attention, and instruction. Their teaching gives directions to be followed in order to win approval, and there are fairly clear cut things identified that each individual can do to succeed. Imagine the significance a young person feels, and the sense of belonging and affection attached to it. Under these conditions any young person would feel a profound sense of acceptance for his or her uniqueness.

In a time when there appears to be more people living isolated lives, we are seeing the harvest of this error in more mistreatment and violence. We have failed to teach such people that the highest level of individual achievement they can aspire to is not money, fame, or power. Instead, the highest goal is to be successful in high-quality relationships.

By the time we are grandparents, most of us have learned some things about money, fame, and power. We have seen that our careers and other efforts to achieve these ends are limited in their ability to provide fulfillment. We also understand that while adding spice to our lives, hobbies and recreation also have their limitations.

To grandchildren, we grandparents are messengers of the past who carry with us the solution to one of life's great challenges. Among all the things we choose to do, nothing is more important than improving our relationships with one another. We are the best teachers of this important truth.

When we bring all of our children and grandchildren together (with uncles, aunts, and cousins) we are creating a family village. We also do this when we take our grandchildren to church, ball games, Saturday-night concerts in the park, the circus, and on picnics. These activities bring our grandchildren into contact with others who are also members of the "village." Because we are there, we crown the moment with importance. We meet people that we know there, and we communicate that friendships are among the best things in life. They learn that we have relationships we value—and so should they.

Even in illness and in death we teach this lesson. Our roles in these are personal, of course. Nevertheless, we show our grandchildren about the importance of the family village and its ceremonies. Whether in joy or sorrow, when they recognize common feelings and common purposes they feel the importance of "belonging." They are included and they learn that they are significant. Many people have reported their greatest motivation in life came from these experiences.

Is our role as grandparents unimportant? Does it end? No, it is not unimportant, and it does not end, but goes on whether we are around are not. Further, whatever we do, good or bad, will be added to our grandchildren's store of memories. Since we are not a neutral force in the lives of our children and grandchildren, we should fill our time with things that help and contribute.

The very best way, in my opinion, is to understand that we, our children, and our grandchildren are developing, changing, and growing. Development never stops for us, and it never ends for them. Therefore, at any moment, and in many different ways, we can contribute to the most important parental task if we understand the real power of parenthood. ❀